NUMBER
96
Leunig

'Once, when I was a kid, I was walking down a suburban street at night, when I noticed a rhythmic flickering of light from inside the houses. Though screened from view by the drawn curtains, the lights from a row of separate houses were all pulsing in time. And then I heard the music and I knew: everyone was watching the same show … *Number 96*.'

— McKenzie Wark

Celebrities, Culture and Cyberspace. Annandale NSW:Pluto Press Australia, 1999

'I believe that the television serial provides a surrogate sense of community and that many viewers are more involved in *Number 96* than they are in their own community.'

— Phillip Adams

The Age, July 17 1974

'It's a social disgrace in some grades not to be able to watch *Number 96*.'

— School Headmaster

TV Week, 30 June 1973

'When Shakespeare was writing his plays, people queued up for Shakespeare because they wanted Shakespeare. Today they're queuing up for *96*. So, in my opinion, *96* is today's Shakespeare.'

— John Singleton

Barry Humphries' Flashbacks. ABC, 1999

Australian TV's Most Notorious Address

NUMBER

Nigel Giles

M

MELBOURNE BOOKS

Published by Melbourne Books
Level 9, 100 Collins Street,
Melbourne, VIC 3000
Australia
www.melbournebooks.com.au
info@melbournebooks.com.au

Images courtesy of the author's private collection, the collections of those noted in the acknowledgements and the National Film and Sound Archive of Australia.

Title: Number 96: Australian TV's Most Notorious Address
Author: Nigel Giles
ISBN: 9781925556001

A catalogue record for this book is available from the National Library of Australia

Page 1 image courtesy Michael Leunig
Back cover image courtesy Chris Keating

For my parents.

Thanks for letting me stay up late.

Strictly for adults

The management of 0 Melbourne would like to make it clear that tonight's premiere of 'Number 96' is a very adult programme. In fact, more adult than Australian television has ever been before. Its realism may surprise you. Its bluntness may anger you.

'Number 96' is the frank, honest story of 14 people who share not only an apartment block, but each other's lives. It's a new kind of television. You might love it. You might not. But you must watch it tonight, and decide for yourself. After the kids are tucked in.

'Number 96', 0 Melbourne tonight at 8.30.

Foreword

I must confess, when I first heard that my friend Nigel Giles was writing a book about *Number 96* I had serious doubts about its viability. It seemed to me that in the forty-odd years since 'Television lost its Virginity', everything that could possibly be written and reported about the series had already been done, and this included my own memoir on the subject.

Therefore, it comes as a complete and pleasant surprise to find that Nigel has taken a refreshingly different approach, by letting the people actually involved in the series tell the story in their own words. He has painstakingly assembled an astonishing verbal narrative of actual quotations that brings to vivid life this groundbreaking period in Australia's television history.

For myself, reading this book has been an intensely emotional experience. It was like being in a room filled with all those talented people who helped make the series such a memorable success. Hearing their voices again, reliving those incredible, exciting times had me reminiscing, laughing and — at times — reduced to tears for those of them who have passed away.

This entertaining and informative book is a fitting tribute to them all, and a valuable addition to the *Number 96* legend.

David Sale, creator of *Number 96*
Sydney, May 2016

Introduction

You're Not Allowed to Watch *Number 96* Tonight

I was eight years old when I started watching *Number 96* in 1974, two years after it made its spectacular debut on Melbourne's ATV0. While most of my grade three classmates were tucked into bed by 8.30pm, I was allowed to stay up on school nights and watch this adults-only soapie. My parents' reasons for letting me stay up and watch *Number 96* are still a mystery to me. I'm just thankful that they did. *Number 96* was, and still is, my favourite TV show.

Unfortunately, this made it a powerful weapon to use against me one time when I misbehaved. I don't recall what I did, but it must've been bad because Mum, who was always a softie when it came to discipline, decided to put her foot down. 'Right,' she said, 'you're not allowed to watch *Number 96* tonight.' At the time at least, this was harsh punishment and I was devastated.

Up until that moment I thought I was lucky having the parents I did. Most of my friends at school weren't allowed to watch *Number 96* and now I knew how they felt (even if it was only one episode I was missing out on). I had two other school friends who were allowed to watch and this common thread with one of them, Jacinta, cemented a friendship that still exists to this day.

The other friend was a classmate named Wendy who not only watched *Number 96*, but had an older brother who knew one of the stars, Josephine Knur. Josephine played Lorelei Wilkinson, a favourite character, and I entertained thoughts of meeting her. Maybe she'd turn up at my school one day. It was always fun discussing the previous night's episode with friends at school the next day. Those kids who weren't allowed to watch, because their parents thought the show too laden with sex, would listen in awe.

I can't recall the first episode I ever saw, but some of the earliest storylines I remember are Maggie Cameron being tied up and held hostage and a fire in Jack Sellars' flat. I also remember Carol Raye as Don's zany Aunt Amanda, aka the Baroness Von Pappenburg, who came to visit *Number 96* from Heidelberg, Germany. One day my family drove past a signpost to the Melbourne suburb of Heidelberg and I was thrilled at the prospect of being in Amanda's territory. So what if we weren't driving through Germany. Heidelberg Victoria was good enough for me.

Then there was the milk bar in Lilydale at 96 Main Street that modelled its street signage on the *Number 96* logo. I would crane my neck to check it out every time we drove by even though I knew I wasn't going to see Aldo, Roma or Arnold serving behind the counter. The logo above that milk bar was there for years, long after the series had closed its doors.

As much as I loved *Number 96*, it never occurred to me to write to the actors and ask for their autographs, though my dad once helped me out in this regard. In 1975 he was marching with the Croydon Citizen's Band in Melbourne's Moomba parade. I got up early on the Monday morning of the parade before Dad left home and asked him if he could get me some *Number 96* cast members' autographs. I knew they would also be in the procession as they were every year. When Dad came home he told me he hadn't recognised many of the actors as it had been a while since he'd watched the show, but he handed me a scrap of note paper and on it were the autographs of Bunney Brooke, Jeff Kevin, Joe Hasham and Elaine Lee. I marvelled at them. Those were the first autographs I ever collected and I still have that precious piece of paper to this day.

That same year our family moved house and I was thrilled to discover our new neighbours, Gordi and Lilian, the girls next door, were also fans of the show. Gordi was five years older than me. She impressed me because she had watched the series from the start and was able to fill me in on some of the stuff I'd missed. One Sunday at the Croydon Flea Market she generously gave me forty cents to buy a second-hand copy of *Marriage of Convenience*, one of the novelisations based on an early storyline of *Number 96*. It took me years to find all the other books and complete the set. But what impressed me the most was that both Gordi and Lilian had been to see the *Number 96* movie at the cinema. I was too young for its M rating and had to wait patiently until it screened on telly.

I was sad when *Number 96* came to an end in 1977. I vividly recall watching the final episode and saying goodbye to my favourite show. Week after week I began scouring the TV guides in search of repeats of the show or a screening of the movie, ever hopeful of finding an opportunity to re-live the *Number 96* magic.

One memorable day in 1981 I was let out of high school early and got home in time to watch *The Mike Walsh Show*. Brian Phillis was the afternoon talk show's director and he was celebrating a career milestone. Apart from many other experiences, such as working with Graham Kennedy at GTV9 in Melbourne, Brian had been one of the directors of *Number 96* throughout its five and a half year run. Mike Walsh announced that joining him in a tribute to Brian would be Johnny Lockwood, Joe Hasham, Sheila Kennelly and Pat McDonald. I couldn't believe my luck. Brian and the former *Number 96* cast members spent a rollicking time recalling their days working on the series and several clips were shown to highlight various storylines and characters.

• • •

Many years later I was in the Melbourne office of the National Film & Sound Archive (NFSA) when Helen Tully, the Broadcast Curator, made a passing comment about the Archive having just acquired some old episodes of *The Mike Walsh Show*. I mentioned the Brian Phillis tribute to her and thanks to Helen's expertise she managed to locate the episode. I recently got to see it again for the first time in over thirty years. It now sits safely in the NFSA Collection and I hope Brian's family get to see it one day too. Initially I wanted to make a documentary about *Number 96*. Had that eventuated I would've used footage from *The Mike Walsh Show* as well as some other great *Number 96* related footage that I've discovered; stuff that hasn't been seen in decades.

With the doco in mind, the ball got rolling many years ago when I first wrote to Elaine Lee. She was touring regional Australia in a production of *Steaming*, the wonderful play by Nell Dunn set in an English bathhouse. The play features plenty of nudity although, ironically, Elaine was playing one of the few characters who kept her clothes on. In my letter I told Elaine I believed it was time *Number 96*'s achievements were recognised and its story celebrated. I wrote about my desire to place the whole phenomenon of the show into context.

A couple of weeks later I was thrilled to receive a reply. Elaine thought it was a great idea and was willing to discuss my plans further. She gave me her telephone number and told me to call her when she was back in Sydney. I was excited and nervous when I made the call, but it was a magical starting point. It turned out Elaine had kept in touch with dozens of her former colleagues and she was happy to forward letters to them on my behalf. I got busy writing to several cast members. Elaine also suggested I contact David Sale, the show's creator. You'll discover as you read this book that David's contribution is pivotal. He's still surprising me with fresh anecdotes.

Elaine put me in touch with so many of her former colleagues. Others I tracked down through various contacts or just by looking in the phone book. The easiest person to find was Norman Yemm who just appeared at my block of flats one day! (He was visiting a relative.) Incidentally, Josephine Knur was the hardest, yet it turned out her brother had attended the same high school as me! It was a privilege to hear these people's stories. I'd travel around with my dictaphone, mini-cassettes and a list of questions. Over the course of the journey I was fortunate to discover treasure troves of *Number 96* memorabilia and to make some lasting friendships with the people I met.

For one reason or another the doco never came to fruition. I had a nibble from the ABC and a meeting with the TEN Network in Sydney, but that's as far as things got. In the meantime I'd been lugging equipment all over the country recording oral histories for the NFSA's oral history program. Many of the people I interviewed had worked on *Number 96* so I was accumulating more and more material. I still had a passion to tell the whole story and when it became obvious a documentary wasn't going to happen I decided to write this book.

My use of the oral history style of storytelling throughout this book came about partly because this project began as a doco, but it also best serves the multi-perspective take on things. This style of storytelling provides a platform for a diverse range of voices where some anecdotes are recalled differently from one person to the next. I've done very little editing, and made corrections for the sake of clarity only. This style of storytelling also allows for the voice of each interviewee to come across in its own rhythms and idiosyncrasies.

I hope you'll feel very much as if you're part of a conversation with all these wonderful people. Sadly, I've said goodbye to too many of them. Thank goodness their stories are told here along with all the others that bring this book to life. I've tried to present as many of the memorable and most loved characters as possible. And as well as hearing from the actors, I'll introduce you to some of the brilliant behind-the-scenes people who often get less recognition than the performers. I hope you get not only a true sense of the triumphant success of the show, but an understanding of what it was like for those at the heart of *Number 96*, including the fans.

I could tell you dozens more stories about the show that left its indelible mark on me, but that's enough of my recollections for now. It's time to sit back and relax and hear some of the stories from those who experienced *Number 96* firsthand.

But first a confession. I never did miss that episode all those years ago. I went to bed early that night with a plan. Unbeknownst to anyone, I switched on the black and white television beside my bed, turned the picture/brightness way down so the screen was black and I ran an earphone from the set, under my pillow and into my ear. It was just like listening to *Number 96* on the radio! At one point my mum came in to check on me so I pretended to be asleep. She had no idea, but drastic times called for drastic measures. All these years later I'm still watching.

VOLUM.
TONO
INT.
UHF
BRILLO
CONTR.
UHF
VHF
LAVIS

Chapter 1

How It All Began

I believe that no other TV show anywhere in the world had such an impact, nor broke so much ground in such a relatively short time as *Number 96*. It's a shining example of daring to be different and succeeding. Australian audiences took *Number 96* to their hearts and as the show hit the top of the ratings its stars and the characters they played became household names. But there's a lot more to the story than what was reported in the newspapers and magazines. To understand the lasting impression *Number 96* has made, not only on viewers, but on our television industry — specifically production techniques and content — we need to go back and look at what came before.

The arrival of television in Australia in 1956 brought with it a suitcase full of imported comedies and dramas. In the early days, shows such as *I Love Lucy*, *Father Knows Best* and *The Beverly Hillbillies* all came from the US, while the UK gave us *Coronation Street*, *On the Buses* and *The Rag Trade*. They proved to be popular with local audiences but reflected a lack of Australian content. When we did produce our own shows it not only provided our screen practitioners with an opportunity to hone their skills, it also gave viewers a taste of their own culture and many of these shows were very well received.

Bandstand, a local version of an American format, came along in 1958, hosted by Brian Henderson. Each week it presented established singers and musicians alongside up-and-coming artists and became one of the most popular shows of the period. *Bandstand* enjoyed great success alongside other perennial homemade favourites: notably the quiz show *Pick-a-Box* hosted by husband and wife team Bob and Dolly Dyer, and *The Mobil-Limb Show* hosted by Bobby Limb. Also featuring Dawn Lake and Noel Brophy, this hour-long, weekly variety show was produced by NLT for the Nine Network. Together with *IMT* starring Graham Kennedy and a succession of other hosts, home-grown television variety was alive and kicking.

Television soap opera began in Australia in 1958 with the morning melodrama *Autumn Affair*, which was produced in the studios of ATN7 and screened for fifteen minutes three days

above: The cast of *Bellbird*, the ABC's first soap opera

a week. The series starred radio veterans Muriel Steinbeck, Len Bullen, Diana Perryman, Queenie Ashton and Owen Weingott and ran for two years. The Seven Network made other attempts at producing daytime soap operas with *The Story of Peter Grey* in 1961–62 and *Motel* in 1968–69.

It wasn't until the arrival of the ABC's rural drama *Bellbird*, which began in 1967, that viewers across Australia had an ongoing evening series to follow religiously. *Bellbird* was produced in Melbourne and screened Monday to Thursday as a lead in to the nightly news. Each episode ran for fifteen minutes and the show became extremely popular with country viewers. During its ten-year run its cast included such luminaries as Elspeth Ballantyne, Maurie Fields, Peter Aanensen, Terry Norris, Gerda Nicolson, Dennis Miller, Alan Hopgood, Maggie Millar, Anne Charleston and Lynette Curran.

Melbourne-based Crawford Productions was one of the most prolific providers of television drama at a time when networks were required to screen a mere six hours of local content per month. They pioneered local content with their successful, long-running police shows *Homicide*, beginning in

below: Gordon Chater, Carol Raye and Barry Creyton in *The Mavis Bramston Show*

opposite left: Cast members of ABC kids' show *Adventure Island*. Courtesy Mary Kennedy

opposite right: The cast of *The Rovers* from left, Noel Trevarthen, Grant Seiden, Rowena Wallace and Eddie Hepple. Courtesy Chris Keating

1964 on the Seven Network, and *Division 4* in 1969 for the Nine Network. They were two of the most popular shows on the small screen and in 1971 were joined by a third Crawford cop show, *Matlock Police*, for the 0/10 Network, which also became a hit.

Australian comedy came of age in the 1960s with the groundbreaking *The Mavis Bramston Show*. The sitcom, *My Name's McGooley, What's Yours?*, starring Gordon Chater, John Meillon and Judi Farr also proved to be popular. And for kids of all ages there had been numerous shows from *Play School*, *Romper Room* and *The Magic Circle Club* to *Here's Humphrey* and *Adventure Island*, as well as the international hit *Skippy*.

In 1969, *The Rovers*, a family adventure series based in the Queensland tropics, began on the 0/10 Network. This series, starring Eddie Hepple, Noel Trevarthen, Rowena Wallace and child actor Grant Seiden, contained classic elements of the Australian outdoors, with cute and cuddly animals and lots of ocean adventure. *The Rovers* was inspired by the success of *Skippy* and made with an eye on the international market by NLT, the production house founded by Jack Neary and entertainer Bobby Limb with financial backing from Les Tinker.

Working on *The Rovers* as executive producer was expat American, Bill Harmon. He was born in Poughkeepsie, New York, in 1915 and had worked on Broadway and in US television before coming to Australia to join NLT. He arrived in 1961 with his wife Del and young sons Mark and Paul. Throughout the 1960s Harmon produced TV shows for Sydney-based entertainers Bobby Limb, Barry Crocker, Dave Allen and Don Lane.

Also working on *The Rovers* as a producer was Don Cash. He was born in England in 1910 and began his career producing stage shows and RAF training films during World War II. Cash

would eventually find work on films such as *The Lavender Hill Mob* and *Pandora and the Flying Dutchman* before becoming an American citizen and spending nine years in New York, where he produced and directed television shows for NBC and ABC. In 1968, Cash was invited to join NLT in Sydney and arrived with his young wife, Nancy, in May of that year.

> *'In 1971, Australia's population reached 13 million, Television was fifteen years old, still came in black and white and was present in ninety percent of homes.'*

Although Don Cash and Bill Harmon had both worked at NBC in New York, they didn't work together until *The Rovers* in 1969. It was a fortuitous meeting of two experienced and visionary men. That same year, they worked on the little-known film *Squeeze a Flower*. Then in early 1970 they teamed up again to work on the seminal Australian feature, *Wake in Fright*. Less than a year later, change was brewing.

In 1971, Australia's population reached 13 million, Television was fifteen years old, still came in black and white and was present in ninety percent of homes. It was a different world to today where nearly everyone has their own pocket-sized screen as well as multiple TV channels and other platforms to choose from. Australia was under a Liberal government that had been in office for twenty-two years and was headed, at the time, by Billy McMahon. We had troops in Vietnam, you had to be twenty-one to vote, we measured the temperature in degrees Fahrenheit and *Cleo* magazine was still a year away.

below: Don Cash and Bill Harmon. Courtesy Nancy Cash

opposit top: Cast members of *The Group*. Courtesy Don Storey

opposite bottom: Writer David Sale, 1971

But the country and society were changing; we were becoming more permissive. By the beginning of 1971, Don Cash and Bill Harmon had departed NLT to form their own production outfit, Cash Harmon Productions. In time they were joined by others from NLT including writer Lynn Foster and producer Bob Huber.

As Nancy Cash remembers, Cash Harmon started out in the corner of her living room with a number of projects on the boil, including screenplays for seven feature films. With plenty of ideas to keep them busy, their first successful venture was a TV sitcom called *The Group*. Mike Harris wrote the pilot episode, based on an idea by Anne Hall, before Bruce Gyngell, then head of ATN7, commissioned a further thirteen episodes.

The Group first aired in August 1971. Based around the lives of five young flatmates, the cast featured Ken James, Greg Ross, Gregory de Polnay, Jenee Welsh and Roslyn Wilson with Terry O'Neill as their busybody landlord. One of the writers was David Sale who, a few years earlier, had risen to prominence as a writer and executive producer of the top-rating satirical program, *The Mavis Bramston Show*.

DAVID SALE (writer): I worked for Bill and Don for the first time doing *The Group* and from wanting me to write three episodes, I ended up writing eight and a half. 'Half' because I re-wrote somebody else's script.

NANCY CASH (wife of Don Cash): *The Group* was a great show. It won a Logie Award for Best Comedy and people seemed to like it, but it wasn't renewed by the network after the initial thirteen-week season. And that's the thing, being successful never guaranteed anything in the television industry.

Long before *The Group* went to air, the Cash Harmon team was already working on other proposals. They moved from Cash's lounge room to an office above a funeral home at 293 Pacific Highway, Crows Nest. Friend and fellow producer John Collins let them have use of the office rent-free while they got themselves established. They were working from there when, in April 1971, they approached David Sale once again, this time with a completely radical concept.

Chapter 2

Take a Walk Down Any Paddington Street ...

preceding: Moncur Flats, Woollahra, in the street where Don and Nancy Cash were then living

DAVID SALE (writer): I was just about to go back to England for the publication of my first novel, *Come to Mother*, and three days before I left for London my agent rang me and said, 'Bill and Don want to take us to lunch tomorrow to discuss you doing a treatment for a continuing series.' Well, I was about to leave for England, so I wasn't really interested. Anyway, I said, 'Where are we having lunch?' And he said, 'Beppi's.' And I said, 'Okay, I'll come,' because Beppi's is my favourite Italian restaurant. So we had this lunch and they said they had an idea and they wanted me to see this block of flats. So after the lunch they took me to see a block of flats in Moncur Street, Woollahra. And it was *the* block of flats.

BOB HUBER (producer): Ian Holmes and Peter Skelton from Channel 10 had come to us and said, 'We want an adult show to be screened two or three nights a week.'

It was crucial for the 0/10 Network to come up with local content, as questions were being raised in Parliament about their efforts to meet the current Broadcasting Control Board quotas. On top of this, the six-year-old network was consistently left floundering at third spot in the ratings behind the other two commercial stations. It was make or break time.

'It's got to be an adult series and there's got to be plenty of sex and nudity.'

DAVID SALE: They said, 'It's got to be an adult series and there's got to be plenty of sex and nudity.' I was allowed to put whatever characters I wanted to in the block of flats so I went home to the friend's apartment where I'd been staying. It got to about nine o'clock and I thought, *well, I'd better get on with this treatment.* I opened a bottle of scotch, sat down on the floor in the corner and wrote and by midnight it was finished.

In his treatment Sale created characters with surnames he found randomly in the phone book and others he invented. He wrote a few pages of story ideas for future episodes, setting the action in the inner Sydney suburb of Paddington.

DAVID SALE: I started it off by saying, 'Take a walk down any Paddington street and you'll see so-and-so. You'll hear this; you'll smell the food. Look! Here we are at this block of flats. Let's go in.' And whoever was reading this treatment, I led them in, starting at the ground floor flat and continuing up to the top. Because of the time element I didn't even think up characters. I put in everybody I knew, slightly disguised. And I think this is probably why they all became so identifiable — because I knew them.

Sale sent his treatment to Don Cash and Bill Harmon and flew to England. It wasn't long before he received word from Australia that Channel 10 had given the go-ahead for a pilot to be made.

DAVID SALE: Bill Harmon rang me in London and said, 'Jesus David, they love it. Write the pilot on the way home.' So I wrote the pilot episode in Athens and Bangkok and typed it up on the hotel typewriter in Hong Kong.

BILL HARMON (producer): David sent over a pilot, which, in David's own words, was diabolical. He didn't think it was going anywhere. He sent it over and it was terrible. So then we sat down and began working on it.

'When I wrote the original pilot episode it was dreadful.'

DAVID SALE: When I wrote the original pilot episode it was dreadful. Bill said, 'David, you've tried putting in all this stuff,' and it was, 'way too complicated.' It was dreadful. It was Bill who said to me that I needed to start the whole thing at episode 3 and then go back and establish. Of course he was right — I didn't need to set the whole thing up, just let it unfold gradually.

When it came time to cast *Number 96* the producers had certain actors in mind for some roles, but generally went for unknowns. The diverse cast was one of the largest ever assembled for a local production.

NANCY CASH (wife of Don Cash): Bill and Don did most of the casting, if not all of it. They didn't have a casting director at Cash Harmon Television but they were both very good at casting.

One of the most well-known actors cast was Johnny Lockwood, who had appeared on many stages throughout Australia, including the Tivoli circuit and in hit productions of *Oliver!* and *Canterbury Tales*. He was also seen regularly on TV programs including *Revue '62*, *The Mavis Bramston Show* and Don Lane's *Tonight Show* out of Sydney.

DAVID SALE: I wrote Aldo for Johnny Lockwood, who'd been marvellous in *Mavis Bramston* and absolutely no trouble to work with, which is saying a lot for a comedian.

bottom left: Johnny Lockwood as Aldo Godolfus

bottom right: Johnny Lockwood (far right) in *Mavis Bramston* days

NANCY CASH: Johnny Lockwood's casting was interesting. I don't think he'd ever done drama before. He was a stand-up comic really, a comedy performer. They were very keen to have Johnny. I don't know whether it was hard to talk him into it or not. They were certainly thrilled that he accepted the role.

JOHNNY LOCKWOOD (actor): I'd known Bill Harmon a very long time when he asked me to go to lunch. He told me about *Number 96* and offered me this role of the deli owner. He told me we'd be doing three shows a week and I laughed at him. I'd only just come out of the *Bramston Show* so I knew how hard it was to do one a week and I refused it. Then he called me to go to lunch about a week later with Don Cash, his partner, and he tried to convince me, but I said no. And again they took me out and again I said no. About three weeks after that I was in Surfers Paradise. I kept getting calls from my agent and eventually *he* convinced me that I should do it. I was in a bit of a commanding position so we agreed on money and that was that.

DAVID SALE: I wrote Aldo as a Greek and Johnny rang me up and said, 'David, I can't do Greek …'

JOHNNY LOCKWOOD: I said, 'I can do Jewish … can I make him Jewish?' And he said, 'Yeah, sure.'

DAVID SALE: We forgot to change the name. Aldo Godolfus. Greek! And he's playing more or less a Hungarian Jew. Nobody ever picked that up. Of course the Jewish people loved him. He was very popular in the Jewish community because, for once, a Jewish businessman was being presented as a lovable character.

Another cast member whose role was written especially for her was Bettina Welch. Originally from New Zealand, Bettina had enjoyed a successful stage and radio career in Australia since the 1940s.

above: Publicity shot of Bettina Welch from her theatre and radio days

DAVID SALE: Bettina Welch as Maggie Cameron. That was written especially for her because when we were doing *The Group* I'd written an episode and had gone along to a reading and there was Bettina, whom I admired very much, playing a very minor part. I said, 'The very next show I do, I'll write you a marvellous part.' She loved it. She was an actress and she loved something to get her teeth into. It was the first real bitch on television. It was before Alexis Carrington. It was before Pat the Rat. It was a juicy part and totally against type. Bettina was the loveliest lady you could ever hope to meet.

ELEANOR WITCOMBE (writer): She was supposedly pretty tough, so we had her being tough about things and, you know, she could curl her lip beautifully when she felt like it, but underneath, eventually, we got this vulnerable person, you know, who'd get drunk. And we could give her other dimensions because Bettina was such a good actress.

Another actress spotted during a guest stint in *The Group* was Elisabeth Kirkby. In the episode 'This Week She's Liberated', English-born Kirkby played an overwrought mother with a handful of kids and another on the way.

ELISABETH KIRKBY (actress): The cameo in *The Group* was funny and appealing and it pleased the Cash Harmon team, so when *Number 96* was being written, David Sale introduced the character again in a different setting. At *The Group* wrap party Bill Harmon told me that Lucy would be in *Number 96*. So, the pregnant mum in *The Group* was my audition.

Joining Elisabeth Kirkby as Lucy in flat 8 was Scottish-born actor, James Elliott, as her husband Alf. The pair had an instant on-screen rapport.

JAMES ELLIOTT (actor): I heard about the role through my agent and I was sent along to do an audition. They got a number of actors in the running for the role, I think about five people tested. I was asked many years ago how the role came about, and what I said was none of the actors interviewed wanted the part of Alf Sutcliffe — they rejected it — until the tea lady at Cash Harmon said, 'What about James Elliott? He'll do anything for money.'

'the tea lady at Cash Harmon said, 'What about James Elliott? He'll do anything for money.''

DAVID SALE: I put my own parents in it. Alf and Lucy Sutcliffe — Lancashire migrants. The only way they differed was that both my parents adored Australia, but I made Alf a whinging Pom just to keep it interesting. And I even called Lis Kirkby's character Lucy, which is my mother's name. I didn't even bother to change the name.

Below the Sutcliffes in flat 6 lived aspiring actress Janie Somers, played by recent NIDA graduate Robyn Gurney. Her flatmate was Sydney Harbour tour guide and part-time model, Bev Houghton, played by another newcomer, Abigail.

ABIGAIL (actress): I first heard about *Number 96* from my agent. She telephoned and said, 'Get over to Channel 10. There could be something there for you.' 'What exactly?' I asked. 'I'm not too sure,' she said, 'but it sounds like something out of *Coronation Street* spiced up with *Peyton Place*.' I wasn't very enthusiastic when I went to the studios. I wanted to break through, but I didn't see the audition for *Number 96* as being the big chance. I didn't think any more about it until the telephone rang at the Double Bay flat I had moved to and my agent said, 'Congratulate yourself, honey, you've got the job.'

Downstairs in flat 4, school teacher Mark Eastwood and his pregnant wife Helen were newlyweds, just moving in under the

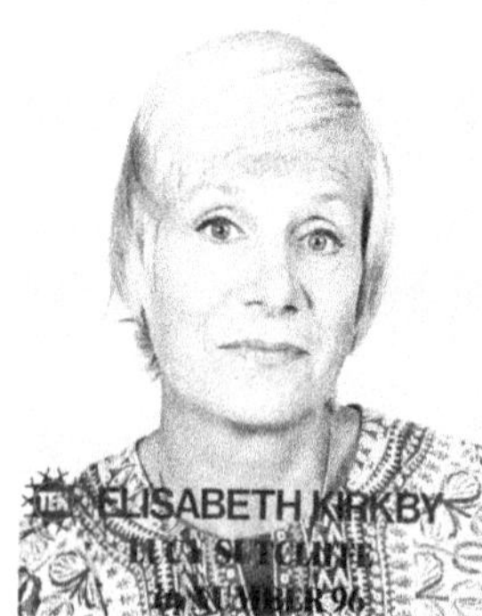

top left: Elisabeth Kirkby as Lucy Sutcliffe. Courtesy Mick Pratt

middle left: James Elliott as Alf Sutcliffe. Courtesy Mick Pratt

middle right: NIDA graduate Robyn Gurney as Janie Somers. Courtesy Mick Pratt

top right: Abigail as Bev Houghton. Courtesy Mick Pratt

bottom: (left to right) Briony Behets as Helen Eastwood, Martin Harris as Mark Eastwood and Vivienne Garrett as Rose Godolfus. Courtesy Mick Pratt

watchful eye of their neighbour from flat 3. The role of Mark went to NIDA graduate Martin Harris, and Briony Behets, who had recently arrived from England, was cast as Helen.

On the ground floor, also living in flat 2 behind the delicatessen, was Aldo's daughter Rose Godolfus, played by NIDA graduate Vivienne Garrett.

VIVIENNE GARRETT (actress): On the last day of NIDA you get up in front of casting directors, like a showcase. At the end of the showcase there was a little bit of a whisper that there was an American TV producer and another guy who were casting this TV series. They were looking for a young cast of people to be in this show so everyone started getting excited about this. Denny Lawrence came over to me and said, 'Those TV guys want to meet you.' I remember walking towards them, these big producers, and I felt nervous and very special and everybody was watching me. I was standing in front of them and Bill Harmon had this big fat cigar hanging out the side of his mouth

and said, 'Oh no, not *her*. I wanna meet the good looking red-head.' My heart sank, and I went and got my bag and I left.

Garrett spent early 1971 on tour with a theatre-in-education company and also travelled to Melbourne to appear in some Crawford productions.

VIVIENNE GARRETT: Then my agent called and said Cash Harmon want to see you. I went, 'Oh yeah. I've met those guys.' I remember going to this room in North Sydney one day. I went in and these two guys — these guys who'd humiliated me in front of my classmates — were sitting there and I was so angry, but I wasn't nervous. I went in there with attitude and I sat there and read this thing and they said, 'Thank you very much,' and I said, 'So, is that it?' They said, 'Yes.' I said, 'Okay.' I didn't say thanks or anything. I walked out. Now if you look back and see what sort of girl Rose was — or how they envisaged this character — she was a rebellious teenager. I think I came in with attitude that was right for the part. So lo and behold I get a screen test.

But she still had to wait to find out if she'd been successful.

VIVIENNE GARRETT: I go out to Channel 10 and do the screen test with Martin Harris and I knew the scene very well. And I knew Martin; he wasn't a complete stranger. Anyway, we did this scene and that was it. I rang my agent and said, 'Did I get the part?' And she said, 'Oh, look, they're doing call backs and your name's not on the list.' I said, 'It must be. I don't understand. Can you check?' She said, 'Oh Vivienne, I'm not going to check. Your name's not on the list, honey.' I was really perplexed. I couldn't believe it. Anyway, she rang back about a week later and said, 'You've got the part. They just wanted to see a few other people, but you were their first choice.'

On the top floor in flat 7, next door to Lucy and Alf Sutcliffe, was the mysterious Vera Collins.

DAVID SALE: Vera Collins was actually based on someone who was quite well known at the time. She always picked the wrong fella.

ELAINE LEE (actress): I was sent along to this screen test where I met them all and I remember we were in this huge dressing room at Channel 10. My screen test was Dorrie and Vera together. So I was sitting with this woman — I don't know who she was, this reasonably elderly woman — and we were just going through the lines and I thought, *well my test must come up in a minute*. Well, the door swung open and in flounced Hazel Phillips, and she said, 'I don't know why everybody's here. The part's mine.'

After being called back the following week for a second test, South African-born Lee, who at the time was unknown in Australia, won the role of flat 7's Vera Collins. Below Vera, in flat 5, lived a couple of young men. NIDA graduates Joe Hasham and Paul Weingott were cast respectively as gay law student Don Finlayson and his bisexual lover, photographer Bruce Taylor. Depicting two men as live-in lovers was a unique situation not only for Australian television, but television around the world.

'Depicting two men as live-in lovers was a unique situation not only for Australian television, but television around the world.'

DAVID SALE: I said to Bill, 'Do you mind if I put two homosexuals in one of the flats?' He loved the idea. He said, 'Give me homosexuality without any deviations.' Whatever that's supposed to mean!

top left: Elaine Lee as Vera Collins. Courtesy Mick Pratt

top right: Paul Weingott and Joe Hasham created television history as lovers Bruce and Don

bottom: Bruce and Don from flat 5 visit Janie and Bev next door in flat 6. Courtesy NFSA

PAUL WEINGOTT (actor): I don't think I was very politically or socially aware, and I got caught up in the excitement of being in a new series, not realising what it might become and maybe I didn't really question it. I just took it and ran with it.

JOE HASHAM (actor): My audition for the role of Don was, if anything, unremarkable. Both Bill Harmon and Don Cash were present. I read opposite another actor whose name escapes me. I honestly thought he was probably more suited for the role and I was convinced he would get it. He didn't and the rest is history.

above: NIDA graduate Joe Hasham as Don Finlayson

opposite: Joe James as Gordon Vansard and Lynn Rainbow as Sonia. Courtesy Joe James

DAVID SALE: Joe Hasham's character was based on a guy I had met who was a solicitor with an oil firm and I couldn't have picked that he was gay.

JOE HASHAM: I was an actor and I was playing a role. That was my initial reaction. As time passed, however, my feelings toward what I was doing changed enormously. I began to realise the profound effect *Number 96*, and particularly my character, Don Finlayson, was having on the viewing public and I realised that I had a huge responsibility in playing a gay character.

So the gay guys were in, but there was another character who never made it beyond the first draft.

DAVID SALE: Bill only made one change to my ideas. In my original treatment the shop next door to the deli was an antiques store, which was to be run by Terry O'Neill. Bill Harmon didn't really see the potential in that and said to me, 'Let's leave it vacant for thirteen episodes and then let's have somebody move in.' So we decided to have the chemist shop with Sonia and Gordon. Everybody thought they were brother and sister but they were really waiting to be married.

Enter Joe James as Gordon Vansard and Lynn Rainbow as Sonia. Joe James had been a regular in the popular adventure series *Barrier Reef* and his performance in the film *Demonstrator* had impressed Don Cash, while Lynn Rainbow was another performer who had made a guest appearance in an episode of *The Group*.

LYNN RAINBOW (actress): My character in *The Group* was written by David Sale. David wrote this character called Valerie Venski and she had verbal diarrhoea. It was great fun and that led to my being cast in *Number 96*.

JOE JAMES (actor): I recall my agent saying, 'They're making this thing called *Number 96* and they'd like to see you for a part

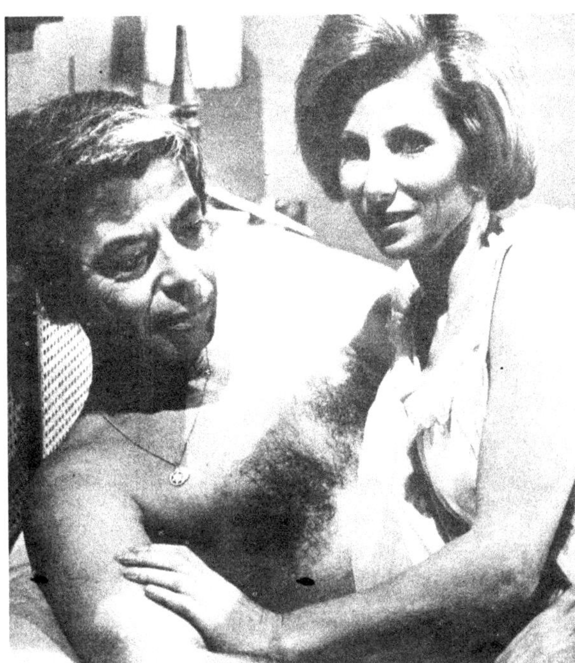

in it.' My agent wasn't very happy about it. She didn't want me to do it. She said, 'It'll be a disaster because it's going to be too shocking,' and all this sort of thing.

The premise of *Number 96* was that the block of flats had been built on the site of pensioners Dorrie and Herb Evans' former home at 96 Lindsay Street, Paddington. The elderly couple now occupied flat 3.

DAVID SALE: I wrote the character of Dorrie Evans based on this busybody neighbour I had at one time. I was living in a block of flats in Neutral Bay and they were all retired people there except me. I was the only single person there and there was this old guy and he always wanted to know what was going on. I thought there's one in every building, but I'll change the sex. So he became Dorrie.

NANCY CASH: I remember they were very keen to get Pat McDonald. They'd seen her acting on the stage at the Ensemble

top left: Pat McDonald, 1970

bottom left: Ron Shand as henpecked Herb Evans

right: Pat McDonald and Ron Shand as Dorrie and Herb Evans

Theatre and thought she was an excellent actress. They approached her directly to be in the show.

DAVID SALE: When Bill had cast *Number 96* we had a cocktail party to meet each other and my first words to Pat McDonald were, 'Oh but you're far too young,' because she was a smart lady and I'd imagined a little grey-haired lady with a bun. But of course Bill was absolutely right.

Pat McDonald was an experienced stage actress who had done a small amount of television work, and appeared in early Australian feature films *Seven Little Australians* and *Wings of Destiny*. With major casting complete in September, a pilot episode was scheduled to be shot in October 1971.

JAMES ELLIOTT: Ron Shand wasn't in the pilot. I remember the writer saying to Pat McDonald, 'You're going to get a husband, you know. He's only a little fella and you'll have a lot of fun', and sure enough, a couple of weeks later, there popped up Ron Shand playing the part of Herbie.

DAVID SALE: It was decided to give her a henpecked husband, and I remembered Ron Shand because I'd worked with him in *The Wizard of Oz* when I was acting, and I loved him. I thought he was a marvellous little guy and I thought he'd be wonderful as the henpecked husband.

Ron Shand was born into a theatrical family and made his professional debut aged fourteen. He'd worked as a dancer and a comedian and had performed on stage in everything from vaudeville to Shakespeare. He'd also appeared in early television dramas and at the age of sixty-five was the oldest member of the cast.

BILL HARMON: We wrote the third episode as the pilot, as the way to get into it. Then we wrote the preceding hour for it.

TED JOBBINS (floor manager): We made the pilot and everyone was very enthusiastic about it.

BILL HARMON: Within the week of our shooting it they picked it up. It didn't take them long to make a decision on it. Then Ian [Holmes] came to us and said he wanted to do three a week and we thought that was too many, but we thought we could do that.

DAVID SALE: I had recommended Johnny Whyte because when I left *Mavis Bramston* he had come over from England to replace me as executive producer. He loved Australia and he was very easy to get on with. Also, he had worked on *Coronation Street*. When they phoned me in London I said, 'Listen, if you're going ahead with this you'll need some kind of story editor.' I said, 'I'm staying with Johnny Whyte,' and actually Don Cash and Nancy were in London so they came around and met Johnny and signed him up. So Johnny came over as story editor.

TED JOBBINS: I got the job of floor managing because I was senior floor manager at Channel 10.

Most of the original cast of *Number 96*. Courtesy Cash Harmon

KEVIN POWELL (production manager): June Cann said, 'Bill Harmon and Don Cash have heard you are passing through and they want to talk to you', and I went out and I had breakfast with Don Cash at his house in Woollahra, and he said, 'Kevin, we've got this little show called *Number 96*. It's a piece of cake.' He said, 'We'd like you to production manage it for six months; that's all it'll run.'

Ted Gregory directed the pilot, and then once the series was given the go-ahead Cash Harmon, in conjunction with Channel 10 executives, hired directors Brian Phillis and Peter Benardos. Although both men had extensive production experience, this new style of television would present a unique set of challenges.

BRIAN PHILLIS (director): In 1971, having just returned to Australia after some years in Los Angeles, I received a phone call from Ian Holmes, then running Channel 10 in Sydney. He asked if I would be interested in coming up to Sydney to talk about a radically different show in development. Ian mentioned at our meeting that this new show to be titled *Number 96* was to be a fast-paced, prime time drama/sitcom kind of production with no constraints on content. The show was to be produced by two Americans, Don Cash and Bill Harmon, whose offices in Crows Nest were above a funeral parlour. Ian arranged for me to meet them.

PETER BENARDOS (director): I had this phone call from Don Cash, who was part of the Don Cash/Bill Harmon situation, and he said, 'Can you come in and have lunch with me?' So I did. And he said, 'Now we'll just go down to this little restaurant somewhere in North Sydney.' He said, 'It's just down the road.' And he said, 'I won't tell you what's on my mind until we get there.' Anyway, we finally got to this little restaurant and he said, 'We have an idea of doing drama and producing five episodes a week. What do you think?' And I said, 'Well I've never done drama.' He said, 'But you know enough about cameras and the correct method of using cameras and not crossing the line,' and

'Nude' show to go ahead

The show that stirred up all the noise because of the nudity clause in its contracts, No. 96, goes into fulltime production on January 24.

No 96 is being made for the 0-Network by Cash-Harmon Productions, who turned out The Group earlier this year.

TEN-10 will screen it sometime early in 1972 at a date still to be announced.

Fifty half-hour episodes are to be made for the show, described by producer Don Cash as "more of a serial, like Peyton Place." There will be a continuing story, set in an apartment building numbered 96.

The new show, to be given an AO rating, is "strictly for adults," says Cash.

"We felt there were enough shows for family viewing. This will be strictly sophisticated, adult entertainment.

"There has been too much fuss about that nudity clause.

"We asked some of the actresses to sign contracts saying they would be prepared to strip if the story called for it. But we do not plan to introduce nudity just for nudity's sake.

"If anything offends people's sense of morality, then I'm sorry. They have the right to switch off and watch something else.

"All the actresses we have signed understand why we had to do it. The only reason we put in the nudity clause is because we didn't want a situation where we could be up to, say, episode 12, and all of a sudden someone says they don't want to do a nude scene. We would have to respect their wishes, if that happened. By writing in the clause beforehand, we have just done some intelligent advance thinking.

"Only one was offended by it, and turned the part down."

Johnny Whyte, who was with the early Mavis Bramston shows, has been appointed script editor. A team of half a dozen top writers has been working on the serial, set in a Paddington-Woollahra type area.

Johnny Lockwood plays the owner of a delicatessen. Joe James is the other shop-owner, a chemist. Others in No 96 include Vivienne Garrett, Pat McDonald, Martin Harris, Briony Behets, Abigail, Robyn Gurney, Paul Weingott, Joe Hasham, Elaine Lee, Hames Elliott, Elizabeth Kirkby, Lyn Rainbow and Joe James. Norman Yemm from Homicide has a guest role in seven or eight episodes.

A second TV series is in the planning stages by Cash-Harmon Productions.

Said Don: "It's Bill's idea. Everyone we've talked with has been very excited about it, as it's never been done before.

"As soon as we can get room to breathe, we plan to commission a pilot."

Vivienne Garrett

above: Newspaper article announcing that *Number 96* was to go into production on 24 January 1972. Courtesy Joe James

all this. And I said, 'Oh yes, I know all about that. Did that in Canada.' Peter Skelton, the production manager of Channel 10 at the time, was a very dear friend of mine, and he came out to Bilgola Plateau where I lived to fill me in on how we would work and do five half-hour shows a week. And I said, 'What kind of money are you offering?' and he said whatever it was and I said, 'Gee, it's not much money.' He said, 'Oh well, it's an experiment for us. We don't really know whether it's going to work or not.'

BILL HARMON: Before it went to air we had some kind of a party at the network and Ian pulled me aside and said he wanted five episodes a week and I told him he was crazy, but he insisted on it.

TED JOBBINS: Management decided that perhaps we'd better put this on more often. They said that they wanted five half-hours a week and everybody threw their hands up in horror.

JAMES ELLIOTT: I was told it was going to be five nights a week and I thought, *well that's impossible* — actors can't do that sort of thing.

DAVID SALE: I said, 'Oh God, it'll never work.' I said, 'Nobody's going to stay in five nights a week.' Well, of course — famous last words.

‘I said, ‘Oh God, it’ll never work.’ I said, ‘Nobody’s going to stay in five nights a week.’ Well, of course – famous last words.’

11 DAILY MIRROR, MONDAY, MARCH 13, 1972

Chapter 3

Tonight at 8.30 Television Loses Its Virginity … er Innocence

DAVID SALE (writer): There was a big launch. The first episodes were being shown to the rent-a-crowd people of that era and the critics. All these people were standing around drinking and talking and nobody was paying a bit of attention to the screen, and when they did they'd just laugh and sneer.

TOM GREER (publicist): We just wanted to get bums on seats for episode 1 and we started off flogging sex, sex, sex, sex, sex, and it wasn't really there.

BILL HARMON (producer): David Sale even got sex into the title.

preceding: Adverts hyping the debut episode of *Number 96*. Different versions were produced as some papers would not publish one version

above: The lavish launch. Courtesy NFSA

opposite: Publicity shots of the sexy girls from *Number 96*

DAVID SALE: The sexual connotations of the title never occurred to me. I could make myself look very clever and say, 'Yes', but it was just *Number 96* and that came about because it was midnight and I was getting very tired and a bit pissed too. I suddenly thought, *now what can I call this?* I can't call it a street because there's *Coronation Street*. So I thought, *I'll give it a number and then I'll think of a clever title later*. Well, even a number has to roll off the tongue alliteratively and I thought 19 and I thought 29 then I got to number 96. Ah, *Number 96*, that sounds good.

The initial newspaper headlines heralded this new era in Australian television with a catchcry that has endured to this day.

TOM GREER: I decided on the two things — 'virginity' and 'innocence'. The advertising agency came up with the wording. One of the young copywriters from the agency wrote it in some general copy and we said, 'Wow what a headline that would make!'

VIVIENNE GARRETT (actress): The publicity machine at Channel 10 was incredible. There were ads in the paper every day and photos. It was really provocative. It was a huge campaign so it caught on pretty quickly.

TOM GREER: We decided to take a full-page ad in the two afternoon papers, *The Daily Mirror* and *The Sun*. Back in those days it was great to have two afternoon newspapers. We booked a full page in both papers in a very good position, right up the front. We had four plates made — two saying 'Tonight at 8.30 Television loses its virginity!' and two saying 'Tonight at 8.30 Television loses its innocence!' We gave 'virginity' to both of them. *The Mirror* took 'virginity'. *The Sun*, being a bit prudish, knocked it back and we gave them 'innocence'. Now that was ideal because that was going to keep people talking.

NUMBER 96

The famous *Number 96* logo

right: TV guide listings for the debut episode

opposite: Two early reviews

PICK OF TONIGHT

The Snow Goose, 7.30 pm, Channel 9.

A one-hour drama adapted from Paul Gallico's moving novel about an English lighthouse keeper who befriends an injured snow goose. Stars Richard Harris and Jenny Agutter.

No. 96, 8.30 pm, Channel 10

This is the premiere of TEN's much publicised night-time serial about the people and their doings in a Paddington apartment house. To get you into the story, tonight will consist of three half hour episodes rolled into one. Stars Johnny Lockwood and 28 others.

8.30 Number 96: A new adult drama series portraying the lives of people living in a block of flats in an inner Sydney suburb. The characters include the caretakers of the flats, a law student, a photographer, an aspiring out of work actress, a fortune teller and a "whinging Pom."

In Sydney, on Monday 13 March 1972, *Number 96* went to air for the very first time in the adults-only time slot of 8.30pm. The special ninety-minute presentation was preceded by an announcement from Channel 10 personality Jeremy Cordeaux, warning viewers that what they were about to watch was not suitable for all members of the family.

NANCY CASH (wife of Don Cash): I saw the first episode and remember thinking it was absolutely terrific. It just seemed to be very strong on drama, story and characters and it was certainly different from anything that I'd seen in Australia.

DAVID SALE: The critics lambasted it.

ELAINE LEE (actress): I thought it was appalling. My mother came out from South Africa to watch the first episode but when

TV WEEK VIEWPOINT

THIS SERIES IS A GREAT LITTLE NUMBER

IT'S SO REALISTIC, SAYS IAN DOUGALL

NO. 96, the new series on the 0-10 Network has the potential of becoming cult viewing with its down-to-earth realism.

A combination of drama, sex and everyday domestic situations makes it first class adult viewing.

Some scenes will shock. Others are on a lighter note depicting ordinary people's

but shares her life with the other tenants—and to earn extra money she tells fortunes on the side.

Abigail plays Bev, a young swinging girl in love with men of all ages. She shares a flat with Janie (Robyn Gurney)

No. 96: what a reaction!

THE TELEPHONE has stopped ringing at last! A peacefulness, broken only by the chatter of typewriters and copy boys, has descended around my desk. And I don't want to think for at least a month about Channel Ten's new daily serial, Number 96.

The phones started jangling as soon as I arrived at work yesterday morning. Everyone had an opinion on Monday's premiere of the show — and everyone, it seemed, wanted to tell me about it.

Viewers' reactions were mixed. But at least they did react. Some called it the worst show ever produced in Australia. They said this, keeping in mind such atrocities as the Link Men, Whiplash and Barrie Howard's television commercials.

Main criticism was aimed at the script. "Number 96," said one indignant viewer, "is a few sordid scenes strung together by cliches."

Other phone callers thought the acting was about on a par with a Christmas pantomime played and produced by inhabitants of a primary school.

"They say the show is keeping actors in work," said a male voice — which sounded as though it belonged to an actor. "I reckon they would be doing the public a service by digging ditches instead." And some people liked the show. One woman said: "I know that's how they go on in Paddington. I used to live there, and I could tell you a lot more."

My opinion remains unaltered. I said, after sitting through a morning watching several episodes, that Number 96 would not win any awards. But it will score well in the ratings. And Monday night's premiere will probably have the highest ratings in Channel Ten's history.

Only one person I spoke to did not watch the show. And he was an out-of-work actor who spent the night drowning his sorrows in a pub.

it went to air we just sat there. There was this stony silence from my ex-husband, my mother and myself and when it finished I just got up. I didn't even ask them what they thought of it. I just thought, *this is a dog.* And I thought, *well Elaine, you've been in flops before so you just ride it through, you know, so what's new?*

RITA JAMES (wife of Joe James): The first night that *Number 96* went to air, a group of us was at our unit in Bronte. We all sat and watched the television and they were all cheering and thinking it was wonderful. So then they decided they'd all ring up Channel 10 and say how much they enjoyed it and pretend that they were the public, trying to get the ratings up. It was Joe Hasham's idea to ring up.

TED JOBBINS (floor manager): When it went to air, the first week it wiped the arse off everything on television and everyone

above: After its initial screening in Sydney, this scene featuring Mark Eastwood's attempt at seducing his pregnant wife was cut

bottom: The infamous nudity clause. Courtesy Elaine Elliott

opposite top: Hippies played by Chard Hayward and Cathy Jones strip off in Lucy Sutcliffe's laundrette

opposite bottom: Johnny Lockwood, as Aldo, in the bath

Control Board orders censorship of sexy Australian TV show

was so amazed. It came in, I think, at mid-thirties, which was an unheard of rating in those days and it maintained it right through the week. Kerry Packer from Channel 9 sent a telegram to the manager at Channel 10 saying 'Congratulations. You've beaten us this week'.

When the series debuted on Tuesday March 14 in Melbourne, the Broadcasting Control Board had cut controversial scenes. One deleted scene showed Martin Harris as Mark attempting to seduce his pregnant wife, Helen, played by Briony Behets. Two other scenes featured Martin Harris with Vivienne Garrett.

Dear Sir,

Following examination of the programme "Number 96" televised by station TEN on Monday, 13th March, the Board has directed me to inform you that three scenes in the programme are regarded as being entirely unsuitable for television. The first scene, early in the programme, showed Mark the husband, attempting to put his hand up the dress of his pregnant wife; the other two scenes showed Mark in bed with the daughter of the local grocer.

VIVIENNE GARRETT: It was the first episode and I was found in bed with Martin Harris. I was the slutty little girl from the delicatessen who had been swept off her feet by this school teacher who'd moved in with his young pregnant wife. Oh dear! And while she'd been at the shops I ducked into his room and we'd had sex.

One issue which confronted many of the actors was the well-publicised nudity clause in their contracts, which stated that if the script called for it the actor had to disrobe.

7. If, for legitimate and dramatic reasons, the producers are convinced that a scene demands that the Artist should appear nude within the realms of good taste and within the restrictions of the Australian Broadcasting Control Board, the Artist agrees so to do. Such appearances would never to full frontal nude shots and all such scenes would be shot in a closed set.

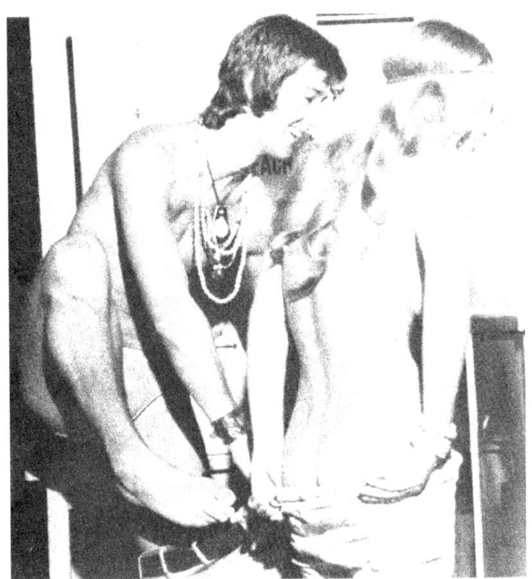

VIVIENNE GARRETT: So we're about to do this scene and I didn't know that my breasts were going to be exposed. Bill Harmon came up to me and said, 'When [Briony] walks into the room I want you to jump up and let the sheet drop and we want to see your breasts.' I looked at Martin and I looked at Bill Harmon and I went, 'You're kidding?'

DAVID SALE: Bill said, 'If they go to bed, we see them getting undressed, if they hop into the shower, again, we see them nude.'

VIVIENNE GARRETT: We were all made aware of the nudity clause. I wasn't naïve about the nudity clause, but when I spoke to my agent she said, 'There are certain things that the censors won't allow,' but I think they allowed a lot more than we thought they would.

LYNN RAINBOW (actress): There was never any problem. I was brought up in a family where the body was a body and nothing to get your knickers in a twist over. So I don't think it totally registered that I'd actually signed a nudity clause. It didn't bother me. Pretty soon after, we were going topless on the beach. It never bothered me.

JOE JAMES (actor): I think everybody had to sign it. Even Johnny Lockwood.

JOHNNY LOCKWOOD (actor): I came out of the cinema one day and saw the newspaper headlines. It said 'Aldo strips at last'.

ELISABETH KIRKBY (actress): I did *not* have a nudity clause in my contract.

JAMES ELLIOTT (actor): The nudity clause was something I wasn't asked to sign and my agent told me I would probably be the last card in the pack to be looked at in the bollocky.

ABIGAIL (actress): Nudity has never worried me. When we were discussing the nudity clause in our contracts at the start of *Number 96* there were some actresses who said the whole business was diabolical, but I didn't have any hesitation in signing. I felt there was just too much fuss.

VIVIENNE GARRETT: When people think of *Number 96* they think of Abigail, but mine were the first breasts ever shown on Australian television and very few people know that. It's been wonderfully disguised and I'm very happy about that [*laughs*].

ELAINE LEE: We'd get our scripts two weeks in advance and for a week I stewed on this one scene where I had to be nude. I said to Garth [Meade], my then husband, 'I can't do it.' And I said to Bill Harmon, 'Look, I'm really sorry about this, I know I've signed a contract, but I'm going to have to break it.'

NORMAN YEMM (actor): The day we were going to shoot the scene where I had to rip the nightie off Elaine Lee — and you really didn't see anything at all — we were sitting there and she said to Bill, 'I don't think I can do it.' And then I started to get a bit apprehensive — I've got to take *my* clothes off on television.

ELAINE LEE: I'd given my notice but Bill wouldn't accept it. I said, 'Well, I can't do the scene.' So he said, 'I promise you it'll be an absolutely closed set.' Bill was true to his word. It was an absolutely closed set apart from the cameraman, the wardrobe girl, Norman and I, and Bill.

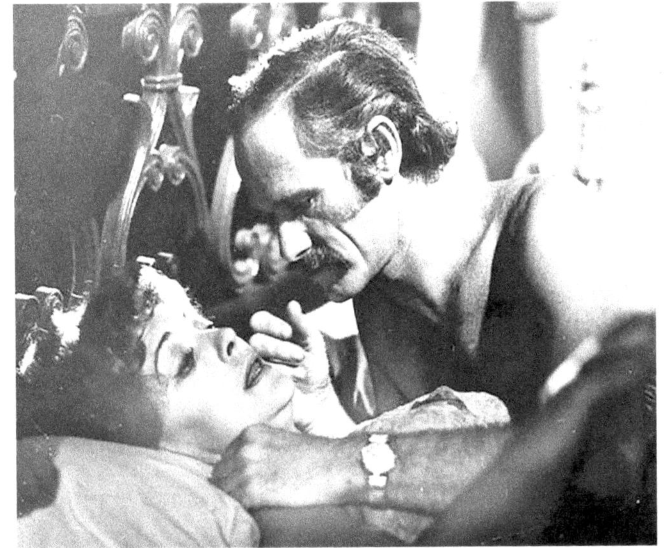

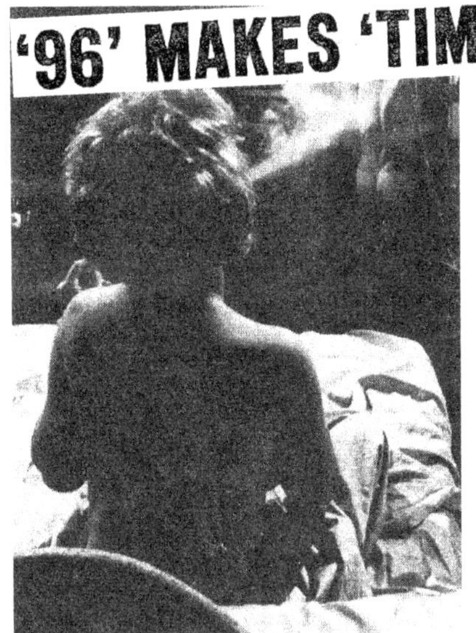

opposite: Abigail was one of many stars who signed the often-exercised nudity clause

top left: Elaine Lee and Norman Yemm as estranged husband and wife Vera and Harry Collins. Courtesy NFSA

top right: *Number 96* even made the headlines in *Time* magazine for its provocative content

BRIAN PHILLIS (director): The closed sets were a formality in name only. Visitors were asked to leave the studio, but every TV monitor inside Channel 10 was tuned in loud and clear while a scene was being shot.

NORMAN YEMM: The funny part is, in Queensland I think, there was a dentist up there who was anti-pornography — anti anything that was against the rules — and when the show went to air in Brisbane they put a black strip across my backside, which is strange because you only see me with my back to the camera, in a long shot, just getting into my dressing gown and it's something that one had to laugh about more than anything.

The scene causing so much concern for Lee and Yemm (and the dentist) was controversial, not just because of the nudity, but because it depicted the taboo subject of rape in marriage. The storyline made news in *Time* magazine and caused more headaches for the censors. Rape was just one of a wide range of taboo subjects that *Number 96* would depict on our screens.

VIVIENNE GARRETT: [There was a scene in which] Rose was being gang raped by a group of bikies. When we came to film it

top: Vivienne Garrett, as Rose Godolfus, often played the victim

bottom: Joe James as Gordon Vansard

opposite left: A nude scene featuring Ron Shand

opposite right: Part of a memo from the Broadcasting Control Board ordering a deletion

I took actor Vince Gil aside and said, 'I have problems in doing this scene.' We'd rehearsed the scene and the director said, 'Rose is really enjoying this.' I said, 'Sorry, no way,' and I shut the set down basically, with the support of Vince and a couple of the other guys. Anyway, they re-wrote the scene and we shot it with Rose as a victim, being abused and hurt.

In future episodes Rose would find herself pregnant, which brought the controversial issue of abortion into the storyline. Joe James, as Gordon Vansard, was also embroiled in this hot topic.

LYNN RAINBOW: Everybody used to say Joe James's character was the chemist. I said, 'No, no, I was the chemist. He was the struck-off doctor.'

JOE JAMES: I was a struck-off doctor who performed abortions, apparently.

The pro-abortion storyline came at a time when the practice was still illegal in many parts of the country, and resulted in irate church groups picketing the front of Channel 10. More taboo situations were tackled in other early episodes, once again involving troubled Rose Godolfus.

VIVIENNE GARRETT: I was always playing the victim. Things happened to Rose. She was the girl that got hooked on marijuana. I did a scene where I was supposed to be stoned. I'll never forget it. I played the whole scene like I was stoned. In the delicatessen.

The Broadcasting Control Board stepped in once again. Rose was not permitted to be shown enjoying the marijuana. It was from this point — for the first time in the history of Australian television — that the Control Board invoked Section 101 of the *Broadcasting and Television Act*.

KEVIN POWELL (production manager): I remember, at one point in *Number 96*, we got to the stage where maybe things had been taken a little beyond the thin red line as far as the powers that be in the government departments were concerned and they slammed us down. I think it was called a 101, which meant that every single episode had to be viewed before it could go to air.

TOM GREER: We were, at one point, censored and they sent this darling religious man up from Melbourne every week, from the Control Board. The first thing I said to our people was, 'We'll introduce him to the glamour of show business.' So we did. We took him on a tour of the studio and he met some of the loveliest people, like Pat McDonald and Joe Hasham.

JAMES ELLIOTT: The censorship people were always watching very carefully that we didn't overstep the mark. Swearing was not allowed. Even mild swearing such as 'bugger' and 'damn' and so on. They weren't allowed in those days.

TOM GREER: For the censorship guy's first couple of trips we didn't make it too hard for him with what was in the content, but he'd see a week's worth of tapes and of course he'd get involved with the story. We just got around him. There were a couple of times when he'd be sitting in there watching and a few awkward things would come up. When they did — like a word or something — the tea trolley would arrive: clack, clack, clack, clack, bang, bang, bang. It really was a case of total distraction. It was rehearsed.

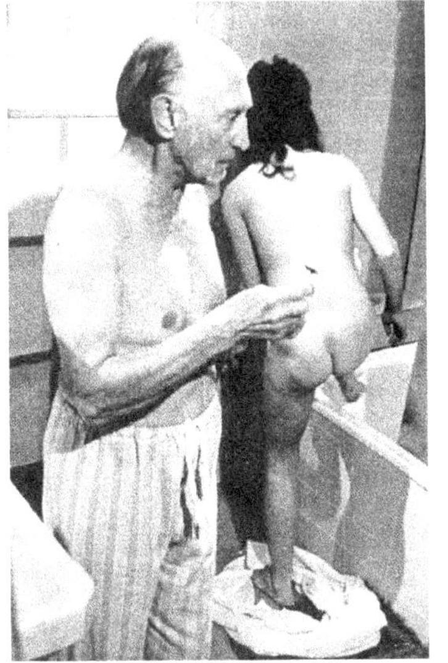

SHEILA KENNELLY (actress): With the blow-up sex doll that Herb was trying to flog, Megan McGlashan, one of the

EPISODE 373 MAY BE TELEVISED SUBJECT TO THE FOLLOWING DELETION:

SCENE: SUTCLIFFE'S KITCHED ARNOLD, ALF AND LUCY FIRST SEGMENT OF EPISODE DELETE THE EXPRESSION 'GET STUFFED' UTTERED BY ALF.

STAR NUDE IN BLACK MASS SCENE

ONE of Australia's leading actresses has stripped for a black mass scene in the 0-10 Network's **Number 96.**

The actress is Elaine Lee, who appears in the soap opera serial as fortune teller and mystic Vera Collins.

The nude scene is the latest in a long series which have been featured in the controversial program.

The black mass scene was filmed last week at the Sydney studios of TEN10.

Before shooting began producers ordered everyone not connected with the series to be cleared from the studio. Press photographers were not allowed to attend.

The scene shows Elaine (as Vera Collins) entering into a black mass ceremony conducted by a high priest, played by Peter Reynolds.

Vera is wearing a long, sheer robe and is apparently in a deep hypnotic trance.

As she enters the black mass circle, comprising Toni Lamond (Karen Winters) and Alastair Duncan (a hypnotist), the "high priest" reaches out and slips the robe from her shoulders, showing her to be naked.

TV WEEK understands that executives of the 0-10 Network were uncertain about including scenes of such strange rituals in the series.

They gave the go-ahead after insisting that not all of the actors and actresses should appear in the nude, as normally happens in black mass ceremonies.

For several weeks TEN10's art director John Northcote did extensive research on black masses and re-created the location for such a ceremony in the channel's Sydney studios.

For Elaine Lee the nude scene was her second since she began appearing in the series at the start of the year.

Her first was in an early episode when she was involved in a love scene with her estranged husband, played by former **Homicide** actor Norman Yemm. — **TONY FAWCETT.** #

● **Elaine Lee . . . in the raw.**

OCTOBER 21, 1972—TV WEEK—Page 5

above and opposite: Articles discussing a scene depicting witchcraft and nudity

producer's assistants, tells a lovely story. She said, 'The era was still quite prudish because even though it was only a blow-up rubber doll they had to paint undies on it according to the censors.' So, although there was all this nudity, it wasn't allowed to be full frontal even on a rubber doll.

Further risqué content was followed by more complaints. One storyline in particular was the last straw and led to *Number 96* remaining under Control Board scrutiny for two years.

DAVID SALE: I was due to go to London for the publication of *The Love Bite*, my second novel, when I put this idea up at a story conference. We'd heard about the Cross and all this Rosaleen Norton stuff in the past. And I'd read *Rosemary's Baby* and loved it. So we had this thing with the witch moving in. I was practically on the way to the airport. My bags were packed and I was waiting for a taxi, and I rang Bill and said, 'When you're casting that witch, we don't want a Morticia with black hair and all this sort of thing.' I said, 'Get Toni Lamond to do it.'

ELAINE LEE: I loved all that black magic stuff. I mean, as an actress I loved the drama of it. For weeks Vera'd been trying to give up cigarettes, so she went to this hypnotist who happened to be the head of a coven — Vera didn't know that, of course.

BLACK MASS SEGMENT WAS NOT GOOD TASTE!

Jerry Fetherston warns Number 96 producers

ELAINE LEE, in a hypnotic trance, steps towards the altar and begins reciting the Lord's Prayer backwards.

Slowly the robe slips from her shoulders and she crumples to the floor behind a discreetly held cloak.

It is, of course, the now notorious black mass scene from **Number 96**—the scene

beyond the bounds of good taste.

That may be, although I did not find the particular segment offensive. Just ridiculous.

The writers have shrewdly stirred every social issue,

Vera read the Tarot cards and was quite psychic and susceptible, so the coven was able to influence her and decided that they were going to use her for this black mass.

The day of taping — in October 1972 — was Friday the 13th.

ABIGAIL: At times it was quite amusing. I was almost naked and on cue two boys were meant to lift me onto the altar slab. The cue was meant to come from Elaine who was drinking from the so-called blood cup, but the boys kept missing it. I would have to jab one of them in the thigh each time to get them moving.

ELAINE LEE: Toni Lamond and I got the giggles. We laughed and laughed, we couldn't stop, because wardrobe had made this conical-shaped hat — it wasn't very good — for the High Priest character and he was supposed to be nude, but of course he had his underpants on and they were really baggy old daks. I had to get down and kiss his feet and he had really dirty toenails! When he came on with this conical hat I said, 'It looks like Noddy,' and I just went off.

ABIGAIL: When I was finally placed on the altar, Peter Reynolds, who played the Grand Master, was to chant various incantations while holding this great sword over me. Unfortunately, he kept forgetting his lines, would turn around to get prompted and forget about the sword. It nearly went through the skin. By the time he got around to the chanting he had such a peculiar lilt to

NAKED SACRIFICE ON BLACK FRIDAY:

SATAN COMES TO NO. 96!

IT was Friday the 13th and in the studios of Sydney's Channel 10 weird things were happening.

An episode of **Number 96** was being recorded — an episode that was eyebrow-raising even for that trendy show.

In the station's Studio A, an altar had been erected, and around it several of the show's leading stars were taking part in a black mass.

Draped naked across the altar was the curvaceous Abigail, who plays Bev the perennial virgin.

Poised above her was a sword wielded by the high priest of the mass, played by Peter Reynolds, dressed in his robes of office.

To the side was Elaine Lee, who plays Vera Collins, and she wasn't to be outdone by Abigail.

For as the action began the clothes slowly fell from Elaine's body, revealing her naked also.

And fluttering around in the background was none other than the former darling of Melbourne television, Toni Lamond, muttering incantations and revelling in her role as procurer of virgins.

As the scene got under way the extras leaped and danced to jungle rhythms, taking care not to burn their robes on the flickering candles.

Onlookers were ushered from the studio during the crucial moments of filming, to save the naked actresses from embarrassment.

In the Channel 10 boardroom, specially invited members of the Press had a birds-eye view of the goings on through the transmitting monitor.

For nearly an hour Abigail lay naked on the altar while the scene was being shot and re-shot.

The studio rang with nervous laughter as the cast went through their paces. Although the feeling was light-hearted, a general uneasiness could be sensed.

Most of the stars denied being superstitious, but several of them had said prayers in the dressing-room before being called on to the set.

The idea of filming a black mass on Friday the 13th had some of them worried.

Before the scenes were filmed, TV WEEK spoke with Abigail, who admitted being nervous during rehearsals.

"I don't personally worry about these things as a rule," she said, "although I was upset at rehearsal when Peter Reynolds was holding that dagger over me.

"The dagger is very heavy and sharp — and we were all laughing a bit while rehearsing. If he had dropped it I would have been in trouble.

"It's a coincidence that we were filming the scene on Friday the 13th, and I suppose it's a bit eerie."

Before the scene Abigail slipped into the dressing-room and changed into a flesh-colored bikini, which was removed for the filming.

She was wrapped in a blue silk sheet and lifted on to the velvet altar, her waist-length blonde hair trailing on the ground.

The set had been constructed and modelled on the real setting of a black mass.

The set designer, John Northcote, had spent hours researching in libraries and studying books on witchcraft to authentically reproduce the mystic setting.

Beside the altar was an ornate gold throne and a table equipped with a long leather whip and a silver goblet containing red wine — in place of human blood.

The studio lights were dimmed and the candles lit

Page 6—TV WEEK—NOVEMBER 4, 1972

while extras in their floor-length black capes shuffled around waiting for their cues.

Elaine Lee stood nervously on the sidelines, obviously wishing it was all over.

"I am tremendously worried about this particular scene," she said. "As Vera Collins I play as a mystic and I really identify with the character. I couldn't play Vera if I weren't like her.

"I have brought all sorts of lucky charms with me today — just to keep me calm.

"I don't believe in black magic, but I do definitely believe in the supernatural.

"In the scene I walk on to the set fully dressed, and my clothing is removed before they dress me in my long robe.

"I prefer it if the set is closed when I have to do a nude scene, as I get very embarrassed.

"In the black mass I am supposed to get very worked up and frenzied.

"I'm not really looking forward to doing the scene, but I feel it is essential to the plot of **Number 96**. I wouldn't do it otherwise."

Another cast member who was particularly worried about the black mass scene was Toni Lamond.

She is playing the role of Bev's flatmate who, through hypnotherapy, procures Abigail as the sacrificial virgin.

"I am genuinely worried about the filming," Toni said, "because I have strong feelings about dabbling in things we don't really understand.

"In one scene I had to recite the Lord's Prayer backwards, which upset me very much.

"In fact I have been so concerned that I contacted a friend of mine, clairvoyant Fiona McCallum, and asked her for some advice on how to cope.

"Fiona is very good, and gave me some helpful tips on how to get through it. She said that as long as we were just saying the words, and not feeling any malevolence, everything should be all right.

● ABOVE: Abigail on the altar awaiting sacrifice with Peter Reynolds, Alistair Duncan and Elaine Lee.

● RIGHT: Peter Reynolds as the Grand Master, with Alistair Duncan as the hypnotherapist, Elaine Lee as the medium, and Toni Lamond as the hypnotherapist's assistant.

"She suggested I say a few prayers, and she will be praying for me too.

"But I still find the whole thing very unsettling. I will be very glad when it's all over."

The associate producer of **Number 96**, Ted Jobbins, told TV WEEK that the black mass scene had not upset the cast unduly.

"I think most of them are amused rather than worried about the scene," he said.

"As far as the cast is concerned it's just another job. It is all being treated very light-heartedly, even if it is Friday the 13th." #

NOVEMBER 4, 1972 TV WEEK—Page 7

above: Another article about the infamous 'black mass' scene

opposite left: Ronne Arnold as Chad Farrell. Courtesy Mick Pratt

opposite middle: Lynn Rainbow as Sonia. Courtesy Mick Pratt

opposite right: Chad and Sonia share a groundbreaking kiss

his voice that it was hilarious. It cracked me up. I was trying to keep rigidly still while my body heaved with laughter.

ELAINE LEE: In the middle of a scene I'd be doing something and then go into this hypnotic trance and start speaking in a strange tongue. Michael Boddy wrote the script and I remember it clearly because I was so angry with him. Literally, on the page of the script was something like 'oobli goobli doobli'. I said, 'I'm not doing that. That's ridiculous.' So my ex-husband, who spoke Xhosa very well, just plucked out some African words. Some of them were *filthy*.

DAVID SALE: It was the most unpopular storyline ever. Nobody believed it went on, but it did. They didn't want to know about it. It was too unsettling.

Once again *Number 96* created outrage and divided critics and viewers alike. The Control Board ordered the scenes be deleted and today it seems none of the black mass footage survives.

The series tackled some other pertinent social issues, including racism. During this storyline another groundbreaking moment came in episode 33, with an interracial kiss between Ronne Arnold as Chad Farrell and Lynn Rainbow as Sonia.

LYNN RAINBOW: I think Ronne was quite nervous because he was mostly known as a dancer and hadn't really done much television acting, but he was very good. He's also very good looking and we shared a romantic moment in *Number 96*.

RONNE ARNOLD (actor): Lynn Rainbow was a wonderful and exciting actor to work with. As far as the kiss with Lynn is concerned, it was very natural and real because of our friendship. At first, the thought of it was extremely difficult due to the social situation in Australia. Once it was aired and generally accepted by the viewing audience we both realised it had made an important impact on racism in Australia, and possibly helped to forge greater tolerance of interracial relationships.

DAVID SALE: At the time, you could never have done that sort of storyline on American television. The Midwest Bible Belt would've been up in arms, but we could get away with it. And we did it with a twist. Everyone would've expected Dorrie

Evans to be a bit racist, but we made it so she thought of Chad as a gentleman. You know, he carried her washing up the stairs for her and that sort of thing, and she just thought he was wonderful.

NORMAN YEMM: Ronne Arnold, now there's a delightful guy. I'd worked with Ronne at the Princess Theatre and then met him again in *Number 96*. I had to call him a black bastard or something or other, and I kept apologising and he'd say, 'You're an actor, aren't you?' I didn't want to insult him.

RONNE ARNOLD: Norman Yemm as Harry Collins the racist was very confronting to both of us, at first. Norman constantly said to me, 'Ronne, this is very difficult behaving this way to you.' It was also difficult for me, as we had both become very close and good friends when we performed in the stage musical *Most Happy Fella* in Melbourne. But we both overcame that and performed the situation even better. The other thing that also helped us during the filming was the audience's acceptance of me, as a character, and dislike of Harry Collins for being so unkind to me.

In August 1972, the series dealt with breast cancer. Despite all the sex, scandal and nudity, this storyline would prove to strike the biggest chord with viewers.

ELISABETH KIRKBY: The episodes that gave me the most satisfaction as an actor were the episodes that dealt with Lucy's suspected breast cancer and the relief that was felt by the occupants of *Number 96* — and all the viewers — when the biopsy proved Lucy's lump was benign. I was told at the time that the ratings on the night when the result of the biopsy went to air were over fifty. That kind of rating had never been achieved previously, except for certain sporting fixtures.

ELEANOR WITCOMBE (writer): It was a very good scene to write, where Lucy thought she had breast cancer and was afraid. I remember that as one of the best scenes Jimmy Elliott played.

opposite top and middle: Despite on-screen acrimony, Ronne Arnold and Norman Yemm were great friends

opposite bottom: Elisabeth Kirkby as the beloved Lucy

JAMES ELLIOTT: Because the show was so popular we could introduce a certain amount of informative stuff. Women actually discussed breast cancer on television and what to do about it. This was the sort of thing that *Number 96* could do very well and every now and again it did.

ELISABETH KIRKBY: I was told that after Lucy's breast cancer scare there was a noticeable increase in women going for mammograms. There were many other storylines that dealt with important social issues, but they were never given the prominence of the sex scenes.

TOM OLIVER (actor): It was the same with Norman Yemm's character; they showed both sides of the coin. When Norman Yemm's character was persuaded by Elaine Lee, who played Vera his wife, to go to AA — Alcoholics Anonymous — it had an immediate effect. Norman started getting these letters from wives and from husbands about their partners, saying thank you for portraying it like that. They'd tell him how they'd been trying to get their husband or wife to go to AA for years and how *Number 96* had helped them take it on board and actually start going to AA meetings. It had those wonderful side benefits that nobody ever knew anything about.

Another of those important social issues that was depicted in *Number 96* was male homosexuality, which in 1972 was still a crime.

PAUL WEINGOTT (actor): It did bring homosexuality between two men to the fore. I'd have to look into it, but maybe that was the beginning of something for the Australian gay community. It was still illegal.

JOE HASHAM (actor): My parents thought it was an okay program and were very proud that their son was on national television. That was, until the episode where Don confessed to Bev — Abigail — that he was a homosexual. There was what I can only describe as stunned silence. It took Mum and Dad a

above: A magazine cover warmly welcoming the depiction of gay characters onto Australian television

few weeks to accept the fact that I was playing a gay character, but after a while, when it became obvious that the character was having a marked influence on the way Australians perceived gays, my parents became very proud of their crusading son.

BOB HUBER (producer): To present a young man as normal and loved, as Joe Hasham was, was quite daring and it worked. It really worked.

TOM OLIVER: Joe Hasham would have letters — fan mail — from doctors, lawyers. He would have letters saying thank you for portraying a homosexual that way and I think on some occasions it prompted people to come out.

PAUL WEINGOTT: Joe portrayed Don as a pretty regular sort of guy and I don't think I played Bruce any differently. So it made people think.

JOE HASHAM: I can only recall positive viewer reaction. The Australian viewing public took the character of Don Finlayson to their hearts. There was a survey taken, by Sydney University I think, which showed that *Number 96*, and specifically the character of Don Finlayson, did more for the gay-lib movement than all the gay-lib movements put together. This, of course, is testament to the genius of David Sale and the producers of the show.

DAVID SALE: We had two gay guys living together, but we didn't see them doing anything.

TED JOBBINS: There were executives at Channel 10 who were very homophobic. One in particular thought it was disgusting that we even had two gay guys in the show, let alone anything happening. Now, there were instructions — fine, they were in it, but they weren't allowed to touch, they were never allowed to be in bed together and everything had to be all above board.

TOM GREER: We had the homosexual stuff, which didn't get too much copy because, while it showed that homosexuals could also be ordinary, very straight acting members of the community, the press didn't like to talk about that sort of thing. It was a bit taboo, that subject.

DAVID SALE: At one stage Channel 10 wanted us to turn Don straight. I said to Bill, 'It's impossible; it can't just happen like that. It's ridiculous.' And he went back to them and said, 'You turn Don straight and we go to Channel 9.'

JOE HASHAM: They protected the character of Don and were very careful not to put him in harm's way.

ELEANOR WITCOMBE: It had to do with integrity. Nobody has ever thought of *Number 96* with integrity, but I'll tell you what, it wouldn't have been what it was if there wasn't integrity in the professionalism of the people concerned.

In contrast to the gay characters, young heterosexual characters who fell in love became cause for celebration and front page news. June 1972 saw *Number 96*'s first wedding. In episode 78, wayward Rose Godolfus married a respectable Jewish doctor, Julian Myers, played by Lew Luton.

VIVIENNE GARRETT: We had this wedding. I had the wedding gown fittings. It was a beautiful dress. It was blue, pale blue, because I was tainted. I was second-hand Rose. I couldn't be in white.

TOM GREER: That was a beauty, the Rose Godolfus wedding. We decided to run a press reception and to bring journalists to the wedding. So we ran a wedding reception in the ballroom at the Sebel Townhouse. Now, remember Godolfus was poor. We ran a lavish wedding, you know, fit for royalty. The Godolfuses couldn't afford this.

AT the reception (from left): Lucy (Elisabeth Kirkby), Alf (James Elliott), Mrs Lubinski (Phillipa Baker), Aldo (Johnny Lockwood), Rose (Vivienne Garrett), Julian (Lew Luton), Janie (Robyn Gurney), Jack (Tom Oliver), Claire (Thelma Scott).

WEDDING BELLS FOR No. 96'S ROSE

above: Rose Godolfus weds Julian Myers in *Number 96*'s first big wedding. Courtesy Elaine Elliott

opposite: A news article reports on the TV wedding as if it were real. Courtesy Joe James

With 250 guests, the wedding reception was a great success and no wonder, its budget was reported to be $5000 (approximately $55,000 in today's money).

VIVIENNE GARRETT: We had worked all day shooting the wedding. Then we had to go to this reception. They spent a lot of money and we had to do this mock wedding at the Sebel Townhouse where they had this cavalcade and people lining up and waving and stuff like that. I said, 'Do I have to go?'

TOM GREER: We had a fleet of ten Mercedes Benz in maroon. They drove in convoy to the wedding reception. The bride arrived in her gown with the groom and they sat at a banquet table with all the guests around. We had telegrams from the prime minister and famous people from overseas, which I think

Sucking pigs and caviare — and the band played 'Second Hand Rose' — at the $5000 5½ hour champagne spree — with hangovers to follow

96 fantasy went the whole hog

From ALAN VEITCH IN SYDNEY

Rose, the bride of just two hours, was already two months pregnant so, quite appropriately, the wedding reception band played "Second Hand Rose."

Such was the send-up theme of Australia's strangest non-wedding — the television nuptials of Rose Godolphus and Dr Julian Myer, two characters in "Number 96."

- Above, the "bride" and "groom," played by Vivienne Garrett and Lew Luton, at the reception.
- Left the "bride" tosses her bouquet Lynn Rainbow at the reception
- Far left the "bride" and "Dorrie Evans" played by Pat McDonald

Johnny Whyte and David Sale wrote. We had the cutting of the cake and the wedding toast. We had bridal marches and the whole bit.

VIVIENNE GARRETT: Peter Carrette was the photographer and I can remember he was there. He offered me a little toke on a joint out the back of the Sebel. I remember having a puff. I didn't get off my face, but I remember thinking the only way I was going to survive the night was to enjoy it and that's when I loosened up.

TOM GREER: The only thing was, when we showed this enormous, beautiful buffet there were two whopping big pigs' heads in the middle, for a Jewish wedding!

ARNOLD GETS A SHINER IN PUNCH-UP

NUMBER 96 TURNS TO VIOLENCE!

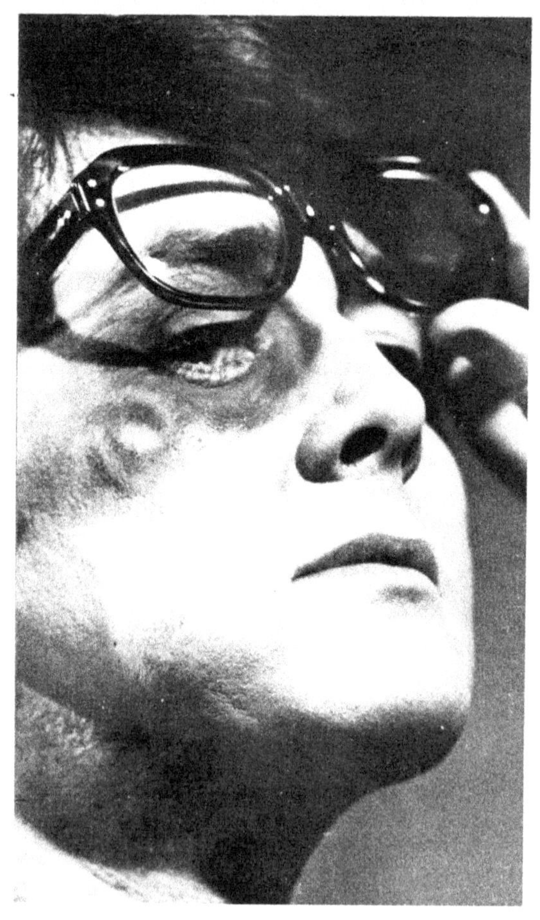

Chapter 4

What's Going to Happen Next?

above: Jeff Kevin as punctilious Arnold Feather was a potential suspect in the early whodunit storyline featuring the kinky Knicker Snipper

opposite: Mark Hashfield was Abigail's partner in real life and Alan Cotterell, the Knicker Snipper, on *Number 96*. Courtesy Mick Pratt

THELMA SCOTT (actress): We had plenty of cliffhangers. That was the whole idea keeping it going.

JEFF KEVIN (actor): The biggest ratings were to do with the whodunits, like the Knicker Snipper — that sort of thing.

DAVID SALE (writer): Johnny Whyte and I loved those sort of Agatha Christie whodunits. So, we introduced them.

SHEILA KENNELLY (actress): Those scripts were so good. Now I've never been in a show that generated such a serious reaction before.

The Knicker Snipper was the first big, sexually loaded mystery at *Number 96*. This outrageous storyline had an unknown prowler sneaking about the building cutting holes in the female tenants' underwear. These cliffhanger episodes became an audience guessing game, and viewers remained on tenterhooks not knowing when the infamous maniac would strike again.

JEFF KEVIN: Arnold was going to come in for three weeks and I think, at that stage, there was some idea that he was going to be the Knicker Snipper.

DAVID SALE: We didn't know who it was. Whoever was in the episodes that week, we'd have things happening to them. How the Knicker Snipper got into the flats and everything, we didn't know. Things just happened.

JOHNNY LOCKWOOD (actor): At least four or five RSL clubs in Sydney had notices out: 'Number 96 — we will announce the identity of the Knicker Snipper'.

JEFF KEVIN: There were bets taken and announcements were made in clubs across the country when it was revealed, so people could actually collect on whoever it was.

DAVID SALE: When we finally decided, it was because we wanted to, shall we say, dispense with the services of whoever was Abigail's boyfriend in the show — who was Abigail's boyfriend in real life — so we just made him the Knicker Snipper. Then people said, 'Oh we knew it was him all the time.' *We* didn't know, not until we came to write the episodes.

TOM OLIVER (actor): Mark Hashfield, Abigail's partner, played a character who seemed all okey-dokey above board. The ladies were finding that their panties were getting snipped and I think they found him under the bed or something with several pairs of panties. They were wild storylines. They really were [*laughs*].

In episode 140, after four weeks of torment, the identity of the Knicker Snipper was finally revealed. The culprit, Alan Cotterell, played by Mark Hashfield, had at one point — in an effort to throw viewers off the scent — organised a vigilante group among the residents of *Number 96* to try and catch the offender. The cliffhanger element of *Number 96* was an enticing device and used to great effect. But maintaining secrecy was seen as crucial in order to keep people watching.

'I think they found him under the bed or something with several pairs of panties. They were wild storylines.'

JEFF KEVIN: We were always sworn to secrecy, in terms of scripts, because we'd have them for so many weeks ahead. You were on an honour sort of thing when you were being interviewed to never give the storylines away.

JOHNNY LOCKWOOD: My doctor used to ring me and say, 'Can you tell me what happens for the next month? I've got to go to England for a conference.' I'd say, 'I'll tell you when you get back.'

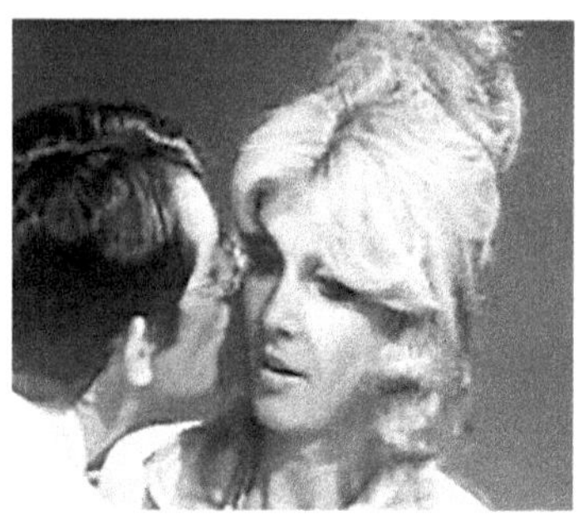

above: Arnold Feather attempts to kiss Les Girls legend Carlotta as Robyn Ross. In order to conceal her identity, Carlotta was billed as Carolle Lea in the closing credits of the show

It was never more important to keep storylines secret than when Carlotta joined the *Number 96* cast. The portrayal of a transgender character on television was another world first, and the producers were determined to keep Carlotta's identity a secret so as not to give away the plot.

JEFF KEVIN: I can't remember how many people in the wider world would've known that Carlotta was transgender. I remember Johnny Lockwood running around saying, 'Cor, look at that. Gorgeous.' He had the hots for her and we were all looking at him saying, 'Don't you know?' But he didn't know. So, maybe other people didn't know either.

CARLOTTA (actress): I had an interview with Bill Harmon. He told me the storyline and away we went, but they wanted to keep it a secret. They didn't want the plot to get out so they kept me in a hidden dressing room.

LYNN RAINBOW (actress): Carlotta! That was very risqué. I don't think she was allowed to go into the canteen for lunch. They took her lunch on a tray into her tiny little cubicle dressing room. They were trying to keep it under wraps as much as possible.

JEFF KEVIN: Of course, Arnold didn't know and that was the big thing. He'd fallen in love with this character, Miss Ross, who turned out to be Mr Ross. There was a scene where that was revealed.

At certain times the producers of *Number 96* would order a closed set and at one point they banned all press from the studio — there are varying reports as to how well-enforced this rule was.

DAVID SALE: At one stage the newspaper critic, Veritas, who was our sworn enemy — he used to knock it every week — got hold of the synopses for the week and he printed it all. He was basically saying, *there, now you don't have to watch it.* It didn't make a tad of difference.

As well as nightly cliffhangers, a big end-of-year cliffhanger was crucial to keeping viewers interested over the summer break. When the series resumed the following year, the cast were just as surprised as audiences to discover the outcome. For actor Joe James, 1972 ended with his character, Gordon Vansard, involved in a drunken car accident. With his life left hanging in the balance over the break, there were just enough episodes in the can for him to return in the new year lingering in a coma, before his character was killed off.

JOE JAMES (actor): It was coming up to Christmas and I said to Bill or Don — I can't remember which — 'Am I okay for next year because I'd like to make plans if I'm not going to be in it.' 'Oh yeah, yeah. Everything will be fine', I was told. Then I found out I wasn't coming back when I read it in the script. I was quite angry, so in a fit of pique I blurted this out to *TV Week* and made a big thing about it — said I was really disappointed that they'd told me I had a secure tenure and then they turned around and said I'm out. Bill was furious. He thought I'd been disloyal to the company. I had this big scene with him in his office.

'I was quite angry, so in a fit of pique I blurted this out to TV Week and made a big thing about it.'

KEN SHADIE (writer): A lot of them got their scripts with apprehension because they didn't know if they were going to be killed or strangled or thrown out of the building or wander off into the sunset. They were kept in the dark as much as anyone, I think.

JOE
IS SHOCKED
OVER 96
AXING!

ACTOR Joe James is shocked and upset at

sad to think I won't be re-joining them in the new year.
"Regular work isn't easy to

above: Joe James expressed dismay to the press at his surprise axing from the show

opposite top: (left to right) Bill Harmon, Johnny Whyte, Lynn Foster and Margaret Gowanlock

opposite bottom: Elaine Lee and Joe Hasham read a script to discover what's in store for their characters. Courtesy NFSA

DAVID SALE: Each writer would do a week's scripts — five episodes — in a block. We worked eleven weeks ahead and every eleven weeks we would have a brainstorming session on a Saturday in a hotel somewhere. We would go through each flat and offer suggestions.

KEVIN POWELL (production manager): I was over at the Ramada Inn in Crows Nest in Sydney sitting with Bill Harmon, Johnny Whyte, David Sale, Eleanor Witcombe and three or four other writers in my first writers' conference for *Number 96*, which happened every month thereafter.

KEN SHADIE: We went into the Ramada Inn or whatever at Crows Nest and had the top floor to ourselves. We were there all day around a big table and everybody would be throwing in ideas or throwing them out. Then somebody would grab an idea and run with it. These meetings were all notes taken by the secretary and hours wasted or hours spent throwing ideas around.

ELEANOR WITCOMBE (writer): There'd be about twenty to twenty-five people around this table. We'd start with coffee and tea and whatever. I think we'd start at the top flat and work to the bottom. Every so often we'd try it the other way round, but whichever flat came last in the meeting was in trouble because they would bring on the lunch, you see, round about one

o'clock. We'd all have lunch and then a long drinking session, so by five o'clock we didn't know where we were. But I must say, we managed it pretty well.

KEN SHADIE: Out of that meeting Johnny Whyte would then call you in for your set of five scripts you had to write. You'd spend all day with Johnny at his hotel over in Kings Cross and knock out the synopsis, scene by scene.

ELEANOR WITCOMBE: Johnny Whyte was a brilliant editor. So was Ken Shadie when he took over and so was Lynn Foster in the time she was doing it. They melded it all together because we worked as a team — it really all went back to the big meetings we had every five weeks.

DAVID SALE: My scripts; everybody said, 'Oh David, your scripts are so easy to learn and so easy to say,' and I said, 'That's because I say every line out loud.' You know, I sort of acted it out. And if I couldn't say a line then I'd change it.

JAMES ELLIOTT (actor): The writer's name was taken off the script. We'd be handed three or six scripts at a time and nowhere would you find the writer — that was after the show had been running for about a year or so — because the actors knew there were some good writers and some pretty awful writers.

ELAINE LEE (actress): We used to complain and say, 'We can't bear so-and-so's scripts.' They stopped putting the writers' names on the scripts, but I'd know. I'd say, 'That's David's,' or, 'That's bloody so-and-so's.' You'd know. The two best writers, I think, were Eleanor Witcombe and David, without a doubt. There was another writer, Bob Caswell, he wrote well too.

VIVIENNE GARRETT (actress): The scripts were unbelievable and I mean unbelievable, but Bob Caswell's scripts were the ones that stood out. I always knew there'd be something really sort of catastrophic or somebody'd be asked to take their clothes off — there'd always be *something* in a Bob Caswell script. He had a way of extracting the titillation or drama from the piece.

'The scripts were unbelievable and I mean unbelievable.'

JEFF KEVIN: Looking at some of the scenes today and in today's assessment, they are hilarious, especially the drama scenes. I had the good fortune to mostly play comedy, but I am in awe of people like Elaine Lee, Bettina Welch and Joe Hasham for their professionalism delivering dialogue that, in some cases, was unsayable.

TOM OLIVER: You've got to roll with the punches when they come up with those outrageous sorts of plotlines. You know, open your mouth and say the lines and try not to bump into the furniture. And try to believe what you're saying.

SHEILA KENNELLY (actress): There was a writer called Derek Strahan who was very wordy and repetitive, which made for good playing scenes, but very difficult to remember, so I always knew his. David Phillips's scripts were quite brief, but with a sharpness to them. It wasn't as sharp as David Sale's, but then there were other scripts where I really couldn't tell who'd written them.

ELEANOR WITCOMBE: I was famous for what Bill used to call tender little scenes, and wherever I could chuck in a tender little scene we'd chuck it in.

SHEILA KENNELLY: Eleanor's scenes showed particular compassion for the female characters such as Norma and Mrs Lubinski. They were written with great love, humour and depth. She really got into the skin of Norma and I loved playing her lines.

KEN SHADIE: Cash Harmon used everybody that was anybody and a lot of writers that weren't anybody came in. But they would try anybody. They had Ross Napier from radio. They had Derek Strahan. They had Eleanor Witcombe. They had Lynn Foster. They had … God they tried everybody that *The Mavis Bramston Show* tried. They had heaps of people. Michael Boddy, I remember. They had Michael Pascoe too. Bill would try anybody and Johnny would try anybody or anything. There was just a stable of writers and they just grabbed them and used them as best they could.

ELEANOR WITCOMBE: Most of the writers were ex-*Mavis Bramston Show* people and this is one of the keys to *Number 96*'s success. We all knew how to write taglines. It was essentially a tag show. A lot of writers, including some very well-known names, wanted to be in this team, but they couldn't do it.

DAVID SALE: We went through a lot of writers because, basically, a lot of them were unsuitable. If they could write drama, they couldn't do comedy. If they did a fair fist of comedy their drama was awful. We really needed somebody who could do both.

top left: Writer Eleanor Witcombe. Courtesy Eleanor Witcombe

top right: Writer Ken Shadie

bottom: Writer David Sale, adept at both drama and comedy. Courtesy Ken Shadie

ELEANOR WITCOMBE: We had a core of about five writers, David, Ken and Lynn Foster, who was a brilliant writer. She started so many things in the early days of radio. She was very good. Bob Caswell had been a gag writer for a comic, so he was into gags and tags. Michael Boddy was the full intellectual with a wonderful sense of humour and came up with some fantastic ideas.

JOE JAMES: I ended up back at *Number 96* as a writer. I knew the characters well enough to know how they'd speak. I was good on the dialogue but not good on ideas.

KEN SHADIE: Johnny Whyte was a great friend and a great mentor as far as, 'Don't worry about it. You'll handle it okay. We're all comedy writers here and we'll all band together,' was considered mentoring. So I was happy with that, but then they gave me the synopses for those first five episodes. I worked over those day and night to try and get them right. They were such sticklers for the characters and their sayings, their particular ones, that I overloaded them with that.

TED JOBBINS (floor manager): Johnny Whyte would allocate episodes to writers, but in a lot of cases, when they submitted their scripts, he would go through and change fifty percent of them. He could see points of character motivation that really weren't right, and if the script wasn't doing what he could see happening he would re-write it.

KEN SHADIE: I tried to do the Pommy accents for Alf and Lucy and I thought, *my God, can I ever handle this?* And the way Arnold Feather spoke — it had to be the way Johnny saw him. So I was pretty worried about whether this was going to work for me. I kept ringing Johnny up when I'd put the scripts in — 'Are they alright? Are they alright?' — not knowing that Johnny re-wrote everything, more or less, that landed on his lap.

'Johnny re-wrote everything, more or less, that landed on his lap.'

SHEILA KENNELLY: Johnny Whyte wrote the most hilarious scenes. They were very, very funny and David was particularly good on the drama. At the end of a scene you'd think, *oh! What's going to happen next?* And you couldn't wait for the next scripts to arrive so you'd know.

ELEANOR WITCOMBE: They were very well-constructed scenes. If anybody took it apart now they would see just how well-constructed — in a variety show type format — those scenes were. Bill Harmon used to say, 'If they don't fucking well like that scene they've only got ten seconds and then they're into the next one.'

WENDY BLACKLOCK (actress): *Number 96* was so successful because there was a really good mix of characters, so you didn't have too much of one couple. You had some scenes and then it jumped to somebody else's apartment so there were cliffhangers all the time. That kept you wanting to go back and kept the interest going.

ELEANOR WITCOMBE: We had to time it. I was with a stopwatch all the time. You had to time it exactly or Johnny would jump up and down and scream. Writing an episode was, in that way, a technically difficult thing.

KEN SHADIE: The thing that sticks in my mind about *Number 96*, writing-wise, was the bloody timing. You had twenty-two minutes or something. My wife and I would be reading the parts and trying to time the damn thing, and I'd come out at twenty-four, then she'd get twenty-one; all this sort of thing. Then I'd give it to Johnny and he'd say, 'No, this is twenty-seven.' It was all over the place, so to get the timing right was a major concern of mine.

ELEANOR WITCOMBE: You had established writers who were comedy writers, which meant they were very disciplined and could write tags, move things along and also write character. Now it's no good writing character if you haven't got actors who can play character, so thank God we got this fantastic lot of character actors.

DAVID SALE: We'd introduce characters and if they made us laugh, if we loved them, we'd bring them back, like Thelma Scott's character, Claire Houghton. We loved the whole idea of this pompous socialite.

THELMA SCOTT (actress): David Sale wrote the role for me. I was more than happy. I jumped at it. She was a very dominating lady and the daughter didn't like her.

ELAINE LEE: My ex-husband and I actually had a flat in Kirribilli and it was right next door to Thelma and Gwen Plumb. Thelma was thrilled to get the role of Abigail's mother, Mrs Houghton, who was this Point Piper sort of lady. She was very, very good and she loved being in the show, she really did. She was essentially a stage actress and she was one of the best radio actresses this country's ever seen.

top: By the end of 1972 the *Number 96* cast was well established

bottom: Thelma Scott joined the cast as Claire Houghton, a wealthy Point Piper socialite and mother of sexy Bev Houghton

Thelma Scott made her professional acting debut in 1931 at the age of eighteen. Her remarkable career covered film, television, radio and theatre. Claire Houghton was one of several characters that were introduced in the early days who made a lasting contribution to the show.

DAVID SALE: We brought in a sympathetic woman for Aldo to talk to because he was having problems with his daughter, Rose. So Roma came into the deli and they became friends.

PHILIPPA BAKER (actress): I was given a script a day or two before the interview. There was a scene with a charming, mature, cultured and sophisticated woman. I fell in love with her. I'd been playing neurotics and misfits for so long I couldn't believe I had a chance for this.

After successfully auditioning for Bill Harmon, Baker was signed to play a Russian widow.

right: Johnny Lockwood as Aldo Godolfus is joined in the deli by Philippa Baker as widow Roma Lubinski. She eventually became Mrs Godolfus. Courtesy NFSA

opposite top: Sheila Kennelly as Norma Whittaker in her trademark blonde wig. Courtesy NFSA

opposite bottom: Scottish-born actor Gordon McDougall as Les Whittaker, Norma's husband

PHILIPPA BAKER: They gave me a four-week contract. Implicit in this was the knowledge that they wrote so close to deadline in those days that if my character didn't 'work' they could drop me in a week if necessary.

DAVID SALE: Vivienne Garrett wanted to leave and we had to write Rose out. Well we had to give Aldo something, so we continued with Roma Lubinski as his love interest and it became a very charming sort of elderly love story.

JOHNNY LOCKWOOD: Philippa is a very, very fine actress apart from being a very nice lady. She was so professional and so uninhibited. It was a wonderful rapport we had between us and I think that showed.

PHILIPPA BAKER: It worked. They offered me a continuing contract. My agent said, 'You don't want to do that, it'll never run. Besides I've accepted an ABC TV play for you.' Another neurotic part. 'Get me out of it,' I said, 'I want to do *Number 96*.'

ELEANOR WITCOMBE: Philippa. She was very good. God, she was good, you know. It had to do with character writing and it brought out the best in people who had just had small roles in things. Now they had something to act. They had proper dialogue and when you can write for good actors it is fantastically satisfying.

Aspiring actress Sheila Kennelly joined the cast as barmaid Norma Whittaker, but had her doubts about being seen in a sex and sin soap opera.

‘when you can write for good actors it is fantastically satisfying.’

DAVID SALE: When she was working in the pub she always wore this big blonde wig and then when she got home she'd pull it off. It just became a thing. I don't know how that evolved. Sometimes it can just happen with the actress.

SHEILA KENNELLY: The idea of donning the blonde wig came from me. That was because I didn't want me, the serious actress, to be associated with a show like *Number 96*. I said, ‘Why don't I wear a wig?’ I forget which associate producer it was who said, ‘We'll try it.’ So in the middle of a scene I pulled the wig off and all my own black, messy hair was underneath and they thought that was hilarious. I think it might've been Bob Huber. So the wig was allowed to stay. But that was my scheme for not being completely identified with this rather shocking show.

ELEANOR WITCOMBE: Norma was a fun character. She was an upright, jolly character and I thought the relationship Sheila set up with Gordon was very good. They worked. They worked together.

Gordon McDougall had spent time working as a radio actor as well as having performed in theatres all around the country. In addition to appearing in the ABC's *Pastures of the Blue Crane*, written by Eleanor Witcombe, his television credits included a guest role in Cash Harmon's sitcom *The Group*.

SHEILA KENNELLY: I'd done a show for the ABC called *Pastures of the Blue Crane* and had a running character role in it. Gordon had a one-episode character role and when I saw that played I thought, *he's very good isn't he? Where did he come from?* It turned out to be Gordon McDougall and I played his wife in *Number 96*.

GORDON McDOUGALL (actor): I had no idea when I first went into the show that I'd be in it for so long. My agent told me a job was coming up in a new series and it just went from there.[1]

TED JOBBINS: Everybody knows a character like Les with all the junk and the crap that was in their flat. Everybody knows somebody that's a collector like that. They had to be married to someone like Norma who didn't care.

'Everybody knows a character like Les with all the junk and the crap that was in their flat.'

ELEANOR WITCOMBE: The characters in *Number 96* had dimension. I particularly liked the character Les Whittaker. Whatever happened, he was going to make a fortune.

The *Number 96* writers also introduced Les and Norma's son, Gary Whittaker, and a daughter-in-law.

SHEILA KENNELLY: They were casting the whole Whittaker set-up and they were thinking of having Gary Whittaker, the angry soldier son, marry a Vietnamese girl, but they didn't find anybody quite right so they went instead for an Italian girl.

MICHAEL FERGUSON (actor): I remember the audition. It was a one-on-one with Bill Harmon. Curiously enough I was trying out for the part of Arnold Feather, subsequently played by Jeff

left: NIDA graduate Michael Ferguson as Gary Whittaker. Courtesy Mick Pratt

right: Les and Norma Whittaker surrounded by clutter. Courtesy NFSA

Kevin. I remember Bill was very happy with my reading, but told me I wasn't nerdy enough for the part. Anyway, he said he'd find another part for me in the show, which turned out to be Gary Whittaker.

SHEILA KENNELLY: He was a problem boy. He used to beat up his wife and just generally be nasty about it. He brought a bit of conflict into Les and Norma's, rather, contented lives — a bit of drama into what was basically a comedy couple.

MICHAEL FERGUSON: I didn't know Sheila or Gordon prior to being cast in the show. They were both wonderful to work with — very supportive and professional. I had a soft spot for Sheila, she was like a mother to me. One time she had to slap me hard across the face and she simply couldn't bring herself to do it. She ended up sort of shove-punching me, which hurt a hell of a lot more and almost sent me hurtling into the next set.

SHEILA KENNELLY: We moved into a flat upstairs. Les worked at the hospital and Norma worked at the pub. The pub scenes became difficult because we had to pull real beer. All the scenes in the pub were recorded in one block. Now that meant they had to start very early in the morning because there were lots of extras and lots of scenes in the five episodes. So there I'd be pulling real beer because you couldn't fake it — ginger ale looked flat and cold tea didn't look like beer. It had to have a head on it. So it was actually pulled through genuine pipes. By about ten o'clock the actors'd be full of good will and bonhomie, the lines would be slipped and they'd say, 'Oh never mind. We'll do it again.' They'd all be quite dipsy-doodle by about midday and they might still have scenes to do from another block later on. It just didn't work. That's why they created Norma's Bar where wine was mostly served, so they could just serve coloured water and that made life a lot easier.

'They'd all be quite dipsy-doodle by about midday and they might still have scenes to do from another block later on.'

Another character who came into the show in the early days was roguish Jack Sellars, played by Tom Oliver. Tom had also had a guest role in an episode of Cash Harmon's sitcom *The Group*.

DAVID SALE: Jack Sellars came into it as a breath of fresh air and sort of stayed. Sometimes you'd think, *oh, a couple of weeks*, and then they'd take off almost without your participation. They seemed to have a life of their own.

ELEANOR WITCOMBE: Tom Oliver. He was very funny. He's a very good actor who is a funny person himself. Jack Sellars was the one who was supposed to take Abigail's virginity.

TOM OLIVER: I was paid to go to bed with some of the most gorgeous women on Australian television at the time. There was Robyn Gurney and then Abigail.

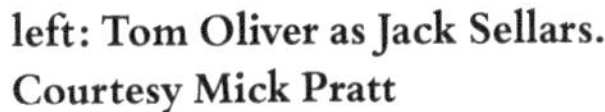
left: Tom Oliver as Jack Sellars. Courtesy Mick Pratt

right: Tom Oliver in Norma's Bar

In April 1973, Jack Sellars opened Norma's Bar at *Number 96* where the Vansard chemist once stood. In real life actor Tom Oliver and his wife Lynn Rainbow opened a bar of their own. They went into partnership with an American entrepreneur and opened Jack's Cellar Bar in Kensington, New South Wales. Both establishments featured a nude portrait of a reclining Norma.

SHEILA KENNELLY: When they wanted to have this nude painting of Norma in the bar, which was a copy of Chloe in Young and Jackson's in Melbourne — it was very similar to that. I wouldn't pose even in my undies for that. So I posed in a full-length caftan and my wig and poor Eunice Dyer, who did the painting, did the body from imagination and gave me a very nice bosom I thought — very pleasantly pointed little boobies. Very nice indeed and I was quite pleased! [*laughs*].

Owen Weingott, father of cast member Paul Weingott, had appeared in a very early episode as Maggie's husband, Victor Cameron, before being re-cast as an artist.

‘poor Eunice Dyer, who did the painting, did the body from imagination and gave me a very nice bosom I thought’

above: Owen Weingott as the artist responsible for the famous nude portrait of Norma Whittaker. Courtesy NFSA

opposite top left: Bunney Brooke as Flo Patterson. Courtesy Mick Pratt

opposite top right: Bunney Brooke with co-star Pat McDonald

opposite bottom: Jeff Kevin as Arnold Feather was as loved by fans as he was by writer Johnny Whyte. Courtesy Mick Pratt

OWEN WEINGOTT (actor): He wasn't actually mad, he was a little eccentric — let's put it that way — this artist that they wanted to paint Sheila Kennelly's character, Norma, in the nude. When they told me I said, 'You're kidding?' They said, 'No, no. You're going to paint her with her clothes on and she doesn't know, but you're going to finish up having her in the nude.' Anyway we did it and it was a lot of fun.

SHEILA KENNELLY: There was a copy made for Jack's Cellar Bar in Kensington and I've got an old black and white one — a copy with cast signatures on it.

In 1972, Bunney Brooke made her first appearance as Flo Patterson, a long-time friend of Dorrie Evans.

ELEANOR WITCOMBE: I think Patti got Bunney Brooke in because she was looking for work.

DAVID SALE: I was in the office when Pat McDonald came in. She wanted to see Bill. Johnny Whyte and I were there and she came in and said, 'Oh I'm glad I've caught you. A very dear

friend of mine,' — we didn't realise they were in an emotional relationship at that stage — 'Bunney Brooke, wants to come … I'd love Bunney to come into the show.' I said, 'I know Bunney from Melbourne and she's a very good actress.' So we had a talk about it and then came up with the character of Flo Patterson.

After a number of guest appearances, Flo earned a permanent spot in the cast and moved into flat 3 with Dorrie and Herb. She brought her pet budgie Mr Perky with her.

BUNNEY BROOKE (actress): When I first took the part, Flo was a very bitter woman. She was lonely and all she had was memories. And then the scriptwriters changed her. It was marvellous. I just followed what they wrote and it was so easy because Flo is such a believable person, someone you can identify with completely.[2]

After David Sale's initial characters had been created, script editor Johnny Whyte introduced a few of his own, including nineteen-year-old deli assistant Arnold Feather, played by twenty-seven-year-old NIDA graduate Jeff Kevin.

DAVID SALE: Johnny Whyte, I think, was actually in love with Arnold Feather.

‘Johnny Whyte, I think, was actually in love with Arnold Feather.’

TED JOBBINS: Arnold Feather was a creation purely of Johnny Whyte’s. Johnny knew exactly what he was, what he would do and would give Jeff a bad time at times.

JEFF KEVIN: Johnny completely took the role over, in a sense. He became extremely protective of the character and somewhat obsessed by it. He was a fantastic writer and he would carefully watch anything I said, and if I dared change any of the lines … It seemed to me that the line between the character and me blurred in some sort of way with Johnny. It did become quite a problem there for a little while.

TED JOBBINS: I can take credit for Don’s Aunt Amanda, Carol Raye. We were at a production storyline meeting and got to the stage where they said, ‘Look, there’s really not much more we can do with Don, storyline-wise.’ I said, ‘Why not have a girlfriend, a crazy fag-hag type girlfriend?’ I said, ‘Every queen you know knows somebody like that; these wonderful women.’ And of course Johnny said, ‘Oh, Carol would be marvellous for that,’ and it clicked and went around the room, and all of a sudden it became an aunt that comes back from overseas. They rang Carol almost immediately on the Saturday afternoon.

CAROL RAYE (actress): I was in London. I’d left Australia and gone to England. The phone rang and it was Bill Harmon, who I’d never met. Bill said, ‘Carol, we wondered if you’d come back and do a guest run in *Number 96*. We’ve got this leading character playing a lawyer …’ which was Joe Hasham, the actor, but his character had become more and more solemn. Joe’s character had got into a sort of rut and they suddenly had the brilliant idea that they’d bring a mad Auntie Mame into his life to jolly him up and introduce a whole new element — they thought that I would fit that role.

above: Former *Mavis Bramston* star Carol Raye joined *Number 96* as Don's Aunt Amanda

TED JOBBINS: She said, oh yes, she could be back for a part. All they had to do was just keep some sort of storyline going for Joe until Amanda arrived. From the moment she arrived his character then took on a whole new element because it was floundering at that point. Dudley came in almost at that same period.

CAROL RAYE: There was a new character who'd come into the shop below the block of flats, a wonderful new young man, Dudley — Chard Hayward. He was so good and he was meant to be homosexual as, it turned out, Don was also. Aunt Amanda, far from disapproving, loved both these young men, thought they were gorgeous and promoted this relationship for all it was worth.

But the introduction of Dudley was not well received by *TV Week* critic Frank Crook, who wrote:

> Poor old Don has been very much out of the limelight recently, doing all the bookwork for Jack Sellars' development company. So to get Don back on top in the popularity stakes the writers have provided him with a little friend, Dudley the grocer boy, who is another of the limp-wrist set. At the moment Don and Dud are circling each other warily, but no doubt love will find a way. Their friendship is being outrageously encouraged by Don's

left: Chard Hayward as Dudley Butterfield. Courtesy Mick Pratt

right: Dudley and Don in a scene together

Aunt Amanda (Carol Raye) and one begins to wonder just where bad taste ends and outright smut begins.[3]

CHARD HAYWARD (actor): My initial contract was for ten weeks. Fortunately my character became very popular, almost immediately, and that was extended.

DAVID SALE: He was gay too and it was a good balance. Again, he wasn't a nasty stereotype. He was campy without being offensive. Chard actually appeared in that earlier scene, this disrobing scene in the laundrette. I think when he came in as Dudley we just needed an assistant for Norma and Les. Johnny came up with the idea.

CHARD HAYWARD: It was obviously very exciting to be cast in the most popular television program in the country, but I hadn't really worked out at that time how I was going to play such an outrageous character.

DAVID SALE: Johnny Whyte swears he modelled Dudley Butterfield on me. Dudley was a movie buff and was always talking about MGM musicals.

CHARD HAYWARD: I think he was created by Johnny and David Sale. When I finally met and got to know them they were both so witty and funny that I realised this was the key to playing Dudley — to do it with a great sense of fun. I wanted the audience to always wonder what kind of outrageous thing he would do next.

JOE HASHAM (actor): Chard was a real hoot and one hell of a ladies' man. Tall, handsome, charming, witty and a fine actor. He was a real pro when it came to work and an absolute joker when it came to play.

It didn't take Dudley long to endear himself to Don Finlayson or audiences. With his camp humour, he was a perfect foil for the more serious Don and they became a long-time couple at *Number 96*. Though occasionally Dud would stray between the sheets with other residents like Jill Sheridan, played by Candy Raymond. Like many of the characters, Dudley had his signature sayings.

CHARD HAYWARD: The obvious one that springs to mind is, 'Did you see it? Ooh, it was ever so good.'

Another of Dudley's was, 'Stop it or I'll slap your wrist.'

TOM OLIVER: In between speech paragraphs there was what we call the big print, and it said: JACK GIVES BIG DIRTY LAUGH. And further down the page: JACK GIVES HIS BIG DIRTY LAUGH AGAIN. I thought, *what's with this dirty laugh business*? So I thought, *okay*, I thought, *who's got the dirtiest laugh I can think of? Sid James, from the* Carry On *movies*. So first day I sent it up basically, not knowing Bill Harmon was sitting in the corner of the studio, and at the end of my first day he came across with his big cigar in his mouth and he said, 'Great characterisation, Tom. I love the laugh. Keep it in.' So I was stuck with it.

above: Dudley and Norma were two of the characters who had memorable catchphrases

opposite: A competition requiring fans to match characters to their catchphrases

In addition to his dirty laugh, 'Jolly' Jack Sellars was also known for his catchphrase: 'I kid you not.' Other characters' catchphrases included Flo Patterson's, 'Tickety-boo,' Herb Evans', 'More or less,' and Les Whittaker's, 'All in good time.'

JEFF KEVIN: Arnold's catchphrases were, 'In point of actual fact,' and, 'If I may be so bold.' Norma addressed everyone as 'Ducky'.

SHEILA KENNELLY: Norma's, 'G'day Ducky,' followed me for years after the demise of *Number 96*.

CAROL RAYE: 'It's quarter past a daffodil,' Amanda would say. Catchphrases do strike a chord.

DAVID SALE: Thelma Scott's was 'Allow me to be the best judge of that.' Then there was, 'Why wasn't I told?' and 'beresk' from Dorrie.

'He's cutting off his balls to spite his face.'

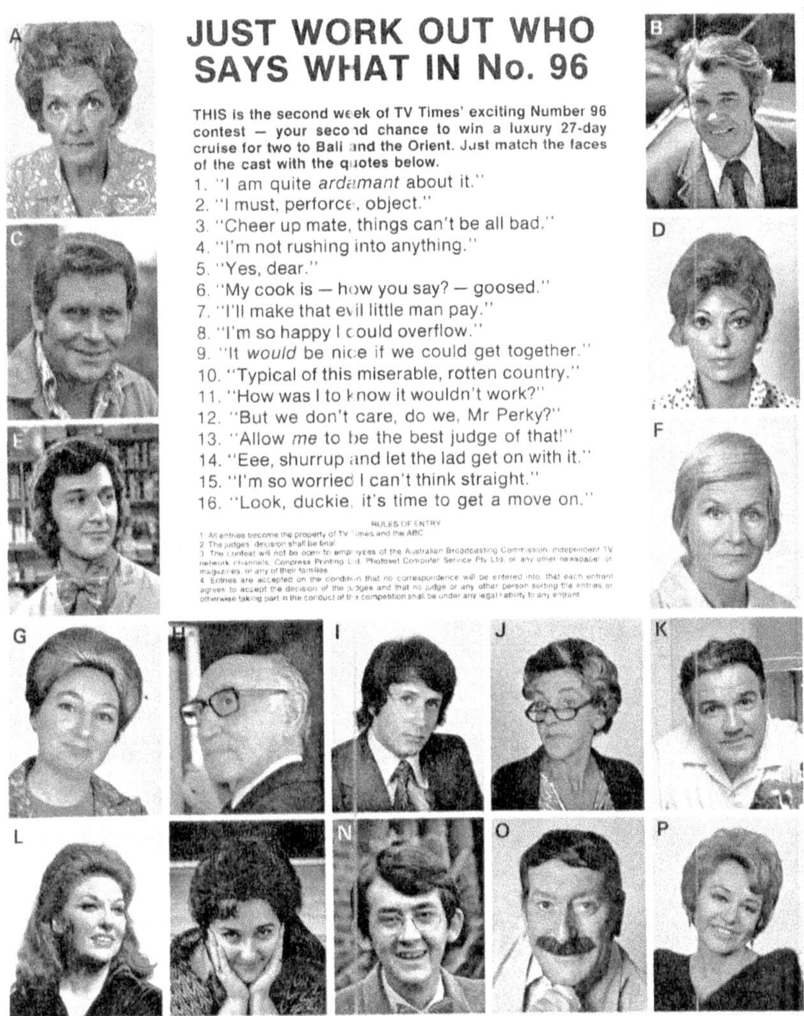

WIN A FAR EAST CRUISE

JUST WORK OUT WHO SAYS WHAT IN No. 96

THIS is the second week of TV Times' exciting Number 96 contest — your second chance to win a luxury 27-day cruise for two to Bali and the Orient. Just match the faces of the cast with the quotes below.

1. "I am quite *ardamant* about it."
2. "I must, perforce, object."
3. "Cheer up mate, things can't be all bad."
4. "I'm not rushing into anything."
5. "Yes, dear."
6. "My cook is — how you say? — goosed."
7. "I'll make that evil little man pay."
8. "I'm so happy I could overflow."
9. "It *would* be nice if we could get together."
10. "Typical of this miserable, rotten country."
11. "How was I to know it wouldn't work?"
12. "But we don't care, do we, Mr Perky?"
13. "Allow *me* to be the best judge of that!"
14. "Eee, shurrup and let the lad get on with it."
15. "I'm so worried I can't think straight."
16. "Look, duckie, it's time to get a move on."

RULES OF ENTRY

1. All entries become the property of TV Times and the ABC.
2. The judges' decision shall be final.
3. The contest will not be open to employees of the Australian Broadcasting Commission, independent TV network channels, Conpress Printing Ltd, Photoset Computer Service Pty Ltd, or any other newspaper or magazines, or any of their families.
4. Entries are accepted on the condition that no correspondence will be entered into, that each entrant agrees to accept the decision of the judges and that no judge or any other person sorting the entries or otherwise taking part in the conduct of the competition shall be under any legal liability to any entrant.

DAVID SALE: Bill was a funny guy. When it came to malapropisms, he was practically Dorrie. About one actor who was causing trouble he said, 'He's cutting off his balls to spite his face.' He always got it wrong.

SHEILA KENNELLY: Bill used to say all sorts of wonderfully inconsistent things. One of his comments, for example, was,

above: Thelma Scott as Claire Houghton was the catalyst for Dorrie Evans becoming the self-appointed 'concerge' of *Number 96*. Courtesy Messenger Press

opposite: 'Mrs Malaprop', otherwise known as Dorrie Evans, was famous for mangling her words. Courtesy NFSA

'There's not enough broads in this show. We need more sex. This is a family show. I don't want to offend anyone.' And it was all said in one breath. He was like that. He'd rattle off and say all sorts of weird and wonderful things. But he was very loveable. We were all very fond of him.

DAVID SALE: We adored Thelma. Honestly, she was funnier off-camera than she was on because she had these things we'd call Thelma-isms, you know. Claire Houghton was the first one to ask Dorrie, 'Are you the concierge?'

THELMA SCOTT: That was very funny. The door opened and there was Dorrie, so I said, 'Excuse me, but is the concierge there?' and she said, 'Well, it's me.' Then she went dashing down the stairs saying, 'I'm the concerge, I'm the concerge [*sic*].'

DAVID SALE: Dorrie, after that, became 'the concerge'.

Dorrie's constant, often screeching, chatter was spattered with many other malapropisms, including 'ardamant' (adamant), 'nave' (naïve) and 'beresk' (berserk). 'Beresk' found its way into the Macquarie Dictionary and became part of the Australian vernacular, while her signature line, 'Why wasn't I told?' became synonymous with busybodies across Australia. Some viewers hung on every word while others wondered if she'd ever shut up. For actress Pat McDonald it was a lot of dialogue to learn, but she was in good company.

JOHNNY LOCKWOOD: Arnold! Poor Arnold was in everybody's flat, every week. He had not only all those lines, but all those hours. I admire that boy so much.

TED JOBBINS: I don't think anybody else could've played Arnold. Jeff did such a fantastic job with it.

JEFF KEVIN: If Arnold had to say one line, and it was a simple line, it was turned into ten, which had all of these ifs and buts.

Verbal diarrhoea. He and Dorrie had the biggest load of lines to learn.

TED JOBBINS: Poor Jeff. No-one ever went around like Arnold Feather, talking like that, so he would have to really work hard on his scripts.

JAMES ELLIOTT: Bill Harmon insisted that he didn't want to see any scripts on the set at all. The actors had to learn their lines at home beforehand and this kind of threw a few actors.

CHARD HAYWARD: I was fortunate to be blessed with an almost photographic memory and could remember lines by virtually just looking at the page. Sadly, that ability has now left me.

PHILIPPA BAKER: In those days I had no trouble learning lines. In fact, they used to sink in at rehearsal more often than not.

JOE JAMES: I got in trouble. I was quite notorious for trying to change the script, for trying to change lines to make it work for me. I just went too far one day and Bob Huber said, 'Why don't you write the fucking thing yourself?'

DAVID SALE: Johnny Whyte was of the very old school and said, 'If they don't like it — we're short of writers and we value our writers — we're not short of actors. They're pounding the doors to get in. So if there's any problem we get rid of the actor and keep the scriptwriter.' He was very firm on that. Any change, any slight change, would have to come in and be OK'd. Nobody could change anything on the floor. It had to be OK'd. Johnny was a real stickler for that.

CONTINENTAL
DELICATESSEN
QUALITY SMALLGOODS
96

Chapter 5

An Immense Operation

preceding: Jeff Kevin and Pat McDonald get ready to tape a scene in the studio. Courtesy Dennis Livingston

opposite: Filming in the *Number 96* deli

ELAINE LEE (actress): You had to be word perfect on Monday because it really was an immense operation. You would rehearse Monday and Tuesday, and I think we'd do locations on Wednesday, and then tape on the Thursday and Friday.

PHILIPPA BAKER (actress): For me it was so easy, so happy. No traumas, no tantrums. Johnny and I were lucky because nearly all our scenes were either in the deli or in the Godolfus flat. Usually they played one after the other, so frequently we were only in the studio two or three days a week.

KEN SHADIE (writer): I'd never seen a production handled like *Number 96*. It was done with military precision insofar as they had people behind the scenes who were able to plot out where the scenes were, who was required, wardrobe etc.

BILL HARMON (producer): Ross Hawthorn was general manager. Kevin Powell was production manager. Bob Huber became executive producer. Peter Benardos and Brian Phillis. Ian Leigh-Cooper was an associate producer, and Ted Jobbins. And four or five girls. It was a fairly large staff.

KEVIN POWELL (production manager): On the studio floor, at one point, we had David Hannay as a line/associate producer, at Channel 10. The production office was basically myself and Shirley Parker, who was my production assistant, and we did the entire scheduling, the entire casting/contracting and everything to do with the artists. Just the two of us. And in a lot of cases the director and I would go out and find the locations.

JAMES ELLIOTT (actor): Kevin was a very nice guy, a very honest, likeable fellow. I liked him very much. He was the one who did the breakdowns of the scripts and the timing — so many minutes to so many scenes — and he could tell you that, out of the thirty-six scenes you were doing the next day, how long you'd take to film them, how long the actor would be in the studio for, whether you could be released before then and at

what time. He had worked all this out beforehand. He was the most valuable person Cash Harmon had. I don't think they realised how good he was.

JOHNNY LOCKWOOD (actor): The producers had a board — it was about ten foot by six foot, something like that — right along the wall in their office. It had dates and the five weekdays and all your call times on there — when you were wanted — and ninety-eight percent of the time they were right.

BOB HUBER (producer): Don and I built the entire production schedule together. We spent weeks and weeks working out every detail; how to get the most out of the actors — who weren't paid overtime. I think we only paid overtime two or three times in the whole run of the series, which was five-and-a-half years. It was a madhouse, but we made it work.

ELISABETH KIRKBY (actress): It was made under onerous conditions. Five episodes a week were shot in two days, including both studio and location shoots. There was minimal time to rehearse; there was minimal time to set up lighting and sets. Yet the two directors, Brian Phillis and Peter Benardos, captured some amazing effects and moments on film that were funny, tender, absurd and heart-wrenching. This is a tribute not only to the directors, but also the editors, sound engineers and vision mixers.

BRIAN PHILLIS (director): Peter Benardos was teamed with Don Cash and myself with Bill Harmon in alternating weeks. After the show was on its feet Don and Bill withdrew from daily visits to the studio as they could see that Peter and I knew what we were doing.

Cast and crew take a break from the 'madhouse', 1973. Courtesy Steve Wakely

PETER BENARDOS (director): The modus operandi, as it were, was if there were kitchen scenes in one apartment you did them all together. Then you'd do anything in the lounge room of that apartment — Vera's or whatever — and then when you stitched it all together it made a half-hour episode.

DAVID SALE (writer): Don Cash worked out a wonderful way of filming that had never been done before. He took the five episodes and it was scheduled so that in those five episodes they might record ten scenes in Vera's flat, ten in the deli and so on. All these scenes would be shot out of sequence, and then at the end of the week you had this enormous roll and it would all be edited and divided up into the episodes.

'Don Cash worked out a wonderful way of filming that had never been done before.'

JOHNNY LOCKWOOD: There were two permanent sets. There was Aldo's shop, and his living room and the kitchen. And the wine bar was permanent too. But of course, the flats — Don's flat was Vera's flat was Dorrie's flat and they used to strip them and change the furniture.

TED JOBBINS (floor manager/associate producer): You basically worked from one side of the flats to the other, and while we were working, if we started in flat 3, we would go to flat 4 on the other side of the studio and the props boy would change flat 3 into flat 5.

LYNN RAINBOW (actress): We would have two sets back to back. My set would be dressed and they would be quietly dressing the other set as I was in my set with Joe James or whoever I was sharing it with.

TED JOBBINS: Getting the set in was just an enormous job. Studio A at Channel 10 was a very big floor area studio. When it came time to doing *96* they had to get two full-size flats in. It worked well because they put them all in together and they took up the bulk of the studio, but we had a lot of room around the outside as well.

BOB HUBER: The sets were permanent and stayed up the entire time. Nobody else used that studio. Well, they couldn't.

JAMES ELLIOTT: It was rather interesting. Having a permanent set is something that's pretty expensive because it's studio space that's all tied up. One time I was on my way to Melbourne or coming back and I met Hector Crawford. Hector said to me at the time, 'That luxury you have at the moment of having sets all permanently there for you to rehearse in as well as to play in, that's a luxury you won't have for too long, you know.' And I said, 'We don't regard it as a luxury, Hector, we regard it as a necessity.'

left: Johnny Whyte on the set

right: The deli was one of *Number 96*'s permanent sets

TED JOBBINS: The staircase was just to the side of the studio near the front door and then across the back of the studio under the control room were the fronts of the two shops and the entranceway. There was one flight of stairs up. You had the two doors and the idea was that each flight would go up once. The numbers changed on the doors. Whatever floor you were on, they changed the numbers.

BRIAN PHILLIS: Ted and I made a good team because we both had the same ideas on how to blow open many scenes — in other words, get the scene out of one particular apartment and cut to the stairs, or the street or wherever. Anything to get away from the same three walls of any given flat. Through it all we had some real laughs — essential for all of us to let off steam at various points during the day.

TED JOBBINS: We started taping about eight o'clock in the morning and went till seven at night, with an hour break, I think it was, for lunch. We had to work within union rules and regulations because once you went over seven o'clock, not only were there the union payments but the crew said, 'Look we don't want the money, we don't want to work because we've got another full day tomorrow.'

BRIAN PHILLIS: Bill had a volatile temper and didn't suffer fools gladly. The first instance of this happened when Joe Hasham was late for rehearsal. Bill chewed him out in front of the full cast and didn't buy Joe's excuses. But the lesson was heard loud and clear — this is business and time is money. Right from the start it was firmly established that because of union constraints there was to be no overtime and no going beyond 7pm, apart from necessary night scenes.

'the lesson was heard loud and clear – this is business and time is money.'

PETER BENARDOS: The cast that came in early in the morning would normally finish their scenes by mid-afternoon, and the latecomers that hadn't started early in the morning were therefore readily available till seven at night. But the crew, of course, had been there all day and the union was pretty tough.

SHEILA KENNELLY (actress): Nobody'd ever done so much television in a week and it was exhausting. There were very few cameramen. They didn't alter them because once somebody was with it they wanted the same ones, and I can remember cameraman Max Cleary getting very angry once about the overtime, the unexpected overtime. There was always some friction.

(left to right) Ron Shand as Herb, floor manager Ted Jobbins and James Elliott, as Alf, rehearse a scene in the pub

opposite: Ian Leigh-Cooper marks a scene featuring Abigail and Tom Oliver

BRIAN PHILLIS: I was amazed when directing a special at Channel 10's studios in Melbourne. I noticed that the Crawford's production *The Box* was still in production at 1am. This was anathema to me, and it reminded me of how our time constraints only added to the momentum, energy and pace that was inherent in *Number 96*.

JEFF KEVIN (actor): *Number 96* was always pressed for time because time was money and you were churning out all these episodes, and you had so much time to get through a day. It was always big pressure.

BRIAN PHILLIS: There were occasional scenes throughout the series, which the audience at home saw unrehearsed, a one-take scene, and no-one knew otherwise. Joe Hasham and Chard Hayward were very good at this and I trusted them. They were tuned into my 'more action, less verbiage' principle. If it was around 5.30pm on a Friday afternoon with seven or eight scenes remaining before the 7pm lights-out it was a critical time. If we failed to have all the scenes in the can then we would go to next Monday's editing session with incomplete shows. Time really was of the essence. But Joe and Chard always delivered. Without even a rehearsal, I would tell them what and where, and then called to roll tape. With those two we sometimes caught seven scenes in the final hour of the day.

NORMAN YEMM (actor): In *Number 96* the emphasis was on doing two-and-a-half hours a week — five half-hour episodes. So you talk about instant television. There wasn't too much of, 'Gee, I didn't like that, I wasn't deep enough.' There were not a lot of retakes. A lot of things got through.

‘There were not a lot of retakes. A lot of things got through.’

SHEILA KENNELLY: We had no rehearsal to speak of. We did have rehearsal, but very little. I can remember one scene with Peter Benardos, who was a fantastic director, of course, and a very quick worker. I said, 'Could we do that scene again?' Because there was something in the scene that was complicated for me and maybe I hadn't learnt my lines well enough either, but he said, 'Rehearsals are for the cameras, not for the actors.' It was that quick. Boom. Boom. No mucking around.

PETER BENARDOS: Lots of times you'd break your heart when an artist would come to you and say, 'Oh please may we do that again, just once more?' And you'd have to say, 'No, because if you do that once more there's one scene we can't even shoot.' And finally they accepted it of course, but it must have broken their hearts. You know yourself when you just need five minutes more.

JEFF KEVIN: When anybody stopped a take it was either with 'shit' or 'fuck'. You said it deliberately because if they were pressed for time they would often leave the fluffs in if you didn't stop it yourself — and we did, all of us, and we always denied it. You'd pretend you forgot your line because you thought, *hang on, that didn't sound right.* So you'd make a mistake deliberately, and the best way to stop a take was to use either 'shit' or 'fuck'.

ELAINE LEE: At the end of every year all the bloopers and bleeps would be edited all together and they would show it at the Christmas party. They were wonderful. They were very funny.

SHEILA KENNELLY: Modern soapies have a pool of directors, but *Number 96* had just two brilliant men who alternated for five-and-a-half years. Peter Benardos was calm and methodical, every shot pre-planned: read through, walk through, rehearse once without script. No time wasted, ever. With five episodes a week, no time *to* waste. A hard training ground, but a very good one. Brian Phillis was volatile and impetuous, ever happy to embrace a new idea, even at the point of recording. This could drive some cameramen to despair or fury.

ELAINE LEE: Brian Phillis would do one week — brilliant, mad Brian — and then very reliable, solid Peter Benardos. Brian was brilliant and his stuff would either hit or miss, but we always had huge fun. Peter was predictable, but his stuff was very solid, good, good stuff when you saw it. And they were both lovely men.

CHARD HAYWARD (actor): They were both terrific guys. Peter was the calm one and Brian was always pushing the envelope. I enjoyed them both.

MIKE DORSEY (actor): Both very professional, both very efficient. You can understand the time constraints of Monday through Friday and you had to finish on Friday.

PETER BENARDOS: It was funny, you know, because there were two directors sure, but I was more interested in my episodes and he was probably in his. We knew what content there was in each other's, but I remember Bill Harmon quite often saying, 'You didn't read Brian's scripts did you?' And I said, 'Yeah I read 'em.' And he said, 'Well you didn't read them too thoroughly.' And he was right. But gee, the pressure of it all. It was pretty tough because while you were in the studio for a week shooting the jolly scenes — you're shooting something like seventy-five scenes in a week — and you'd go home and everything's a bit of a daze, you know, your personal life.

BRIAN PHILLIS: While Peter was in production on his block of five shows, I would be preparing my next week's five shows. Perhaps scouting locations as required or whatever off-set details needed attention. Ted Jobbins, associate producer on my week, would meet with me and talk through anything complicated. As the series progressed I found that off-week crucial to my sanity and seldom went to the production office.

TED JOBBINS: We would work in the studio the first week; second week — Monday, Tuesday nights — we'd be editing and through the day I'd be looking for locations or checking out our

Director Peter Benardos (centre) with (left to right) Sheila Kennelly, Ron Shand, Pat McDonald, unknown, Johnny Lockwood and Bob Huber. Courtesy Benardos family

scripts for the next week. I'd get the scripts a week before. My job, being associate producer, was to actually look for locations and one of the jobs I had to do for this particular episode was find a church. Arnold was getting married or somebody was getting married and it was one of the characters who'd never had anything to do with sex. Now, I found a little church in Hunter's Hill, but soon as I mentioned *Number 96* — 'No.' They didn't care who was getting married. All they worried about was that it was *Number 96*.

PETER BENARDOS: You had one week in the studio, the next two nights of the following week was your editing time, so you'd put the whole show together then.

BRIAN PHILLIS: On the Monday and Tuesday nights Ted, Maggie Powell, my assistant, and I retired to Channel 10's editing suite to put the scenes together. It's important to remember we

‘After a hectic week in the studio I would suffer through a headache for the entire weekend. In the early days, anyway.’

were shooting only two or three weeks ahead of air-time. After a hectic week in the studio I would suffer through a headache for the entire weekend. In the early days, anyway.

TED JOBBINS: So week one, we started rehearsal Monday, Tuesday; taped on Wednesday, Thursday, Friday. Monday night of the next week we had to start of a night time because we needed so many tape machines. We had to wait till the news was finished. We'd go into the control room where they did the news — studio C control room — and work through with a tape boy because you'd have all the scenes from five episodes. You'd have to then start assembling, calling out scene numbers and bumping them all together to make the episode up. It really took a long time.

PETER BENARDOS: Brian and I worked quite differently. He was a bit up and go and good luck Charlie, and I was more gentle, shall we say. But anyway, that was good for the cast because they'd have Brian to work with one week where they weren't quite sure what he wanted and with me they'd know, oh well Pete's fine, and just relax. I was called the gentleman director. And this worked fine. I got on very well with Brian, which was good, and we knew just the rate to play them anyway.

BRIAN PHILLIS: Just before going into production on episode 1, I proudly showed my scripts — five — all marked up with diagrams and notes. Bill took one look, grunted and said, ‘Throw it in the trash.’ It was my first moment of learning to think on my feet, be ready for anything and work around it. Bill's point was right on; preconceived plans and too much

left: The 'gentleman director' Peter Benardos. Courtesy Benardos family

right: The 'brilliant, mad' Brian Phillis. Courtesy Phillis family

blocking were an impediment if things went wrong, as plans locked one into a place with no exit. When knocked off course by unforeseen circumstances, it was a trap. And heaven knows there were plenty of unpredictables in the years ahead.

TED JOBBINS: We had a scene with Les Whittaker and Dorrie at the doorway and there was an explosion in the flat. Brian was a terror. He would've killed all the actors if he'd have had his way. We did the scene once and this little flash came out. It didn't look right and Brian just went to the props boy and said, 'Right, put in three times as much gunpowder.' This God almighty crash went off and scared hell out of everybody, including Dorrie, and they really did react. That was not put on and they screamed. Pat came off the set and she abused Brian because she'd burnt all her stockings; but they loved working with him. He was mad. He did things and you'd say to him afterwards, 'What the hell did you do that for, Brian?' And he'd say, 'Oh well, we got the right effect.'

'Brian was a terror. He would've killed all the actors if he'd have had his way.'

SHEILA KENNELLY: In performance, Gordon coped brilliantly with all the mad inventions that came up in his storylines, some of which taxed his patience. He loved it when Brian Phillis brought a monkey from *The Mike Walsh Show* on to our set and put it hanging in the Whittakers' bathroom to give me a surprise. That was nothing to do with the script, of course.

BRIAN PHILLIS: Les Whittaker, inventor, came up with yet another hare-brained, money-making scheme whereby he would lug an accordion around Moncur Street like gypsy pedlars of old. I immediately said, 'What's an organ grinder without a monkey?' Cut to the Whittakers' bathroom where Les rehearses his bit under Alf Sutcliffe's guidance, while the monkey with the chain about his neck watches every move. Okay, roll tape. All hell broke loose. Something set the monkey off, causing it to bounce off the walls, swing from the showerhead, strew towels about, all the time making those gibbering, high-pitched utterances. It was obvious that this had to be a one-shot scene, and Les and Alf had done a fine job of delivering their lines above the madness in a confined space. Like a Marx Brothers scene.

'Something set the monkey off, causing it to bounce off the walls, swing from the showerhead, strew towels about.'

SHEILA KENNELLY: The Whittakers' flat was like the Tempe Tip — Les's bric-a-brac and bits of inventions filling every particle of space. The inventions were works of art from the props department, creating extraordinary contraptions dreamt up by the writers to inspire Les's catchcry, 'Norma, we could make a fortune.' The sausage-making machine, spewing out sausages of all sizes, left odd frankfurts and Clobassi nestling in the stuffed chairs for weeks afterwards. The exploding vacuum actually melted the nylon on my legs. The baby-washing machine, inspired by car washes appearing in Sydney, produced Les's test doll a limb at a time, dismembered. There was a hunt for stray cockroaches when Les read that if you fed them mashed potatoes they excreted methane gas, there being a petrol shortage in Sydney at the time. The patent wine-bottling machine which popped corks and sent wine gushing actually only worked after we'd finished the dialogue, so we ad-libbed with squawks and imprecations for some time as we were being goosed by the corks.

above: Cast and crew prepare to shoot a scene in the Whittakers' flat. Courtesy Dennis Livingston

'The exploding vacuum actually melted the nylon on my legs.'

BRIAN PHILLIS: In another scene, Les, Alf and Herb were engaged in a plan to scare Andy Marshall, a newspaper journalist, out of his upper flat. Being Halloween, Les thought a pumpkin with candle within might do the trick. Alf went up to the roof in order to lower the pumpkin past Andy Marshall's window. Les and Herb waited down on the pavement in front of the deli when Dorrie emerges from the building. Les made a loud utterance, which Alf above took to be his cue — he let the pumpkin go, which crashed on top of Dorrie's head. The pumpkin broke into bits and it was apparent the prop man had not done a good job of scooping out the pulp inside. The pumpkin weighed like a brick. Pat McDonald was mildly concussed. Pat didn't speak to me for several days after that. It was one of many instances of things not going to plan.

‘he let the pumpkin go, which crashed on top of Dorrie’s head’

THELMA SCOTT (actress): There was that chap I worked with, Richard Lupino, the nephew of the late Hollywood Ida Lupino. He was very attractive, but sadly didn’t inherit his aunt’s acting talent, I didn’t think. He played the American confidence trickster and was having an affair with both mother and daughter; with me and Bev. Later he tried to rob Claire of all her jewellery, which he did, and we had the burglary where they knocked me on the head and stole my jewels.

PETER BENARDOS: Claire was supposed to be dying or whatever, so she had to have her eyelids closed, and the last shot of that particular scene was the camera zooming in to her face. For all intents and purposes she appeared dead. Now, Thelly was an old lady and you could see the eyelids quivering. So I walked down from the control box and I said, ‘Thelly, there’s a bit of a problem here. I’m not quite sure what to do.’ She said, ‘I’ll try Peter, I’ll really try.’ So I went back to the crew and said, ‘Can you just bear with me and we’ll try once more.’ A very simple little scene, but we’re dealing with Thelly and her eyelids are quivering and so on. I said, ‘She can’t do any more.’ The crew said, ‘No.’ And I was stuck with it. I was stuck with this and I thought, *how can I get out of this?* And of course I went home worrying about this and then finally worked out that the moment she is supposed to be out cold, the camera zoomed in, I could do a freeze frame. And that’s what I did, and of course it worked like a charm. I should have thought of it on the day, but you don’t; you’re too busy. And that solved the whole situation.

THELMA SCOTT: I fell unconscious to the floor, came to and found Serena lying motionless. ‘My God, they’ve killed Serena,’ I said, and that was the cliffhanger of that episode. So everybody dashed down the corridors saying, ‘My God, they’ve killed

Thelma Scott with her dog Serena, and Anya Saleky

Serena,' who was my poodle, and she just sort of followed me. Wherever I went she came. She was my dog in real life, Serena, a little poodle, miniature poodle. Then later in the storyline bullets were fired into Claire's window. One of the prop boys fired a real bullet, unfortunately, across my shoulder. He made a mistake. Ted Jobbins has got some funny stories about that.

'One of the prop boys fired a real bullet, unfortunately, across my shoulder.'

TED JOBBINS: I don't know whether I should say this. We nearly killed this poor kid once. I think it was Thelma; yes, Thelma Scott. Claire Houghton was being terrorised by some character — he was actually one of the Lupino family, Richard Lupino, and he was out here and got into the show one way or the other. He was terrorising her or trying to get money out of her or something, but she had this Chinese houseboy and in the scene she had to imagine that there was somebody outside the door. It was a wild and woolly night. There was thunder and lightning and in the scene she was to reach under her pillow, grab a gun, a little revolver, even though they weren't legal in the country, and shoot at the doorway at the back of the set because she imagined there was a character there.

Now there's only one way you can make a bullet go through glass properly and that's to actually do it. So the perspex was taken out, a sheet of glass was put in to this French door at the back of the set and a whole lot of padding and stuff was put up to get the bullet. We had the really good props boy with us at this stage and he had the rifle. The mechanics of it was that she woke up in bed, screamed and carried on and got the revolver and then as she called the houseboy, she shot the gun. At that point the camera was actually on the glass the bullet would go through. We'd see it go and the houseboy would come in. The props boy was a bit worried about the rifle — using live bullets in the set, always a worry. We were shooting the scene; we'd rehearsed it many times. Brian had to cut to the camera at the point where the bullet went so that we actually saw it pierce the glass in time with Thelly shooting it. All was going well except the boy, being worried, had kept the safety catch on the rifle. When the time came, he fired but nothing happened. He realised he had the safety catch on, opened it and fired. In the meantime, the Chinese boy had come in and it missed him by about two inches, I think.

BRIAN PHILLIS: Two more paces and Mutashi the houseboy would have been dead. I broke into a cold sweat and learnt a hard lesson: never, never, never bring a loaded gun onto a set. But the ultimate detail was that even though the bullet went through the window there was no shattering of glass, just a small, pea-sized hole. Ted and I had to shoot around it and concoct a phony window complete with shattered glass to be inserted into the main scene.

above: Cast and crew on the set of flat 3. Courtesy Dennis Livingston

MICHAEL FERGUSON (actor): My second stint in *Number 96* had me as a Vietnam vet who busts a drug ring and becomes a bit of a hero. I remember one scene which took a whole afternoon to do. I had to shoot my wife's brother in the chest with a shotgun. The script had him fall down dead behind a couch, but Brian Phillis thought that was a bit lame when we were rehearsing two days earlier. So he had the props department rig up the French doors in the room, with breakaway hinges and candy glass. The character, Salvador, from memory, was rigged with a harness, blood capsules and wires, and when I shot him he exploded backwards through the doors and lay there in a bloody, pulpy mess … roll credits!

Thankfully, mishaps were not always life-threatening.

BRIAN PHILLIS: There was one day when Ron Shand, Pat McDonald and Bunney Brooke were first up and again my anxiety was to get away to a fast start at 8am. Eight-thirty and no Ronnie. Pat and Bunney started muttering, always an ominous sign with those two — it was a love/hate relationship — two crafty old stagers who knew a trick or two about getting the attention. So there we were, almost nine and Pat and Bunney grumbling about shooting out of schedule. Finally a breathless Ron rushed into the studio, panting out his reason for being late — he seldom was. Living in Kings Cross, he had to face the Bridge traffic, and halfway across en route to North Ryde and Channel 10's studios he realised that he had forgotten to put his teeth in. So he had to detour and fetch them from up at the Cross. Ron was a consummate professional and was always ready to go into a scene.

TED JOBBINS: At times of tension somebody would come up with something and break the tension, and everybody just enjoyed it and went on.

ELAINE LEE: There were a couple of Vera's lovers that came and went that I didn't like. There was one particular fella — I can't remember his name. Peter Harvey? But he wasn't a good actor and he was a golfing buddy of Bill's, and Bill had put him into the bloody storyline. I couldn't bear him. At the end of each scene you were not allowed to break the scene until the floor manager blew his whistle, which was Teddy Jobbins. This particular actor that I didn't like — I loosely call him an actor — and I really didn't like him because when you do a television or a stage kiss there's a way to do it so that it looks passionate and sexy, but it's not. This bloke used to stick his tongue in my mouth and I used to think, *oh I could kill him. That's not the way you act.* But the scene had to end with a kiss. They did this to punish me — the kiss went on and on and on and I thought, *when is he going to blow that fucking whistle?* The scene went on and on. In the end I just pulled away — it's on the goof tape actually — and suddenly I went so South African. I went, '*Blow that bloody whistle, man!*' And everybody just collapsed. He did it deliberately.

'en route to North Ryde and Channel 10's studios he realised that he had forgotten to put his teeth in.'

JEFF KEVIN: We played a trick on everybody in the studio one day. We got into trouble. It was one of those closed sets and I was in bed with Candy Raymond. We were under the silk sheets. So I went and got a half roll of French loaf and shoved it between my legs and then rolled over, you see, and it looked like I had this gigantic hard-on. Somebody said, 'Cut, cut.' We were running close to the wind in terms of time. Brian Phillis was the director and he didn't actually appreciate it on that day. Normally he would've. The crew thought it was very funny. Candy and I did too!

'I went and got a half roll of French loaf and shoved it between my legs and then rolled over, you see, and it looked like I had this gigantic hard-on.'

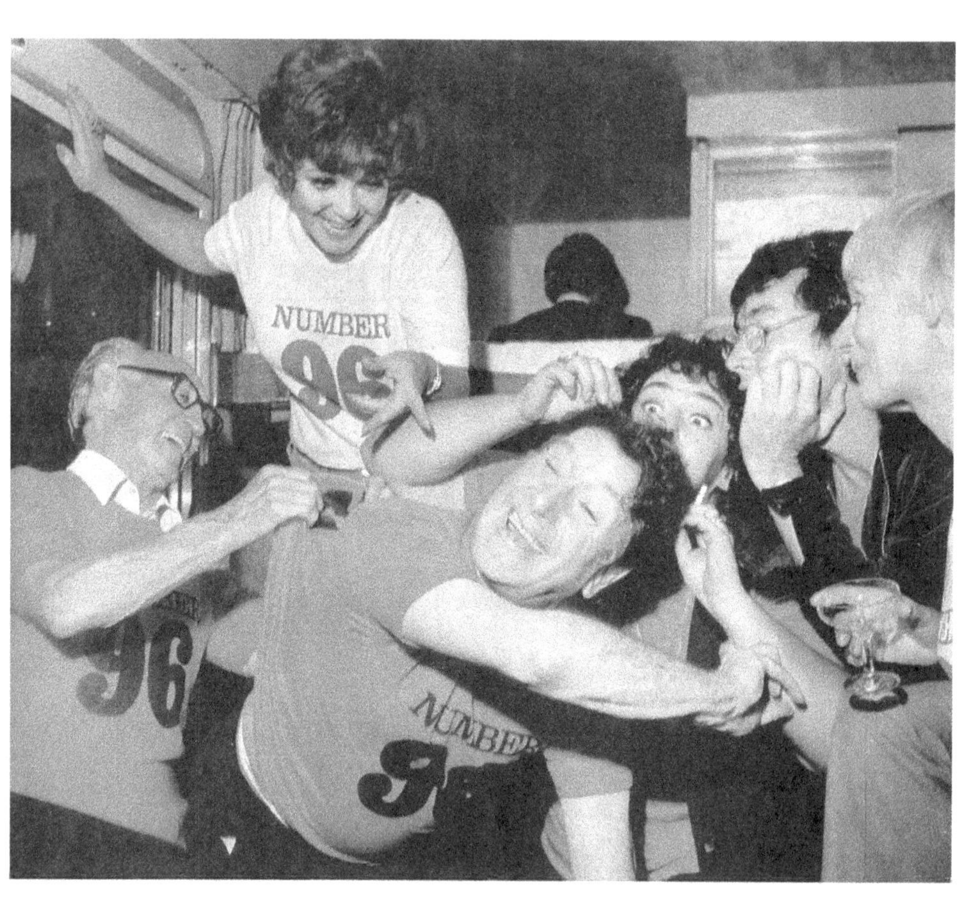
NUMBER
96
NUMBER

Chapter 6

Call the Mounted Police

preceding: Cast members fooling around on the *Spirit of 96*

NANCY CASH (wife of Don Cash): I remember people in the cast started saying they couldn't do their shopping in private anymore, but really, everybody was working so hard on the show, it wasn't until that first train trip to Melbourne for the Logies that anybody realised the extent of its popularity.

TOM GREER (publicist): We received information that the Logie organisers wanted four stars from *Number 96* for their big night. I didn't like this at all as it was an ensemble production with no-one getting obvious publicity treatment over another. I had to keep the peace. I informed the Logie folk that they would have to take all sixteen players in major roles at the time or none at all. They agreed. Now I had to get them there.

JAMES ELLIOTT (actor): We travelled down to Melbourne on the *Number 96* train. This was a creation of Tom Greer, the promotions man. Rather than fly us down there nice and quickly, he hired a train and we had a sixteen-and-a-half-hour champagne party.

'Rather than fly us down there nice and quickly, he hired a train and we had a sixteen-and-a-half-hour champagne party.'

TOM GREER: I wanted the Spirit of Progress with its great silver carriages drawn from Sydney by the great green steam locomotive 3801. The railways were very keen to promote overnight travel from the centre of Sydney to Spencer Street, Melbourne. I had to have a new sign made for the side to cover 'Spirit of Progress' to read 'Spirit of 96'. We had a big farewell from Sydney at about 4.30pm — a red carpet, very large jazz band on the platform.

Spirit of 96, off to the Logies

left: From left, James Elliott, Pat McDonald, Ron Shand and Elaine Lee wave goodbye from the train. Courtesy Elaine Elliott

right: Ron Shand, Pat McDonald and Jeff Kevin inspect the newly christened *Spirit of 96*

BOB HUBER (producer): Dear old Ron Shand. He was unbelievable. He did cartwheels down the platform when we left Sydney, Central Station. I couldn't believe that.

TOM GREER: I had found this crazy piano player, John McDonald, playing in a crummy hotel in The Rocks. I wanted him for entertainment. There seemed to be a problem in getting the piano onto the lounge car. I said, 'Well, they build pianos key by key, put it on key by key.' This they didn't have to do as they just took the side of the lounge car off, put the piano on and screwed the side back on. So simple compared to my rash, but definite idea.

KEVIN POWELL (production manager): We were going down, basically, to look after the cast. But you had writers on board, you had the press, of course. You had a pianist who Tom had told, 'Now your brief is to play between Sydney and Melbourne and not stop,' and it was one great party the whole way.

TOM GREER: The press were invited for cocktails and to see us off, but when the train started to move the press folk were still in cocktail party mode. So they asked where we stopped next. It was Strathfield. They intended to get off there. Well, one or two

above: Non-stop entertainment aboard the *Spirit of 96*

did, the rest stayed at the party till the next stop, Picton. None got off here. The press just continued on to Melbourne. I had one sleeping in my bath.

‘The press just continued on to Melbourne. I had one sleeping in my bath.’

PETER BENARDOS (director): On some little railway station the train had to stop and the local journalist got on board with a bottle of champagne thinking, *I'll get a story out of this*. Well, we wouldn't let him off and he had to come to Melbourne with us. He got his story all right, but he got plastered as well on the way.

JEFF KEVIN (actor): We must've all been pissed out of our minds, but those trips were great. They were really good fun and opulent and quite extraordinary. Tom Greer would organise them and he never thought in a small way. Tom always thought in very big, bold strokes, so consequently, these were extraordinary events. The first one was just unbelievable and I don't think anybody expected the crowds.

TOM GREER: We had enormous crowds at all the stations and the cast were great with them.

KEVIN POWELL: So you'd leave Sydney and the first stop would probably be a couple of drinks down the track — it might be Liverpool — and there'd be kids down the platforms and the cast would get out.

BOB HUBER: In the middle of the night — children in their nightclothes in the arms of their parents. I couldn't believe it.

NANCY CASH: I think everybody — all the actors, all the executives, everybody — was truly amazed at the public reaction to the actors on that train. At two and three in the morning there were a thousand people on a country railway station to see it go through. That was truly extraordinary.

‘I think everybody – all the actors, all the executives, everybody – was truly amazed at the public reaction to the actors on that train.’

ELISABETH KIRKBY (actress): I only realised just how popular the show was when we made the first train journey from Sydney to Melbourne for the Logies, on the Southern Aurora. After leaving Central Station in Sydney, the train took the coastal route, stopping at places like Corrimal and Fairy Meadow before going to Wollongong. The platforms were crowded with eager fans. Much later, when the train got to Goulburn and Albury, the platforms there were crowded too.

above: Ron Shand, Pat McDonald and Elisabeth Kirkby greet their fans

opposite: Hundreds of fans greet the *Spirit of 96* at Benalla

KEVIN POWELL: Ted and I always remember one place — I think it was three in the morning when we got out and there were heaps and heaps of people. Pamela Garrick was in fairly big demand at that point and somehow she got away from the train. Ted and I had to get all the kitchen staff from the train — we linked arms and Ted and I fought our way through the crowd. We managed to get Pamela and locked her in the middle of us and waved a bit like you do when you're drowning off Bondi Beach. The kitchen staff actually pulled us back as though each one of them was a link on a rope. And when we got back, the kitchen staff were putting disinfectant all over Ted and myself. Our arms had been scratched to pieces by these frenzied girls and guys trying to get to Pamela, but it reminded me of the frenzy that I'd experienced with the Rolling Stones at Granada concerts; Gene Pitney, Dusty, Herman's Hermits, all that stuff — this excitement, this crowd.

‘it reminded me of the frenzy that I'd experienced with the Rolling Stones at Granada concerts’

TED JOBBINS (producer): When we stopped at Goulburn, I was responsible for Joe Hasham and several others. They all started signing autographs when we pulled up there. I just happened to look up, and at the back of the platform, standing on some carts that they had there, was a whole group of boys — these were young boys and I would imagine, probably, that they were gay. But they would dare not come down to Joe. All they were doing was staring at him from the distance, and they wouldn't come down to him because in those days to be gay in Goulburn was like being dead. I thought how sad it was that we're still in this situation where those boys were not able to even come down and get an autograph signed or anything. There were about four or five of them, just all staring at him. They didn't look at anybody else and that's why I thought they might be gay. They'd found him and they wouldn't go near him. It was sad.

JOHNNY LOCKWOOD (actor): At Albury we always had to get out and do radio interviews. We were all doing three or four radio interviews.

TOM GREER: A funny thing happened in Albury. We had arranged a radio interview with Thelma Scott. She turned up at 6.30am in a ball gown and fully made up for a radio interview.

‘She turned up at 6.30am in a ball gown and fully made up for a radio interview.’

TED JOBBINS: At Albury station there was a radio interview live from the platform to Melbourne and Sydney, I think, and at six o'clock in the morning they all started to come out looking like death. Thelly came out looking like a million dollars. She knew the radio broadcast was on and no-one was going to see her looking bad. I remember Elaine saying, ‘Look at her. She went to bed rotten drunk and she looks like a million dollars.’

TOM GREER: The next year we did the same thing, except we went down the Illawarra line via Wollongong etc. The crowd at Wollongong station was enormous.

TED JOBBINS: We got off at the station and I had Ronnie and Thelma Scott at my door, along with a few others. Thelma got off the train and said, ‘Stand back, stand back. All autographs will be signed,’ and Ronnie gave her a bit of a look because Thelly was always the grand dame. She was signing autographs and one little kid came up to Ronnie and Thelma grabbed his autograph book to sign it and the kid said, ‘No, no, I don't want yours.’ She grabbed the book off the kid and signed it and threw it back at him. He got an autograph even though he didn't want it.

DAVID SALE (writer): All the girls were after Joe Hasham and Thelma was standing there at the train saying, ‘All books will be signed,’ and then she'd grab an arm, ‘What's your name dear?’ They weren't after hers. They wanted Joe Hasham's autograph.

TOM GREER: When the train pulled out, the word got to me that Thelma Scott was still on the platform and signing autographs. I was standing next to Ian Holmes when we heard of this. Well, he said, ‘Tom, it's your train,’ so I hit the emergency button — always wanted to do that — and we backed up to collect a confused Thelma.

BOB HUBER: Thelma was nearly lost in all of those people and she was shouting, 'All autographs will be signed. All autographs will be signed.' She didn't know what the hell she was talking about. We had to rescue her and pull her back to the train.

DAVID SALE: Johnny Whyte called her the fastest pen in the west. It was really funny.

Massive crowds met the *Spirit of 96* at each stop but there was as much action on the train between stops as off it.

TOM GREER: It was on this trip that I was sitting with Ian Holmes and surrounded by other Cash Harmon and Channel 10 executives. Tom Barnett, our director of news, leant in and said to Ian and me, while looking to the far end of the dining car, he thought there might be a streak. Ian Kennon, the director of sales, said, 'If there is, Tom Greer will stop this train and put them off into the wilderness.' I thought I best go and check.

CHARD HAYWARD (actor): The streak on the train was really just a spur of the moment thing. Streaking was very popular at the time and Jimmy Elliott and I just decided to strip off and run through the packed dining car. I seem to remember that Channel 10's publicity director was also part of it. All those train trips were just great fun.

'Jimmy Elliott and I just decided to strip off and run through the packed dining car.'

TOM GREER: When I got there they were indeed getting ready for a streak, so I thought why not?

JAMES ELLIOTT: It was Tom Greer's idea. Not only was it his idea, he joined in and became one of the streakers. In fact he was right behind me.

opposite: The stars of *Number 96* arriving in Melbourne for the Logie Awards was big news

opposite bottom: Ted Jobbins and Tom Greer assess the scene on the platform at Spencer Street Station

TOM GREER: I stripped right down like the others and we put our clothes into a discreet bag that a lass took to where we intended to end up. Then they chickened out unless I went first. Oh well, as Ian had said, it was my train so off I took, trusting the others were behind me. They were.

TED JOBBINS: They worked it all out, but they didn't tell anyone, of course, and we were all sitting in the dining room. There was enough room in the dining room for everybody; there was no second sitting or anything. So we were all in there and suddenly the door flew open and they just charged through the dining room naked — just raced through. Of course nobody had a chance to see anything. It was all over and a big laugh afterwards.

TOM GREER: When I came to the end of the dining car a waiter came around the corner with two large silver cheese platter trays. I was not going to stop. So the poor guy had his cheese everywhere and was knocked down by three naked men. Needless to say the crowd loved it and it met with great approval.

TED JOBBINS: Now, Tom Greer always took some members of the press with them. He had his favourites and he had two or three journalists who always went with us as his guests. One of them — and I thought what a lousy thing to do. The streak was an in-joke for everyone there, but this journalist couldn't wait to put it in the paper, and of course when it read, the way he wrote it up it sounded like an orgy from Central to Spencer Street.

NORMAN YEMM (actor): That was a sensational trip, from a fun point of view. You needed a week's holiday by the time you got back.

LYNN RAINBOW (actress): We just got stuck into the grog and it was a party from the time we left Central Station till the time we arrived at Spencer Street.

No. 96 CHUGS INTO TOWN!

HUNDREDS of **Number 96** fans greeted the cast of the show when they arrived in Melbourne aboard a special train from Sydney.

As soon as the cast began to leave the Spirit Of Number 96 express, the crowd began to close in around them.

Extra police were on duty to prevent the fans from getting too close to the stars.

Many fans forced their way across the platform giving police a difficult time.

A spokesman for the 0-10 Network said the big reception at Spencer Street Station proved that the program had not lost any of its popularity. #

● ABOVE: Bruce Mansfield interviews Chard Hayward shortly after the Spirit Of Number 96 arrived in Melbourne.

● BELOW: Joe Hasham was given a warm welcome by the large crowd in Melbourne. Here he signs his autograph for fans.

● ABOVE: Elisabeth Kirkby chats to fans standing behind a barrier.

● ABOVE: Always popular . . . Herb and Dorrie put on an act for the crowd.

● BELOW: Bettina Welch and Elaine Lee try their hand in the kitchen of the Spirit Of Number 96 on the way to Melbourne.

ELISABETH KIRKBY: By the time we arrived at Spencer Street Station in Melbourne, around 8am the following morning, there were so many people that I think the organisers were scared.

BOB HUBER: The mob scene in Melbourne was unbelievable at about eight o'clock in the morning. I thought we'd *never* get to the hotel.

ELAINE LEE (actress): When we went to Melbourne on the train — the first trip to the Logies — and the train suddenly stopped at Spencer Street Station; we stopped quite a way, about two kilometres, from the platform. They said the crowds are so immense that they're calling in the mounted police. I don't think one child went to school that day. They were all on the station.

ELISABETH KIRKBY: There were thousands waiting to greet us and they tried to rush the platform to get as close as possible to their favourite characters. The police could not keep the crowds back.

PHILIPPA BAKER (actress): We were mobbed at the station. I will never forget a sobbing woman tearing at my clothes. This was the first time I realised how real we were to many people.

'This was the first time I realised how real we were to many people.'

JEFF KEVIN: I remember Gordon McDougall had his t-shirt ripped off him by a man with a claw hand. He just caught the back of Gordon's t-shirt and he ripped the whole thing off. It was really an amazing scene.

TOM OLIVER (actor): I think it was Lynn. She lost a gold chain round her neck. They just reached forward and grabbed hold of it. Getting from the train to the vehicle to the hotel somebody reached out among the crowd and just snapped it off her neck.

ELAINE LEE: It was scary because people were pushing and one woman had her baby and she's saying to me, 'Kiss my baby, kiss my baby,' and I thought, *oh, this is really off.*

SHEILA KENNELLY (actress): It was just extraordinary. People would be holding up their babies with this moving train and running along and you'd think, *oh you silly woman, what if you trip over in this great crowd*?

BOB HUBER: Dorrie was very popular and Pat McDonald just couldn't believe any of this and she really was afraid. Mostly, Pat was afraid. Of being swallowed up in this mass of people and being pulled apart and trampled to death. It was that wild. It really was.

THELMA SCOTT (actress): That was horrifying. I cannot stand hysteria, and they were about twelve deep on Spencer Street Station and they had children in their arms and they were coming so close, screaming at us and saying hello and everything, and they had to call the mounted police. It was very, very scary.

WENDY BLACKLOCK (actress): I can remember the first time going to the Logies. Mike Dorsey and I weren't invited properly. We were taken to Melbourne, but we couldn't go in and sit with the others because there were only so many seats that the *Number 96* people could have, and I thought, *well that's pretty silly*. Afterwards I thought, *well what did we bother to go for*, you know? But the next year we were considered to be completely part of the team, and it was an enormous eye-opener to travel on a train where you were told that you mustn't open the window or open the door because there was such a large crowd on the station, waiting to catch a glimpse of you, that the people at the back would push forward and smash the people at the front against the train. And you weren't to get out because if you got out onto the platform — this is along the way, at the stops along the way — that you would have trouble getting back in. Well, of course, I'm so small when we finally got to Melbourne they had to lift me through the crowd. They had horses, policemen on horses, trying to hold the crowds back. I'd never seen anything like it and to actually be lifted over people's heads because they thought I'd disappear and not be seen again [*laughs*]. Amazing.

JOE HASHAM (actor): Of course there are many things that took place on the Logies train that I could never talk about; far too outrageous. But Mr Greer's idea of having the entire cast plus the top entertainment journalists on the one overnight trip from Sydney to Melbourne was nothing short of sheer genius. Hot and cold running live music, gourmet food, unbelievable choice of alcohol — enough to out-Hollywood Hollywood. I will never forget the very first Logie trip — whistle stops at country stations at 4am with thousands of people waiting, but the most unforgettable experience was arriving at Spencer Street Station and being greeted by in excess of 40,000 fans, with mounted police attempting to control them. Frightening, but what excitement.

'arriving at Spencer Street Station and being greeted by in excess of 40,000 fans, with mounted police attempting to control them. Frightening, but what excitement.'

One star who missed all the excitement was Abigail. Fifteen minutes before the *Spirit of 96* was due to leave Sydney's Central Station, Channel 10 executives were notified she would not be

THE DAY ABIGAIL MISSED THE TRAIN!

BY TONY FAWCETT

● **ABOVE: Abigail . . . the sex symbol of Number 96 missed the special Logies' train because her gown wasn't ready.**

WHEN the 0-10 Network's special Logie train, the Spirit of 96, pulled out of Sydney's Central Railway Station there was one passenger missing.

It was Abigail, the sexy star of the top-rating Logie award-winning series.

Abigail had missed catching the Melbourne-bound train because of a last-minute hitch in alterations to her gown for the Logies.

Naturally she was worried her fans along the route would be disappointed at not seeing her. And organisers of the whistle-stop tour were similarly concerned.

But they need not have worried.

For Abigail's non-participation in the most ballyhooed rail journey in history has done little to dim her incredible popularity — particularly with the male television viewers of Australia.

As always, she is still among the handful of stars from **Number 96** who receive the most fan mail.

And her on-screen and off-screen happenings—like her coming marriage to fellow performer Mark Hashfield — are avidly being chronicled by the Press of Australia.

Mostly Abigail is portrayed as a sultry blonde siren in the mould of Marilyn Monroe and Brigitte Bardot.

Words like "curvaceous" and "alluring" litter the stories written about her.

But what about the person behind the sex symbol? What about the intelligent young lady who once began training to become a civil engineer? What about the real Abigail — the woman who can no longer go outdoors alone without being mobbed?

Today English-born Abigail can see the funny side of being tagged a sex symbol.

She jokes about the references to her ample physical charms and admits they have helped her get off the ground in one of the most difficult professions in the world.

But like most screen sex symbols, she admits that deep down burns a fierce desire to be accepted purely as an actress.

"She wants to be accepted as an actress rather than as a sex siren — it's the same as Marilyn Monroe," explains her fiance Mark Hashfield.

Abigail puts forward Jane Fonda as a classic example of what is possible for an actress in her position.

"First off Jane Fonda was regarded as a sex symbol and she is one of the few who have been able to be accepted for their acting," she says.

Among her show-business friends Abigail is known as a determined actress who occasionally gets up-tight just before she goes in front of the cameras.

"She doesn't talk a great deal and it's difficult to have long conversations with her before a morning call," says one of her colleagues. "It is probably that she is deep in thought about what she has to do."

But at social functions and when she relaxes, Abigail takes on a completely new side to her character.

She is at times lively and witty and can confidently mix conversation with the most intellectual people.

"I have a bad temper," she says, "but I have learnt to control it. I don't show it first as Mark's is 10 times as bad once he gets going."

Few people believe Abigail when she says she once studied civil engineering.

She first considered the profession, she says, when her parents tried to dissuade her from following in their show-business footsteps.

Civil engineering was the furthest career from show business she could think of.

In England she became one of the few females in a university civil engineering course.

After a year she moved to Australia and began a similar course in Perth—but her studies were short-lived.

Quickly she was bitten by the acting bug and eagerly accepted her first big Australian role in **There's A Girl In My Soup.**

And that's the play in which she met her husband-to-be, fellow English actor Mark Hashfield.

Abigail holds little regret that she didn't finish her course. Acting is today probably one of her greatest loves and it is a big factor in her relationship with Mark.

Both delight in going to live theatre and constantly talk of show business, particularly Abigail's involvement in it.

Mark now manages Abigail's career and is probably one of her keenest fans.

He contends her true acting talents are going unnoticed in **Number 96** and that her forte is in comedies.

One of the greatest influences on Abigail's private life has been **Number 96** and its overwhelming, and at times almost [illegible]fying, influence on the public.

It has meant she can't go out alone without the risk of being pestered. If she does people stare and point at her.

Several times she has almost been reduced to tears because of the obscene things men have shouted at her.

Consequently she spends a lot of time indoors, listening to records or reading.

Both she and Mark have wide interests and share a love of photography.

The pair have a makeshift studio complete with backdrops and lights in their apartment and do most of their own printing.

Abigail is looking forward to marriage, but thinks it will change her life little.

She is keen to continue her career and has the full support of Mark.

"If anything I think our mutual love of acting will help our marriage," she says. #

above: An article reporting on the drama of Abigail missing the *Spirit of 96*

there in time to catch the train because her dress was not ready. Her absence angered the executives, but she wasn't the only star not on board.

LYNN RAINBOW: Tom refused to go. He flew down. He didn't want to be on a train.

TOM OLIVER: I didn't go on it. I flew down the next day. Lynn went on it. She was still playing Sonia. I thought, *well, the Logies are tomorrow night, the train's leaving today. I am going to get some sleep and be perky for the Logies.* The cast that went down on the train were just knackered, absolutely knackered because they were stopping off in the country at two, three, four o'clock in the morning to wave hello to the crowds that were there. They arrived in Melbourne with bags under their eyes and I flew in at four o'clock in the afternoon.

SHEILA KENNELLY: You'd be in a very smart hotel and the Logies would be, say, on the first floor. So you'd go right down to the basement and you'd go out sort of at the back of the building into these limousines just to be driven around the block to the front to make a grand entrance.

JAMES ELLIOTT: Bill had heard we were going to get a Logie. Now at that time none of the channels would allow actors from rival shows to appear — Channel 10 people would not be seen on any other channels. Bill told all the actors from *Number 96* that when his name was announced as the producer of the show that got the Logie, he wanted every actor in the cast to follow him up on stage.

The 1973 Logie Awards were a huge success for *Number 96*, winning Best New Drama and for Pat McDonald who won Best Actress.

PAT McDONALD (actress): I was so shocked that I don't even remember going up the steps to the stage to collect the award. I had talked over with some other cast members what we would

above: Bill Harmon accepts the Logie Award for Best New Drama surrounded by his cast, 1973

say if we were lucky enough to get a Logie. We had worked out that we would say something about how important this award was to the Australian television industry, but when I got there I was so nervous I couldn't remember anything I had planned to say.[4]

Pat McDonald took her Logie Award into the studio and onto the set of flat 3 where in some episodes, if you looked carefully enough, it could be seen in the background. The series by now had hit its stride, with public and industry accolades and consistent top ratings in its time slot in every state. Sadly, Don Cash did not live to enjoy it. *Number 96* received a massive blow when he died of cancer in January 1973 at the age of sixty-two.

NANCY CASH: Don, unfortunately, wasn't able to experience too many highs. He died after the first year of the show being on-air and he was sick a long time before he died. He had a very short time, unfortunately, to enjoy his success, that particular success. And I was always terribly sorry that he didn't.

LYNN RAINBOW: Don was the antithesis of Bill. Bill was, 'Jesus Christ, Goddamn it,' all the time and Don was very calm. He was the very soothing, placating one.

MIKE DORSEY (actor): They were opposites. Bill was the typical American producer: 'Goddamn,' and all that. It was chemistry. They worked extremely well together. Their office had one big desk divided into two. Don would sit that side and Bill would sit the other side and I think they loved each other. They had a very complementary working relationship.

SHEILA KENNELLY: Don — we didn't see much of because he got very ill not too long after we started. So that was very sad. But Bill was a larger-than-life character. He was a chain-smoker and it was all go, go, go.

TOM OLIVER: They were like Tweedledum and Tweedledee, in a way. Like *The Odd Couple*. Bill was the cigar smoking, very loud, 'Goddamn Tom,' and Don was the quiet Englishman, very softly spoken, but they made a great team, great team, yeah, but they were different as chalk and cheese.

'Bill was the cigar smoking, very loud, 'Goddamn Tom,' and Don was the quiet Englishman, very softly spoken, but they made a great team.'

TED JOBBINS: They were two completely different people, though they complemented each other brilliantly. Bill was one of those people who'd fire the bullets first then find out what he was shooting at afterwards. Don was the complete opposite. Where Bill was very brash, Don was a real gentleman.

above: Producer Bill Harmon at the desk he once shared with Don Cash. Courtesy NFSA

ELAINE LEE: Don was a real gentleman. He was very quiet and hard to get to know. Bill Harmon wore his heart on his sleeve and I related to that.

JEFF KEVIN: I had no problems with either of those two guys. It seemed to me that Don was the softer of the two, but he wasn't, he was much more inclined to make harder and tougher decisions. Bill would come in like that cartoon character, you know, the Tasmanian Devil that spins? Bill was always like that. His whole life revolved around turmoil. I got on very well with them.

DAVID SALE: Bill and Don were tough operators. They were buccaneers. They weren't frightened. They fought the network on things.

JAMES ELLIOTT: Bill was a great guy. Whenever Bill got in an argument with someone, Bill always won the argument. He was a great negotiator.

BOB HUBER: He was a very colourful character and a very fair man. He was wonderful with cast members, if anybody had a gripe or whatever, they'd go in and he'd always sort it out.

JOE HASHAM: The remarkable thing about my relationship with Bill Harmon was that I never signed a contract. It was all done on a handshake. This is probably because we clicked from that first audition onward. Our initial liking of each other developed into a strong friendship and this expressed itself in the trust we placed in each other. At the end of each year Bill would approach me with his hand extended and a little hand-scribbled note was passed to me as we shook hands. On the note were words to the effect of, 'See you next season,' with a number next to it. That number was my increment for the following year. It was an unspoken thing. It became an annual ritual of sorts.

JAMES ELLIOTT: Bill Harmon was the sort of father figure and he loved that title: Father Figure to the Stars.

DAVID SALE: Bill would never criticise without coming up with some positive alternative or situation. He was wonderful like that. He became like a father to me. He was terrific.

KEVIN POWELL: Don Cash passed away with cancer and that's when Ross Hawthorn came in, because Don had insisted that Bill get someone who was a lot more business-oriented, in terms of detail work etc., to back him up. Don knew that he was dying.

MIKE DORSEY: Bill cried when Don died. I actually saw the tears. They were that close.

'Bill cried when Don died. I actually saw the tears. They were that close.'

NANCY CASH: Bill did a remarkable job of continuing on his own under very difficult circumstances. I mean, Bill had never intended to do such a show on his own. He was really horrified, truly horrified, when he realised he had to go on alone. And he did. He did it magnificently.

BOB HUBER: It was hard. It was hard for all of us. They had a contract between them, which said if anything happened to one, the other would buy out his half. Bill was very concerned because he didn't know if that was morally right. And he kept Nancy in the Cash side of Cash Harmon when he didn't have to, but he did. We discussed that at length, into the night, many nights, what to do and how to do it. I thought it was very good of him to do what he did.

NANCY CASH: I was quite close, as close as possible without having an actual part in the production, and I often went to the studio and watched the filming — I was always involved in the major things that happened about the show. And with the people — very much with all the people, who became like one big family, which was especially wonderful for me because I was here and I didn't have any family anyway. But once Don died I really had nobody, family-wise, and there was this whole big, huge wonderful *Number 96* family to have. And they were wonderful people, all of them. They were absolutely wonderful people and all became very, very close friends and treasured friends.

> *‘once Don died I really had nobody, family-wise, and there was this whole big, huge wonderful Number 96 family to have.’*

DAVID SALE: It became very familial. It became a wonderful family. Even now we're in touch, quite a few of us are in touch.

TED JOBBINS: It was one of the happiest groups, particularly in the early days. Everyone got on so well together.

JOHNNY LOCKWOOD: We were all good mates and I never had any trouble with anybody.

SHEILA KENNELLY: When people said it was like a family, it *was* like a family. We used to squabble like a family as well.

BRIAN PHILLIS (director): Pat and Bunney were prone to being difficult. They quarrelled and quibbled, usually on the set, with Ron sandwiched between them.

DAVID SALE: Poor Ronnie Shand was in the middle of it. It was a very miserable time for him because sometimes they'd fight, and all this sort of stuff.

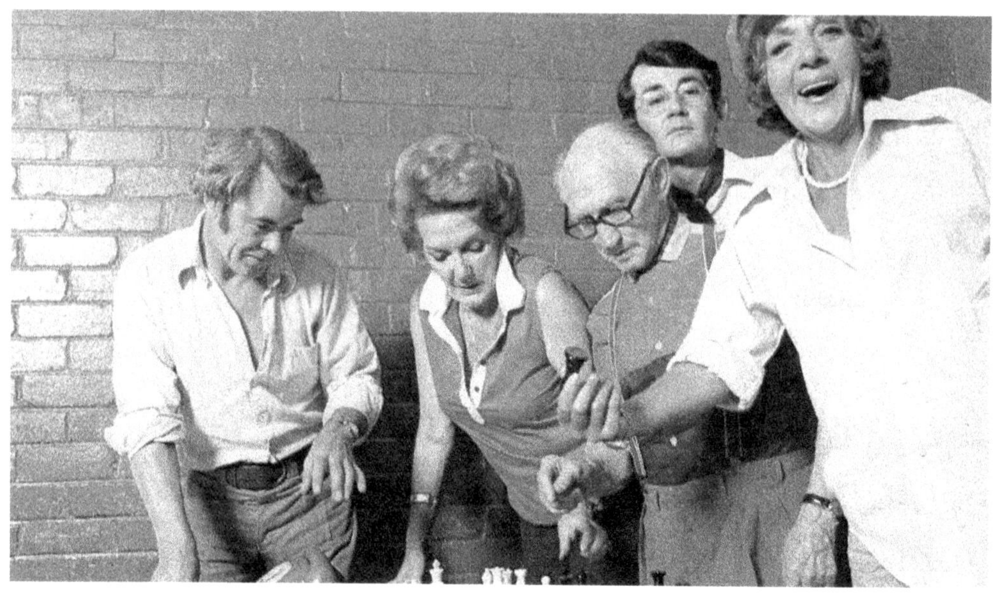

above: The cast get together in the green room

opposite: The ABC's Peter Luck in bed with Candy Raymond during a visit to Channel 10's studio to report on *Number 96* for *TDT*

BRIAN PHILLIS: Ron Shand had immense patience — many of his scenes were played with the 'bookends', Dorrie and Flo. They both possessed the annoying habit of pulling on Ronnie's shirt to get his attention — a tug to the left, a tug to the right, now back to the left. I don't know how Ron accepted it for so long. During a take, Flo, who was a notorious up-stager, always fiddling with something, popping Kool Mints into her mouth, lighting a cigarette etc. In this particular scene the bookends yanked on his shirt once too often and Ronnie had a mini meltdown. I could hear his tirade through the open mic, 'I'm treated like a bloody jockstrap — only here for support.' One of the few times Ron swore.

BOB HUBER: There are dynamics in groups of people and we had the same dynamic that every other group ever had. There were some stirrers. The cast finally divided into Bunney Brooke, who was the head of one camp, and Pat McDonald, who was the leader of the other camp. But it didn't show. It really didn't show. They were all very professional and did their jobs quite well.

DAVID SALE: Bunney didn't have a very good reputation for ensemble-playing because she'd tend to be very divisive, and sure enough when Bunney came into it the cast split right down the middle.

BOB HUBER: There was a time when a lot of people felt Bunney Brooke had to go. She *didn't*. Little did she know, she was very close to going because she was a stirrer.

In 1973, to celebrate the 300th episode of *Number 96*, the ABC's current affairs program *This Day Tonight* took a peek behind the scenes at Australia's favourite address. Peter Luck reported on the phenomenal success of the series and its massive audience. He also drew attention to an alleged feud between Abigail and Candy Raymond. From Peter Luck's *This Day Tonight* story:

> Peter Luck: What's also caused [viewers] to take notice is an amazing publicity campaign. Abigail's lurid memoirs in a Sydney tabloid and a much publicised feud between the leading ladies has made them both household names.
>
> Abigail: At the moment there is an upset between me and Candy, unfortunately, because she wrote that article. I don't think she'd read my book and she made a direct slam at me and at my life.
>
> Candy Raymond: Well, really, you know what newspapers are like.
>
> Abigail: Now I wrote about my life and she implied it was a pack of lies, and she made herself just seem rather bitchy even though she stressed four times in her article that she wasn't being bitchy.
>
> Peter Luck: The carefully choreographed bitchiness between Abigail and Candy only whets the viewers' appetites.[5]

CANDY RAYMOND (actress): Never happened. There was never any such 'feud'. That was absolutely concocted by Cash Harmon — you know, how will we get into *TV Week* this week?

Following the release of Abigail's best-selling autobiography, *Call Me Abigail*, there was talk of a couple of satires. Pat McDonald and Bunney Brooke were planning a book titled *Call Me, Please* that never eventuated, while Candy Raymond responded with an article, 'Call Me Candy'.

CANDY RAYMOND: It most certainly wasn't a dig at Abigail. It was more that a tongue-in-cheek opportunity was presented and I had, by the end of my tenure, become a little disturbed with facing the reality that, no, I was not going to be the nude feminist champion of Australian womanhood.

PETER BENARDOS: I think in any production of any kind somewhere there can be friction. I loved working with Abi, I had no problem at all, but other people had problems, but only little things as far as I'm concerned. Abi was inclined … she had long hair, very long hair and she was supposed to come in early for make-up so they could fix her hair and so forth, and sometimes she wouldn't. She would be late.

LYNN RAINBOW: Abi, apart from her wretched hair, which took an hour to dress and we'd all be hanging around waiting, tapping our fingers, Abi was wonderful.

NORMAN YEMM: She's a lovely girl. And she was our first sex symbol.

THELMA SCOTT: I got on very well with Abigail. A lot of them were sort of rubbishing her a lot. At one stage she turned up and she said she had a migraine, but I think she'd been out all night or something, and I said, 'You kept me waiting an hour, don't do it again or I'm not working with you.' She was great. I met her mother; she introduced me to her mother.

What PM said of the bishop

WHITLAM'S HARSH WORDS CUT FROM TV

The Daily Telegraph

SYDNEY, TUESDAY, JUNE 5, 1973

Swipe at U.S. — 'no harm done'

The Prime Minister, Mr Whitlam, denied last night he had worsened relationships between the U.S. and Australia.

The Prime Minister, Mr Whitlam, was censored last night by the Channel 9 television network.

Four words were cut from an interview with Mr Whitlam recorded last Friday for the television programme A Current Affair.

The words which were cut are reported to have been "liar," "contemptible" and the word "wicked," which the Prime Minister used twice when answering questions about a Roman Catholic bishop.

Before the programme started, it was announced that the cuts had been made because it was feared they might be defamatory.

The interviewer, Michael Willesee, asked Mr Whitlam: "What do you think about the Catholic bishop coming out and saying 'Don't vote Labor because of abortion'?"

'On advice'

Pleased

Praise

Abigail gets the axe from "96"

Abigail the sexy, controversial bedroom girl of Channel Ten's Number 96 has been sacked.

"Dirty"

NSW SCHOOL REVOLUTION—P 3

left: Abigail's axing was front page news

right: A scantily clad Abigail in a scene from *Number 96*

On Monday 4 June 1973, in one of the most shocking moves for Australian TV, Abigail abruptly departed the show.

BOB HUBER: I know that Bill just got fed up and said, 'That's it. That's it.'

DAVID SALE: It was Bill's decision. She was dropped. Abigail's contract was terminated just like that. Bill said, 'We can send you to the kitchen to make a cup of coffee and somebody else carries the cup back out.' Well, that's what happened.

BOB HUBER: Abigail was involved with a man who had great ambition for her and I think he helped screw up a lot of relationships between her and Cash Harmon. It finally got to the point where they said, 'Enough,' and Vicki Raymond came in overnight.

VICTORIA RAYMOND (actress): I got a phone call one day asking me if I could be at the Cash Harmon offices in twenty minutes. I raced in there and they told me they had to replace Abigail. They didn't tell me why. There were various rumours. Then I had to be at the studio the next day.

DORRIE AND FLO WRITE A SIZZLER!

● ABOVE: Dorrie (Pat McDonald) and Flo (Bunney Brooke) at work on their sex saga.

Call Me ABIG

above: An article about Dorrie and Flo writing a satirical response to Abigail's provocative memoir

middle: The cover of Abigail's memoir

right: The media perpetuated the rumours of a feud between Abigail and Candy Raymond

‘Abi, apart from her wretched hair, which took an hour to dress and we'd all be hanging around waiting, tapping our fingers, Abi was wonderful.’

BATTLE OF THE SEX STARS

It's war between the girls from 96

By JIM ORAM

The two sex symbols of Number 96, Abigail and Candy Raymond, are at each others' throats over their literary efforts.

Abigail, author of the book Call Me Abigail, has been sent up in an article, Call Me Candy, by Candy Raymond.

Said Candy: "I think Abigail's book is a disservice.

"Once a person finds fame, as everyone in Number 96 has, I think he or she has a great responsibility.

"They have to use it honestly and with integrity."

Replied Abigail: "I don't think Candy has been in the profession long enough to talk about integrity."

Not 'bitchy'

Candy's article was especially hard at the nude scenes described in Abigail's book.

She said: "Abby talks about 'eyes gazing lewdly in the dark' at her when she did nude scenes.

"The fact is the lighting technicians and sound people in a studio are too busy doing their jobs to worry about anything like that.

"They're blase about it."

Purred Abigail: "They might have been blase about her doing a strip.

"But they were never blase about me."

Candy said she wrote her article not out of bitchiness, but to put the record straight.

Said Candy: "I don't know if Abby really believes what she has written."

CANDY AND ABIGAIL . . . Fight over those nude 96 scenes

CANDY . . . Technicians blase about nude scenes

ABIGAIL . . . They were never blase about mine

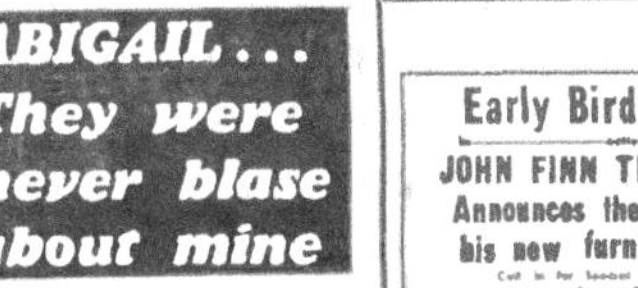

Early Bird Specials

JOHN FINN THE TV MAN

Announces the opening of his new furniture store

NEW

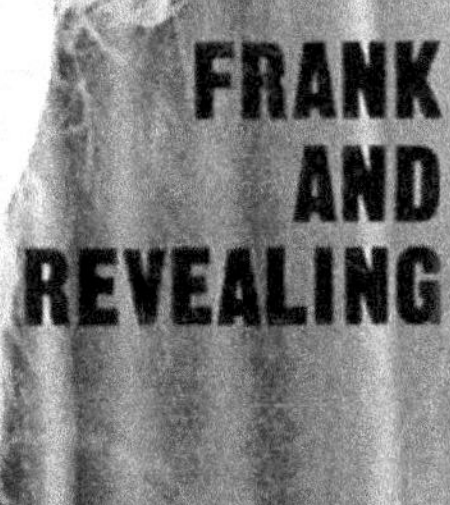

above: Magazine covers of the two actresses who played Bev Houghton, Abigail (top) and Vicki Raymond (bottom)

opposite: Abigail's replacement caused a stir in the media

Vicki Raymond had auditioned for a role in *Number 96* in February 1973 at the same time as her sister, Candy, who had been cast as Jill Sheridan.

Abigail had become Australian television's first and most enduring sex symbol in a very short time, and her sudden departure grabbed the headlines. She'd already been dropped from the series a week after missing the Logies train amid claims the writers were running out of storylines for her character. She was then reinstated, but a few weeks later trouble flared again and she was axed. She was quick to speak out in the press about the poor working conditions on *Number 96* and expressed doubts about viewers accepting Vicki Raymond as her replacement.

ABIGAIL: My similarity to Vicki Raymond is not very great and I think viewers connect me closely with Bev. I may be wrong, but I don't think they will accept it.[6]

Less than five months later a similar situation occurred when Carmen Duncan left the series.

JILL FORSTER (actress): Carmen exited one door as Helen Sheridan and I came in another as Helen Sheridan — I'd never do it again. I'd never take over a role that another actor had started because everybody said, 'Oh, Carmen wouldn't do it this way,' and, 'Carmen wouldn't do it that way.' So I realised I was actually supposed to give a carbon copy of Carmen. I didn't want to and I actually didn't because I thought, *I'm playing the role now. That's me, so like it or lump it.*

TOM OLIVER: I think Carmen had other commitments. Carmen and I go back a long, long time before that. I don't know how we met, but I met her with Jeanie Drynan. They'd just graduated from NIDA.

DAVID SALE: Lovely Carmen Duncan — a delight to work with, loved being in the show — got pregnant and her doctor

OH, BEV—HOW YOU'VE CHANGED!

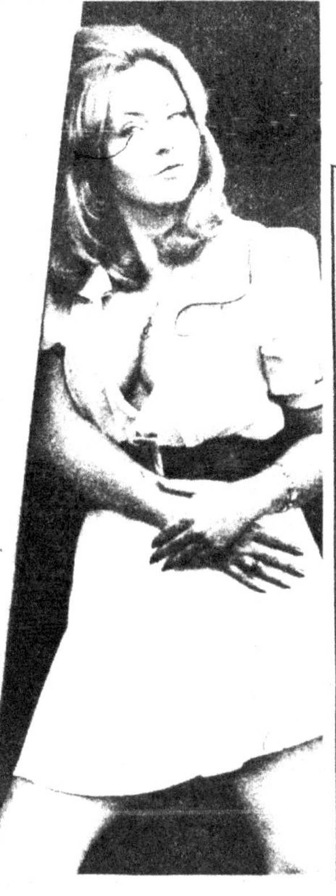

NUMBER 96's least-dressed character, Bev Houghton, will soon undergo a remarkable change.

One night she will look like Abigail. The next, she will be in the form of Vicki Raymond (pictured left).

Vicki is the actress who will replace Abigail fired on Monday for alleged breach of contract.

The producers of Number 96 want to keep alive the character of Bev Houghton, the girl who has difficulty in keeping her clothes on.

Vicki takes it off for Abigail

Vicki, 21, is the sister of Candy Raymond, who has been in the serial for some months playing the role of Jill Sheridan. Vicki has appeared in such television shows as Division 4, Matlock Police and Riptide.

"We believe that viewers will have difficulty in telling the difference between Vicki and Abigail," an optimistic Channel Ten spokesman said today.

But Son Of Veritas calls the change "an insult to viewers." TURN TO PAGE 45 FOR HIS COMMENTS.

VIEWERS WON'T ACCEPT A NEW BEV, SAYS ABIGAIL

ACTRESS Vicki Raymond, chosen as a double to replace Abigail in **Number 96**, does not want to be regarded as another Abigail.

However, she allows one comparison with the top TV sex symbol whose role in Number 96 she took over last week.

"I've never had to worry about my bust line," Vicki said. "So I don't mind competing with Abigail in that department.

"But as far as my portrayal of Bev Houghton is concerned, I hope viewers accept the change in actresses without making other comparisons.

"I don't want to feel like a ghost walking in Abigail's shoes because I'm certainly was like winning a queen-for-a-day competition.

"Any morning I expect to wake up and find it all a sweet memory," she said.

"Candy and I auditioned together for the role of Jill Sheridan last February and Candy got it because I looked too much like Abigail.

"Now I'm in the series for the same reason.

"I was overseas when **Number 96** started and friends wrote to me about Abigail saying she looked and talked like me."

Vicki said she did not know much about the character of Bev Houghton until it was explained to her during her first day of rehearsals on the set.

"You often understudy parts in the theatre, but this sort of thing has never han-

● **ABOVE: Vicki Raymond . . . producers of Number 96 chose her as replacement for Abigail as Bev Houghton in the top-rating**

BEV HOUGHTON'S NEW LIFE IS FOLLY PLUS

BEV HOUGHTON

So the curtain has come down on Abigail's career in Number 96. I will not go into the reasons for they lie entangled in a legal thicket.

But I am astounded at the way in which the producers intend keeping alive the character of Bev Houghton.

What utter folly! What crass stupidity!

Or is it because the producers are so lacking in imagination they cannot dream up a new character.

Abigail was Bev Houghton. Abigail took the character and made her the most important one in the show — in spite of the airy wafflings of producer Bill Harmon who tries to retain the myth that all characters are equal.

And yet Harmon is insulting viewers by keeping Bev Houghton and replacing actresses.

Vicki Raymond, the sister of Candy Raymond, will try to step into Bev's shoes.

Fantasy

No explanation will be given to viewers. Overnight, Bev Houghton will undergo some miracle and personality will radically alter.

And that, disbelieving viewers, is the sort of tawdry fantasy that Harmon expects you to swallow.

BEV HOUGHTON

opposite: Tom Oliver as Jack Sellars with the two actresses who played Helen Sheridan, Carmen Duncan (left) and Jill Forster (right)

said, 'You're not to work.' She wept when she came into the office and said, 'I'm going to ask to be let go,' and she was in tears because she loved being in the show. We loved having her, but it was for her own safety and the baby's safety. So we got Jill Forster to take over.

JILL FORSTER: Tommy Oliver I liked. He's interesting. I remember my first day on set. Most of the others were there and Tommy of course, who I was going to play opposite a lot because he was Helen Sheridan's love interest. He wasn't anywhere to be seen and so I'm having coffee and talking to everybody else, and I suddenly heard this clunk, clunk, clunk behind me. So I turned around quite slowly and looked at him — he's quite small, you know, and I'm tall — and there he was the bastard. He'd got these great big telephone books strapped to his feet. He was coming in like the monster with a bunch of flowers. He was lovely, very nice and fun to work with.

TOM OLIVER: Lovely Jilly. When Jill came in we sort of just picked up where I left off with Carmen. It's no problem at all and you think to yourself, *well, it is soap opera after all.*

Chapter 7

Cranking the Publicity Machine

TOM GREER (publicist): To go to the Logies on those train trips the cast would get one day off. They'd work the Thursday till four o'clock in the afternoon and then they'd be straight on that train and up all night partying. They'd have a big day the next day in Melbourne with press engagements and pictures and then do the Logies. Saturday they'd fly back and be doing their rehearsals on Sunday. So, the day that they were supposed to work, the Friday, was moved to the Sunday. They didn't get a day off. Did not get a day off. And not a complaint.

SHEILA KENNELLY (actress): In 1973, we went to Adelaide for Channel 10's eighth birthday celebrations — smart lunch, even smarter ball, tours of the vineyards, entertainment centre, shopping complex. We travelled through the city in a bus, loud speakers blaring the familiar theme music. We passed a park where a rival TV station was having a picnic for fans of its children's show and the entire crowd of children and parents deserted the animal characters to greet the *Number 96* bus, to the chagrin of the opposition.

NORMAN YEMM (actor): We went to Adelaide to promote the show and that was fantastic. All the characters were taken over and this was right at the boom time when it'd just won the Logie Awards. There was huge publicity over there and we drew more people than The Beatles did when they arrived. We got on this double-decker bus with an open top. It was a beautiful sunny day and we drove all the way from the airport. There were people waving flags, and all that sort of thing, every inch of the way from the airport into the city.

‘we drew more people than The Beatles did when they arrived.’

JOHNNY LOCKWOOD (actor): They reckon there were a hundred-and-something-thousand people lining from the

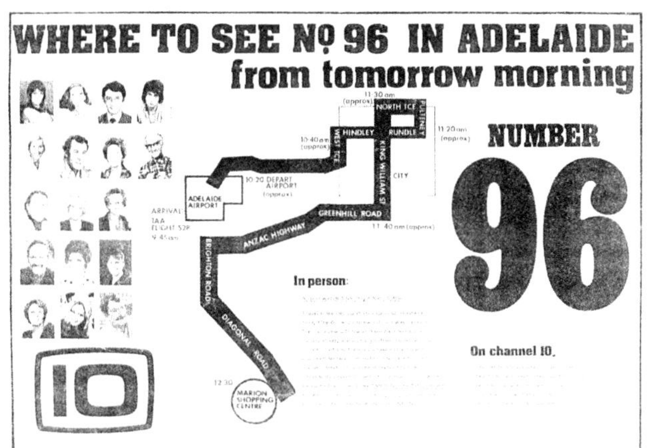

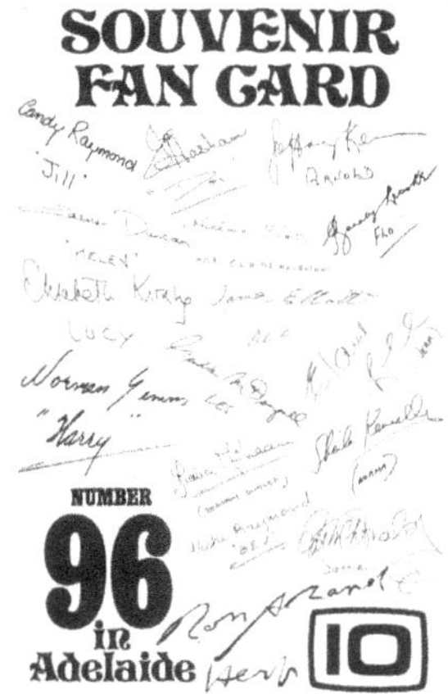

above: Memorabilia and publicity shots of the *Number 96* cast's trip to Adelaide

airport till we got into Adelaide, and then when we got to the shopping centre they estimated a crowd of 6000. We got to Adelaide, but never saw anything of Adelaide. We went to the hotel and couldn't get out; could not get out.

VICTORIA RAYMOND (actress): When we went to Adelaide, I'd been on-air a couple of months in Sydney, but Adelaide was behind Sydney. When we got there everybody was going wild about Dorrie and Herb and Don, but they didn't know who I was.

TED JOBBINS (producer): Vicki Raymond came into the show just before we went to Adelaide. Abigail was still going to air in Adelaide, but Vicki Raymond was on the bus as Bev. Well, there

top: Crowds surround the bus as it makes its way through the streets of Adelaide

bottom: The scene from the balcony of the hotel where the cast stayed in Adelaide. Courtesy Candy Raymond

opposite: Publicity jaunts always ended with a rip-roaring party thanks to Tom Greer. Courtesy Elaine Elliott

were thousands of people around the bus to greet us and Vicki was introduced as Bev, and everyone screamed and cheered and carried on. It was just amazing.

VICTORIA RAYMOND: The next morning I woke up to the sound of my name being chanted because I'd been on the news the night before.

CANDY RAYMOND (actress): In waves they'd be calling. All day and all night there'd be crowds calling in vocal Mexican

waves. They'd go, 'Dorrie, Dorrie, Dorrie,' for about five minutes and then it'd be, 'Jill, Jill, Jill.'

JOHNNY LOCKWOOD: In Adelaide I cut my hand very slightly on a glass that broke, and I'm going, 'Ooh the pain, ooh the pain,' just joking with Bunney Brooke who was a funny lady, so she put a nurse's hat on and dabbed my hand. We were all half shot because we'd been to a vineyard. Anyway, that was that. I took the plaster off when I got home. Two days later Tom Greer came up to me and he said, 'I've got a reporter coming in, go and get some bandages on your hand.'

The press didn't need much encouragement to take a bit of creative licence with the facts in order to produce a sensational headline or story.

TOM GREER: I've got the most wonderful story of Jim Oram. Jim Oram always said, 'I've written more about that bloody *Number 96* show than anything else.' I said, 'Yes Jim, you have.' He said, 'You know what? I've only seen one episode.' And he was dead right. He became great friends with Abigail, the cast members and the people. He was a wonderful man of imagination, and a wordsmith. You'd give him the outlines of what you thought was a good story. 'Oh yes,' he'd say, 'but what you're really saying is this ...' I said, 'That's a pretty dramatic way of putting it.' He said, 'Well yeah, that's what the public want, they want drama.' I said, 'Oh, it's a bit of a beat up,' and he'd say, 'That's fine, that's entertainment.' Great wordsmith. He loved writing about the program, but his innate ability to turn it into something bigger than it really was made him love it more.

WENDY BLACKLOCK (actress): I can remember going to a telethon in Perth and they said, 'Would you mind travelling around the bottom of Western Australia in this six-seater aeroplane collecting money?' So Mike and I set off with a couple of other people and a pilot, and we had buckets so we could ask people to donate money to the charity that the

FLO PROVIDES FIRST AID...

ALDO IN FREAK ACCIDENT!

NUMBER 96 star Johnny Lockwood has had a hand gashed open in a freak accident in Adelaide.

Johnny was touring the streets of Adelaide in a bus with fellow **Number 96** performers when a bottle of champagne he was opening exploded in his hands.

Blood spurted from his hands as glass from the bottle pierced his skin.

An eye-witness said both Johnny and people standing near him in the bus were covered in blood and champagne.

The accident occurred during a promotional visit to Adelaide by the stars of **Number 96**.

While Johnny clutched his bleeding hand actress Bunney Brooke who plays Flo Patterson in the series applied a tourniquet.

"If it hadn't been for Bunney's quick thinking in applying the tourniquet Johnny might have been in a bad way," said an 0-10 Network executive who was on the bus.

"Most of us were so stunned that we just looked on but Bunney went straight into action."

While the drama was going on in the bus thousands of fans of the series thronged the streets waving at the performers.

"Johnny did a marvellous job to carry on after the accident," said the network executive.

"While Bunney was stopping the blood from flowing from his hand he was waving to the crowd with his other hand."

The incident is merely the latest in a series of illnesses and accidents which have beset Johnny in recent months.

Less than a month ago Johnny fell off a stage during his club act and severely bruised a leg.

Since the accident he has had trouble walking, and the bruises are still plainly visible.

For the past six months he has been plagued by partial deafness caused by an ear complaint he has been suffering since the war years.

He has regained some of his hearing through courses of antibiotics and surgery but he still has considerable trouble hearing.

On top of that he has for many years suffered a mysterious illness which makes it impossible for him to go into strong sunlight for long periods.

If he does his exposed skin blisters and eventually bleeds.

Skin ointments and tablets which help the body to screen the sun's harmful rays are of little use for Johnny.

He is a keen golfer but is forced to cover nearly all his body with clothing when he plays. ●

● ABOVE: Johnny Lockwood as Aldo Godolfus in Number 96 . . . dogged by misfortune.

96 STARS IN AIRCRAFT DRAMA

NUMBER 96 stars Wendy Blacklock and Mike Dorsey spent an hour of drama in a light aircraft lost in a violent thunderstorm near Bunbury, Western Australia.

The plane finally made a forced landing at an abandoned airstrip after the storm had closed all available airfields, including Perth airport.

After the forced landing, a shaken Wendy and Mike hitchhiked to the nearest town.

"It really was a terrifying thing to go through," said Wendy.

"We were starting to wonder if we would ever survive — especially when we realised that the pilot appeared to be lost.

"We could hear radio messages coming through trying to guide us to a safe landing spot somewhere, but it seemed that we were just fly-

● ABOVE: Wendy Blacklock.

mally worry me but on this occasion I was terrified. It was jumping and pitching all over the sky."

plane on a whistle-stop tour around the countryside to collect money from the people at the surrounding smaller cen-

● ABOVE: Mike Dorsey.

was closed by the weather and things were starting to look fairly desperate.

above: examples of the 'beat ups' that often sensationalised news related to *Number 96*

telethon was in aid of. And the plane went down in a field, so the headlines were: 'Mummy & Daddy lost in aeroplane crash'. We were perfectly safe, but the plane didn't work so we had to sort of walk. We got to the nearest town and they couldn't get us back in an aeroplane so we had to drive back to Perth, but everywhere along the way we stopped. We'd go into pubs and they'd have the telethon on, but I love the headline, you know: 'Mummy & Daddy crashed in a field'.

TED JOBBINS (producer): The scene that always comes up was when the two boys kissed. That never went to air. Now, what happened that day was that we were shooting in the boys' flat and the scene was just the two of them talking about Maggie and it was a little insignificant scene, but we were running early this day. Bill was on and even though he was always gruff he was always good for a joke. Both boys came into the studio and they were in their pyjamas, and I said to Bill, 'We should do a bedroom scene.'

'The scene that always comes up was when the two boys kissed. That never went to air.'

THE SCENE THEY HAD TO CENSOR

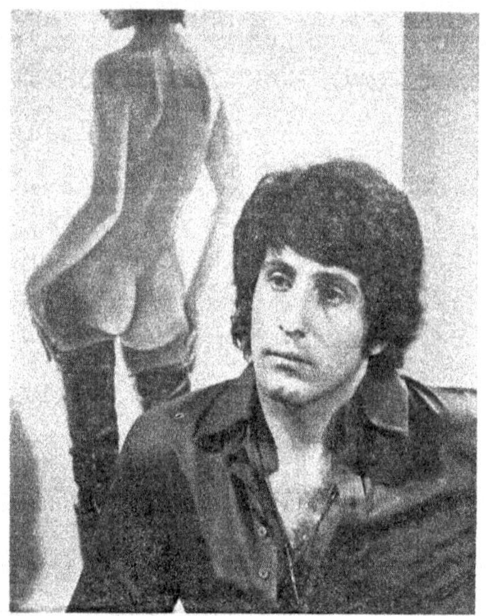

JOE HASHAM is the heart-throb of Number 96. He's the star the girls write to and weep over. But his character, Don Finlayson, is homosexual. And that leads to complications off the set. The shot above, in which Joe and Paul Weingott had to embrace and kiss, had to be left on the cutting room floor.

above: A sensational but false headline regarding an on-screen kiss between Don and Bruce

PAUL WEINGOTT (actor): I remember Joe and I were sitting up in a double bed together, and this was for the Christmas tape or something, and it was fairly spontaneous in a way, you know — let's do what had been suggested — but it was just a bit of fun.

TED JOBBINS: They were just laying in the bed and they played the scene talking about Maggie as if they were making love and talking about each other. They were laying there doing the scene, and then one kissed the other, and they went into this big passionate kiss and that ended the scene. We just waited because we knew the executives were always watching. Well, in about three seconds the production manager came racing into the studio, 'What's this scene? What's this scene?'

TOM OLIVER (actor): Joe Hasham, whether he played a homosexual or not, was the pin-up boy of *Number 96*. The ladies loved him too. He played a homosexual so well, as did Chard Hayward who was one of the randiest actors I've ever known.

CHARD HAYWARD (actor): Strangely enough I didn't get much attention from gay men. Maybe it was obvious that I was just playing a role. The attention from girls was different. They chased us everywhere. I found it hard to believe that it was happening to us.

JOE HASHAM (actor): *Number 96* garnered a legion of fans. Most of the characters had a huge fan base. I used to get anywhere between 300 and 800 letters a week, depending on the storyline. And this fan mail was spread across a very broad spectrum. I had letters from mums who were convinced that their daughters could straighten me out; mums and dads who were seeking advice about their sons whom they suspected were gay; guys who wanted a date; girls who wanted a date; troubled teenagers who were seeking advice about their sexuality, and the list goes on. Not difficult to understand, then, why I concluded that I was carrying a huge responsibility.

SUZY HASHAM (former wife of Joe Hasham): Joe sometimes would have a hard time with the straight ocker men when we were out, but the gay community loved him. He got lots of letters from gay men wanting to meet him and they were always very respectful of me.

CHANTAL CONTOURI (actress): *Number 96* gave the gay community a reason to exist, a reason to validate themselves, when the laws and society and everybody else was against their way of being and against their way of being in love. It was a crime to hold hands with a person of the same sex, mainly male I suppose because women always did, but let's just say men — to kiss, to be affectionate in any way. You were arrested, you were bum-kicked by the police, you were treated like an animal. So something like *Number 96* and the overt showing of homosexuality was such a lifeboat for so much of the gay community, and gave them a bit of courage too. So of course they embraced young actresses like me who were in shows like that. If I went to a gay place I was celebrated.

above: Pat McDonald and Bunney Brooke at home

The popularity of *Number 96* caused problems for many of its cast, mostly regarding a lack of privacy. When local children found out they had Dorrie and Flo living in their neighbourhood, actors Pat McDonald and Bunney Brooke decided to pack up and move.

For actors attempting to conduct a relationship, there was the added glare of public scrutiny. Although the true nature of Pat and Bunney's relationship was a well-guarded secret, Joe Hasham's romance with Channel 10 employee Suzy Phelan was well documented in the press.

SUZY HASHAM: There was a lot of publicity surrounding our relationship. *TV Week* etc. knew about it a long time before we got married, and as I was a staff member the Channel 10 publicity department had a fair bit of control. We also had a lot of control over Channel 10's publicity department, due to my status, but not a lot with the tabloids.

JOE HASHAM: Suzy and I remain to this day the closest of friends. When we first met it was like magic; love at first sight. Corny, I know, but so true.

SUZY HASHAM: We were very careful about our publicity for our wedding, in December 1972, and invited only *TV Week* to cover it, plus a Channel 10 photographer. We had the reception at my parents' home for privacy reasons, but unfortunately the church location got out and it got pretty harrowing. We had the wedding then, as production was in hiatus. Not anticipating the already huge success it was becoming, we decided to downscale and just have a small family affair. It was pouring with rain and the crowds were such that it took ages to clear a path for me to get into the church. They then descended into the church as well, but were well behaved and respected our privacy. We had a big party at Channel 10 with the cast after our return from our honeymoon in Fiji.

JOE HASHAM: As much as I would have wanted all my fellow cast members to be at our wedding I did not want it to be turned into a media circus. This was Suzy's and my day; we wanted to share it with family and friends.

When cast members Tom Oliver and Lynn Rainbow wed in April 1973, it made the news and attracted the attention of hundreds of fans.

TOM OLIVER: We'd known each other long before *Number 96*. We first met at the Independent Theatre in North Sydney while working on the play *The Birthday Party*.

LYNN RAINBOW (actress): I think there was some concern about two cast members having a relationship, but it was never a problem. There was a huge fan turnout the day Tom and I were married at this little church in Double Bay. It was a great, fun day. All the cast of *Number 96* were there, and lots of fans came out to wish us well and see what I was wearing. It was fun.

SUZY HASHAM: Joe was best man for Tom Oliver at his wedding to Lynn Rainbow.

LYNN RAINBOW: Tom was blackmailed by a journalist who can remain nameless. On Logie night, up in one of the rooms afterwards, at an after show party we told our friends in the cast that we were getting married. This particular journalist rang Tom the next day and said, 'If you don't give me the story we will implicate Lynn in your divorce.' That was a bit nasty. However, I have to give the journalist his due. He didn't break the story till Tom gave him the nod.

RITA JAMES (wife of Joe James): Joe and I got married secretly because we didn't want the publicity. So that was very much undercover.

The cast were in constant demand for personal appearances at charity events and telethons. There were handprints and autographs in the footpath outside Sydney restaurant Jason's, and the cast appeared in Melbourne's Moomba procession and other parades around the country.

TOM OLIVER: We came down for the Logies one year, Lynn and I, and we sat with our bums up on the backseat of a sports car — all the people did in the Moomba Parade — and it was just packed, packed with people. It was like a rippling effect, like opposite left: Joe James and his wife Rita. Courtesy Joe James

opposite middle: A magazine cover featuring Joe and Suzy Hasham's wedding

opposite right: A magazine cover featuring the wedding of co-stars Tom Oliver and Lynn Rainbow

top: Tom Oliver and Lynn Rainbow in Melbourne's Moomba procession in 1973. Courtesy Lynn Rainbow

bottom: The 0/10 Network's Moomba float in 1976

the Mexican wave at a football ground. We're slowly motoring down Bourke Street or somewhere, and sections of the crowd would start copying Jack's laugh. So it's like the Mexican wave and this laugh would slowly go down the crowds both sides of the road — everybody having a try at Jack's laugh. It was a very strange experience.

JAMES ELLIOTT (actor): At that time, in the 1970s, there was a lot of rivalry between TV channels and each trying to pretend the other didn't exist. It was really quite silly. One year

during the Moomba Parade in Melbourne — it was something we'd been invited to from Sydney. *Number 96*, at that time, had become famous, a very famous production. It was highly successful and therefore it was hated by the other channels. While we were travelling in a procession of open sports cars during the Moomba Parade, at various points along the route were stationed television cameras — news and so on — and you could easily spot the Channel 9 cameras because as we came abreast of Channel 9's cameras in our little procession you could see that their cameras were pointing at the ground. It was pretty clear that somebody had given direction that under no

opposite top: Abigail makes a guest appearance on 0/10's *The Celebrity Game* alongside Joy Chambers and Joe Martin

opposite bottom: (left to right) Ron Shand on ATV0's *Jackpot Quiz* with Bruce Mansfield; Joe Hasham on Philip Brady's *Password*; Pat McDonald chats to Mike Walsh on his afternoon talk show

above: Cross-promotion: cast members in character on Grundy's *Marriage Game* hosted by Gordon Boyd

circumstances were people who might be readily recognisable from another channel allowed to appear. They didn't want to promote another network.

The cast would, however, be seen making guest appearances on other 0/10 Network programs, including *The Mike Walsh Show*, *The Celebrity Game*, *Jackpot Quiz*, and *The Price is Right*.

WENDY BLACKLOCK: We'd be walking down the corridors at Channel 10 and Mike Walsh would be short of a guest or two and would say, 'Will you just come in and do something?' You got used to it. I went on *Blankety Blanks*. You had all sorts of adventures.

MIKE DORSEY (actor): Mike Walsh was doing *The Mike Walsh Show* at lunchtime. We were often — if he was short of guests — called in to do it, and occasionally I stood in for Mike Walsh if he was sick or on holiday or whatever.

Chard Hayward was another *Number 96* cast member who acted as guest host of *The Mike Walsh Show*. On Grundy's quiz show *Marriage Game*, actors Pat McDonald and Ron Shand,

Elisabeth Kirkby and James Elliott, and Gordon McDougall and Sheila Kennelly paired up and appeared as their alter egos from *Number 96*.

TOM GREER: There was no problem at all with the cast of *Number 96*. They were just delightful. I did not have a problem with any of that cast in that entire period. And we worked them hard.

LYNN RAINBOW: Tom and I spent our honeymoon doing a telethon in Tasmania with Elaine Lee and Johnny Lockwood. That's some way to have a honeymoon!

‘Tom and I spent our honeymoon doing a telethon in Tasmania with Elaine Lee and Johnny Lockwood. That's some way to have a honeymoon!’

opposite: A Tasmanian honeymoon and telethon all rolled into one for newlyweds Tom Oliver and Lynn Rainbow. Courtesy Lynn Rainbow

above left: Publicist Tom Greer. Courtesy Keith Wills

above right: From left, Lynn Rainbow, Pat McDonald, Tom Oliver, Bunney Brooke and Joe Hasham participating in another telethon. Courtesy NFSA

JOE HASHAM: The best publicity trips were the telethons. They were so much fun. You'd get the chance of meeting the top entertainers in the country, while at the same time knowing that you were contributing your time to a worthy cause. There were always such lavish parties associated with *Number 96* publicity. Tom Greer was the master and he made sure that everything we did had the biggest and best impact possible.

MIKE DORSEY: Tom Greer was a brilliant publicist. He'd come up with all sorts of weird and wonderful things. Most of them were fun so you did them with pleasure.

WENDY BLACKLOCK: I remember Mike, at one stage, was invited to go and be a race caller. You'd get all these odd things, and so he'd be at the races, calling the races. I'd say to him, 'You don't know anything about that.' He said, 'Never mind. I'm just filling in,' and people would just be pleased, you know, they'd enjoy seeing you.

CANDY RAYMOND: A fair amount of that 'sisters stuff' publicity happened because: a) it was a good angle; and b) Victoria was just terrific at it.

CHARD HAYWARD: Channel 10 had bought a double-decker bus for promotions and I had a heavy vehicle licence, so I offered to drive it to a party at the Warragamba Lion Park, which Channel 10 owned at the time. On the way back I was about to drive under the bridge at Parramatta when I just had a feeling we weren't going to fit. We later saw that there was a sign, but it was obscured by trees. Anyway, I hit the brakes and we just kind of slid into it and peeled off half the roof. They were always planning to take off the rear half of the roof, but as someone later said, 'Well, let's take off the front half instead because Chard's already done it.'

'I hit the brakes and we just kind of slid into [the bridge] and peeled off half the roof.'

TOM OLIVER: I remember doing a publicity trip to Brisbane with Ronnie Shand. We parked and walked across to the terminal and there was a bunch of fans there, waiting for us, with some newspaper reporters and photographers. Ronnie, being the old ham he was, stepped aside from me and he cartwheeled towards them. A great little guy.

JAMES ELLIOTT: We'd fly down to Melbourne and across to Perth, Adelaide, Brisbane. Those trips were good fun. There was always a rip-roaring party afterwards.

ELAINE LEE (actress): We used to get so pissed.

CANDY RAYMOND: There were marvellous things like *TV Week* deciding to do a snow holiday theme so, bang, you're flown to the snow and put up in a lodge.

ELAINE LEE: We were really on the A-list, so in between working we were invited to stuff everywhere.

● ABOVE: The Number 96 bus . . . extensive damage to top deck and roof.

STARS' TERROR

96 BUS IN BRIDGE SMASH

TWO people came close to death when a bus driven by **Number 96** star Chard Hayward crashed into a bridge at Parramatta, Sydney.

Passengers on the bus said Chard's quick thinking averted what seemed certain disaster.

Number 96 star Pat McDonald got off the bus only minutes before the crash.

Chard, a licensed bus driver, jammed the bus's brakes seconds before its upper section ploughed into the bridge.

Television producer Godfrey Philipp, television pop personality Ian Meldrum, Glenys Long, Dolly East, James Fishburn and Phil Gremub were on the lower deck of the bus.

Ken East was also severely shaken and was helped from the scene.

The bus is the one used by Sydney's TEN10 to promote **Number 96** and other programs.

Also on board at the time was Roger Davies, who manages the pop group Sherbet, and Tom Greer, publicity director of TEN10.

They were returning from a promotional visit and picnic to the Warragamba Lion Park.

"The whole story sounds quite funny," said Chard, "but it was a lot more serious than it sounds.

"Two people came very close to being killed or seriously injured."

Chard said there was no visible sign indicating the bridge's height above the

"I am fairly good at estimating distances, probably gained from my time in the army, and I hesitated—then applied the brakes. We had slowed right down before we hit, but it was enough to smash the top off the bus, which is made of lightweight metal."

After the accident, the bus was reversed out from under the bridge and the rubble was cleared from the upstairs section and from the road.

Looking back, Chard said the accident should never have happened.

"There was a sign indicating it was a low bridge, but we were in the right-hand lane and it was obscured by traffic," he said.

"As it was, we just slid forward into the bridge, but if we had kept on going, it would have taken the tops

● ABOVE: Chard Hayward . . . jammed on the brakes.

when the accident happened," he said.

"I heard a loud crashing of glass and metal," he said.

"Then Chard yelled out.

left: A news article about Chard Hayward driving the *Number 96* publicity bus into a bridge

right: Tom Oliver, Abigail and Ron Shand promoting the show in Brisbane

SHEILA KENNELLY: You'd be invited to open fetes or something, but they'd really be inviting Norma Whittaker, not Sheila Kennelly. Pat McDonald got to the stage — she had so many invitations — she just refused to answer them if they were addressed to 'Dorrie Evans'.

KEVIN POWELL (production manager): It was never, 'Hello Pat McDonald.' It was, 'G'day Dorrie, Herbie.' Tom Oliver was never Tom. It was always, 'G'day Jack.' Every single member of that cast was a real person to that audience and I think that was the success of *Number 96*. People would talk to them about their problems as though they were talking to friends they saw every night over a beer in their lounge room at home.

TOM OLIVER: There're very few avid fans of a show like *Number 96* or *Neighbours* that know your real name. They call you by your character name. Depending on where I am I don't answer to it.

ELAINE LEE: It was always, 'Vera, Vera, Vera,' absolutely. You couldn't go anywhere without being recognised. I used to just wear a scarf over my head and dark glasses and no make-up, but

left: Candy (left) and Vicki (right) Raymond

right: The Raymond sisters on a publicity trip to Mt Thredbo

the minute I opened my mouth they would recognise the voice. I was never Elaine. I was Vera.

JEFF KEVIN (actor): Shopping became a problem and going to the cricket. I'm a great cricket fan. I love the cricket and that was always a major problem. I used to go with my brother. Elaine came with us one day and we told her she had to wear a terry-towelling hat with zinc cream on her nose. Well, she arrived looking like she was going to the south of France. She had the big hat and big sunglasses — extremely stylish. Well, that was just bedlam because people kept coming up to us all day, and once they saw her they looked around to see who else there was. My brother said, 'You'll never come to the cricket with me again.'

SHEILA KENNELLY: One evening Gordon and I went to a club together with other cast members. A lady asked if we were married and Gordon said, 'No, I've got my own little wife at home.' 'Isn't your wife jealous?' she enquired. Then looked at me rather maliciously and said, 'I like yez better with your wig on.'

JOE HASHAM: I could pretend to be cool and say it was extremely difficult, but I'd be lying. True, there were times when

I wished I could just fade into the background and disappear. However, for the most part I enjoyed the recognition. I was appreciative of the fact that I could walk into a full restaurant, without a booking, and immediately get a table.

TOM OLIVER: I recall one night we were in a restaurant in Sydney, and Lynn and I were at a little table for two and I had my back to the wall, and there was a couple over in the far corner and they recognised us and he kept sort of waving to me, and I just ignored him after the initial nod and smile. Anyway, he came across to the table and totally ignored Lynn and just spoke to Jack. 'Come on, Jack. Come on. The wife wants to meet you. Come on over, come on over.' I said, 'No thank you. Go away. I'm having dinner with my wife.' Simple as that. That sticks out in my mind. That idiot.

JOHNNY LOCKWOOD: Actually, Aldo's moustache was my idea because I had been in the *Bramston Show* and I knew what it was like to have people come at you in restaurants and so forth, and I thought, *well, I want to disguise myself*. So I altered my hair — instead of having it back I put it forward and I put a moustache on thinking nobody'll know me. The funny thing is ninety-nine percent of the people recognised me by my voice anyway.

MIKE DORSEY: It was a lot easier for me than it was for some of the others. It was fun. Obviously you get the autographs. I always agreed. I never ever refused. I don't think one should. It's a responsibility if you're a recognisable face to be available to the public. I mean, that's your bread and butter. Because I looked different to what I did on camera I wasn't subjected to as much of it as the others.

'Obviously you get the autographs. I always agreed. I never ever refused.'

ELAINE LEE: The lack of privacy got to me a bit. I hated that.

CHARD HAYWARD: Being recognised everywhere we went was not really an enjoyable experience. We had no privacy whatsoever and it wasn't as if we were earning the kind of money that television actors are earning today, so we couldn't buy huge houses with high walls that we could hide behind.

VIVIENNE GARRETT (actress): I was chased down Bondi Junction by a group of pubescent schoolboys, and I ran into a building society — I remember that — and said, 'Please can you just put me in the back room for a while.' And they did, until the crowd dispersed.

PAUL WEINGOTT: I remember walking with a woman friend in Broadway, outside Grace Brothers, and being mobbed a little bit. You know, three or four young women coming up and sort of going a bit crazy and actually tearing my shirt.

CANDY RAYMOND: One of the things that freaked me out was people asking for photos. That was often an interruption. Somebody would run up to you with a camera and say, 'Can I have a photo with my kid?' Autographs weren't so bad, but photos I kind of freaked out at.

VICTORIA RAYMOND: Actually, a fan took one of my favourite photos of James Elliott and me at the airport. I remember going into a fruit shop and having the fruiterer disappear out the back and come back with all this fruit wrapped up in a basket with cellophane and giving it to me.

CANDY RAYMOND: When Victoria was in the show at the same time, we'd do something like go dress shopping together and people would insist we didn't pay.

ELAINE LEE: If you wanted anything done, the minute they saw you were Vera doors just opened. It's extraordinary.

JEFF KEVIN: If Arnold didn't have anywhere to live, he'd get offers. I had offers of accommodation from all over the country, literally. They were genuine offers. There was a hotel somewhere in the country. They had ten rooms and said I could have whichever one I wanted, free of charge!

'If Arnold didn't have anywhere to live, he'd get offers. I had offers of accommodation from all over the country, literally.'

LYNN RAINBOW: There's a lovely charcoal drawing that a fan did of myself and my dog. They did it from a photo in the paper and framed it and sent it to me. Two other fans sent me the most wonderful handbag that they'd made, a leather handbag. Just out of the blue. I still have it somewhere.

PHILIPPA BAKER (actress): I received a letter from an eighty-year-old woman in a nursing home who wanted to know where she could buy a negligee like one Roma had worn. She said she had always promised herself that one day she'd get one like it. I would have given it to her if it hadn't been the one I had bought myself, many years previously, for my honeymoon.

WENDY BLACKLOCK: They used to send me presents, extraordinary presents. The sort of presents that they'd think Edie would enjoy, and I kept them for some years, like bunches of glass grapes, and they'd send me aprons, embroidered aprons that they'd made.

JAMES ELLIOTT: The people who got the fan mail were mostly the femme fatale type people like Vera, played by Elaine Lee and Abigail. They got a lot of fan mail from fellas. The fan mail that I got was usually from disgruntled Poms because this was the character I was playing.

VICTORIA RAYMOND: My fans were young teenage girls, mainly.

CHARD HAYWARD: Most of the fan mail was from young girls. I used to answer all of it at first, but then it just got to be too much.

CANDY RAYMOND: Lots of fan mail. It was a combination of male and female. There was some perfectly respectful fan letters from males and there was an awful lot of wank mail.

JOHNNY LOCKWOOD: This guy sought out myself and Abigail. We both started to get letters from this guy, who must've been as nutty as a fruitcake. He sent a lot of paper cuttings and one of them would be 'Chocolates, half price' or an advert for a hair-drying machine or something — nothing sensible, nothing at all. One day I got a key. He said, 'I'm going away for two weeks. My address in the Cross is so-and-so. Would you look after the place while I'm away?' So I went and had a look at this place, and lo and behold the key fitted.

Letters poured in by the hundreds and fans flocked to 83 Moncur Street, Woollahra, some even in tourist buses, to see Moncur Flats, the exterior setting for *Number 96*. The real residents must have wondered what hit them as they found themselves answering their doors to total strangers who had turned up hoping to catch a glimpse of Vera, Alf or Lucy, or pop into Norma's Bar for a glass of wine. The block of flats was enchanting. It was eye-opening and exciting, with something for everyone, and some viewers wanted to live there.

BILL HARMON (producer): When the first flat became vacant — I forget who moved out — we put up a question mark on the slide because we didn't know who the hell was moving in next, and we got three legitimate calls asking to rent the place.

Despite being a show for adults, *Number 96* was the second most popular television show with children aged six to fourteen, according to one 1973 report. It sat wedged between *The Brady Bunch* in the number one spot and *Bugs Bunny* at number three.

CANDY RAYMOND: It worried me a little at the time, once I had realised that my grand visions of hippie and feminist ideologies were not being supported. Jill was a pretty one-dimensional character. So it disturbed me a little when I realised I was being a role model for very young girls — or my character, rather than me.

WENDY BLACKLOCK: I remember when my children were at school. I wouldn't allow them to watch, you see, but they'd come home and their friends had told them everything that had been on the night before, but it was so exaggerated. I can remember saying it's better for them to watch occasionally and see for themselves than get the garbled version from the kids at school.

SHEILA KENNELLY: At Busby High School, where I opened a fete, teachers mentioned that getting the students' attention towards learning was difficult at first period as the pupils only wanted to discuss *Number 96*'s latest story. So the English teacher made a point of discussing Dorrie's malapropisms as a way of getting into the subject; the Science teacher, Les's latest invention — why it didn't work, how he could have improved it.

TOM OLIVER: I do remember little Ronnie Shand, who played Herbie. He and his wife, Letty — she passed away, unfortunately — had an apartment in Kings Cross and they knew all the hookers. And so they said at 8.30 at night in Sydney you couldn't get a taxi or a hooker, because they were all up in Ronnie's flat watching *Number 96*.

‘at 8.30 at night in Sydney you couldn't get a taxi or a hooker, because they were all up in Ronnie's flat watching Number 96.’

JAMES ELLIOTT: One time I did meet Mrs Penfold-Russell. She told me that she and her friends were all great fans of the show, but she couldn't go out at night because she had to stay in to watch *Number 96*.

THELMA SCOTT (actress): If we went out, if some of us went to a play or dinner, people would come up and say, 'Excuse me, we had to go out tonight. Would you tell us what's happening tonight?' We said, 'No, we can't tell you that. We probably did that four weeks ago.'

JILL FORSTER (actress): *Number 96* was tremendously interesting because there was this sort of cachet about the show where it was not really the show you watched. So people would recognise you on the street and in cafes and things like that, but they'd always follow it up with, '... but of course I don't watch it myself.'

KEVIN POWELL: I always remember one evening, some people who were friends of my family invited me for dinner. They'd gotten seven or eight other guests, and the lady of the house explained, 'This evening, I hope you don't mind, but we'll have our entrees and then we'll have a little pause, because I want Kevin to have a look at a particularly unusual Australian program that he might find interesting.' We all traipsed in and sat there, and at the end the theme music plays and the credits start rolling, and up comes 'Production Manager: Kevin Powell'. So anyway, over the dinner I suddenly found that, 'We don't actually watch this program ...' but as they had more and more to drink every single one at this table knew exactly where we were in storylines right up to the night before. And that's when I thought, *aha, we've made it!* Our writers used to say that we're writing for Mr and Mrs Blacktown, but it wasn't. It was across the board.

ELISABETH KIRKBY (actress): On one occasion we were being quizzed by the media about the show, and they were telling us

The
National Times
May 8—13, 1972 20c

No 96: PUTTING TV BACK 10 YEARS

A WEEK'S READING

top: A legion of fans of all ages

bottom: Bill Harmon had this headline framed and hanging in his office

that it wasn't even a drama, it was only a soap. I can remember Gordon McDougall saying, 'Perhaps it is only fish and chips, but it's bloody good fish and chips.'

> Gordon Mcdougall (actor): I don't think I've got any right to impose my taste for cordon bleu cooking on somebody. If they like fish and chips it's my job to serve them the best possible fish and chips. And that's what I'm trying to do here.[7]
>
> Ron Shand (actor): That is the key of all show business — entertainment — and we are giving the masses entertainment.[8]

NORMAN YEMM: Bill used to have a framed, full-page newspaper headline at the back of his desk — I can't remember the exact wording of it — where it said, '*Number 96* takes television back ten years,' or something to that effect, knocking it.

NANCY CASH (wife of Don Cash): I think Don was rather amazed that it generated as much comment as it did. I mean, the show was outrageous in many ways and it was intentionally outrageous, so he wasn't surprised that outrageous things got publicity because they were intended to. That's what they had set out to do, and it was happening and it was working and he was very pleased. I should think that Bill was too, but Don's attitude to all that was, 'They're worried about nudity? Well let's give 'em more,' you know, it's working.

ELEANOR WITCOMBE (writer): The shock-horror was there on purpose. Bill always admitted, 'That'll make 'em watch us.'

BOB HUBER (producer): They set out to create controversy. And they did. They wanted to farm the depths of any subject matter and they did. It's remarkable how many people I've met since that show who said they learned about life from it. There wasn't anything like it ever before. Nobody was as daring as Bill and Don in presenting what they did in the storylines. I think they did everything — we did drugs, we did pack rape, we did cancer. I mean, there were so many subjects that were controversial.

'Nobody was as daring as Bill and Don in presenting what they did in the storylines.'

CANDY RAYMOND: There was one storyline where my character had it off with a priest — Hilton Bonner — and that's the only one I can really recall having weird experiences in supermarkets. You know, little old ladies coming up and shaking their fingers at me and saying I should be ashamed of myself.

SHEILA KENNELLY: Veritas said, '*Number 96* has the wowsers in a frenzy. The knockers ring up with their complaints during the commercial breaks or after *Number 96* has finished, but never while it's on.'

TOM GREER: The Veritas column. That was the centrespread of the *Sunday Mirror*. Oh yes, there were no problems. You just had to get copy. Good, bad — it just didn't matter. We wanted to be mentioned in Parliament and we wanted the threat of losing our licence.

MORE OBJECT TO SEX ON TV

CANBERRA—Complaints about objectionable remarks and undue emphasis on sex in Australian television programs increased substantially in 1971-1972, the Australian Broadcasting Control Board said yesterday.

above: A controversial scene involving Hilton Bonner as Father O'Brien and Candy Raymond as Jill Sheridan

NANCY CASH: I think what genuinely puzzled Don was the attitude that so many people had, not in the business, but people in general had, that seemed to say, gee you shouldn't be making a show like this — that there was something wrong with making a big, successful show that generates a lot of publicity for outrageous things. I suppose, perhaps, there was just the element of it never having been done before.

CANDY RAYMOND: Cash Harmon — American boys — they knew how to keep *Number 96* happening. They produced not only the show, but the reaction to the show. They knew how to work the media.

TOM GREER: We entertained *Pix* and all the old scruffy things you'd find in the barbershop. It didn't worry us. *The Catholic Weekly* was a bit difficult. I tell you what, we got stories in there. It didn't matter; copy is copy. It got to the point where *TV Week* and *TV Times* were very important to us, but by God we were important to them. Particularly *TV Week*. *TV Week* was a very aggressive marketer and it had enormous sales. The cover was the ideal thing to have, but *Number 96* would get cover after cover after cover, and all of a sudden we said, 'Hang on, there's some other shows on this station as well.'

TV Week produced two special magazine supplements for eager fans who couldn't get enough of *Number 96*, and *Woman's Day* produced a twenty-four page lift-out.

Whether you liked it or not, *Number 96* could not be ignored. In fact, it seemed everyone was talking about it. On Channel 9's *Graham Kennedy Show*, host Graham Kennedy took great delight in the news that there had been a mix-up of *Number 96* episodes in Melbourne with two episodes screening out of order, causing confusion for viewers. Even the ABC's newly appointed chairman, Professor Richard Downing, admitted that he and his family watched the show. Famous faces of the day started popping up in cameo appearances, such as Mike Walsh, Noel Brophy, Brian Bury, Ron Frazer and Frank Thring (who turned up in the deli to buy a packet of cigarettes).

above: From left Noel Brophy, Ron Frazer (with Elaine Lee) and Frank Thring all made cameos in the show

DAVID SALE (writer): We had Robert Helpmann popping in — Sir Robert Helpmann — and the Duke and Duchess of Bedford. Cameos, you know.

CAROL RAYE (actress): I remember distinctly we had a very unusual guest duo: the Duke and Duchess of Bedford from England. The Bedfords were very high aristocracy. The Duke of Bedford and his wife, who was French, — very vivacious and attractive — came to Australia, for what reason I can't remember, and were co-opted into an episode. They did a cameo scene on the premise that Amanda Von Pappenburg, my character, the Baroness, had known them in England and either brought them to the wine bar or they dropped into the wine bar, and she said, 'Darlings, fancy seeing you.' So there was quite a good scene, but they were so professional and wonderful.

TED JOBBINS: So many people went through in those days. And it was through people like that, you know, in little cameo bits coming in — and really good actors — that all of a sudden people started saying, 'Oh, it's not so bad.'

DAVID SALE: Hazel Phillips begged us to come into it, and then of course I went overseas again on one of my little jaunts for a few weeks and they turned her lesbian. And she was horrified.

above: The real Duke and Duchess of Bedford meet Carol Raye as Baroness Amanda Von Pappenburg

opposite: Articles reporting on *Number 96*'s ratings dominance

She said, 'What will my ladies think?' because she had her audience of old ladies. Bill said, 'She's gotta decide whether she wants to be a fucking actress or a fucking personality.' We weren't very happy with Hazel because she went out of the show and really bad-mouthed it in the press. It's all made up now. It's all water under the bridge.

NORMAN YEMM: I was falling for Hazel and she was in love with Vera, who was in love with me [*laughs*].

Number 96 went from strength to strength, and continually knocked off the competition.

TED JOBBINS: First of all they started throwing in big, major movies, but the problem was it was stripped across the five days and a major movie's one night. Even then, the ratings would drop a little, but it never affected it. Channel 9 gave up. Eight-thirty to nine made a difficult time period. Eight-thirty is prime time. They couldn't throw in something every night of the week. Channel 7 put in odd things, but they didn't seem to fight it as much. They just couldn't do anything.

Rivals fight back: ALL~OUT TV WAR ON '96'

LISTENER IN TV 10c

Vol. 46, No. 27 July 14-July 20, 1973

TV channels are loading big guns to counter the extraordinary popularity of "Number 96."

● GTV9 will give away $20,000 worth of prizes next week in a competition aimed at bribing viewers NOT to watch "96."

IT'S 96'S YEAR!

TWO series, miles apart in themes, have won the drama awards at this year's Logie Awards.

They are the 0-10 Network's soap opera saga **Number 96,** which won the best Australian drama series award and ABC-TV's **Seven Little Australians,** a period costume production, which won the best new drama award.

Seven Little Australians was a Logie triumph with two of its stars Leonard Teale and Elizabeth Alexander winning awards.

Seven Little Australians is undoubtedly one of the finest dramas produced in Australia to date.

But while it's reaping awards in Australia, it's overseas success is no less outstanding.

Currently it is shaping up as the most successful series ever to be exported from this country.

Rights to it have been snapped up in North and South America by the giant 20th Century organisation, and in the United Kingdom it will be screened on the BBC.

The world distribution company of Global has sold it to Sweden where it has already begun screening and sales seem almost certain to Denmark, Holland and Norway.

In Sweden it has won the honor of gaining the biggest rating ever for a children's series, though most might argue its appeal extends well into the adult viewing audience.

The first chance Americans will have of seeing **Seven Little Australians** is when it premieres on the CBS Greater New York Network.

It is being treated by CBS as a trial before it is spread throughout its normal channels.

It will probably be renamed and screened in five hour-long episodes (in Australia it was 10 half-hour episodes)

Seven Little Australians was a co-production between the ABC and Ethel Turner Productions and the Australian Film Development Corporation.

While all three are rightly sharing in its glory much of the individual credit must go to its freelance director Ron Way and executive producer Charles Russell.

In particular, Ron Way treated the entire project as a task of love and his understanding, control and guidance rarely faltered.

At times he had to fight for his ideas, but he won out and few could criticise the end result.

He faithfully brought out via his actors all of the pathos and joy which made Ethel Turner's original book a best-seller.

"It has shown that Australians have the ability to produce drama which ranks among the finest," enthused one critic.

To say **Seven Little Australians'** success was a surprise is probably an understatement.

Equally surprising was the way it brought together a cast of relatively unknowns (apart from Leonard Teale) and welded them together in one of the finest casts assembled.

Overnight it won a giant-size reputation for Elizabeth Alexander and it both destroyed and created a new image for Leonard Teale (See story, pages 20-21.)

For eight years Leonard had checked in weekly as one of the men of **Homicide,**

● ABOVE, LEFT: Joe Hasham . . . the heart throb of Number 96.
● LEFT: The two sisters of Number 96 . . . Candy and Vicki Raymond. Vicki left the show earlier this year.

Page 10—TV WEEK—MARCH 16, 1974

Casualties of the show's success included Tony Barber's *Great Temptation*, and the chat show *JC at 8.30*, hosted by Cash Harmon's old mate John Collins, who'd helped them on their way to success just a few years before. In time the Cash Harmon office would move from the Crows Nest office John Collins had provided, to 35 Grosvenor Street, Neutral Bay.

TOM OLIVER: It was an American company out of New York that did a worldwide survey and found that *Number 96*, pro rata of population, at 8.30 at night, was the highest rating TV show in the world. That's quite something.

JAMES ELLIOTT: It was one of the highest rating programs of its kind in the world — this was a quotation from one of New York's newspapers, *The Times*. So Channel 10 was bumping along on top of the pops. They were really enjoying the fame and fortune, and everybody was very happy about it of course.

With its staggeringly high ratings the series made four consecutive appearances in the national top ten shows of the year, taking the number one spot in both 1973 and 1974. Attracting such a huge audience share enabled the network to finally attract the big advertisers and the big bucks. *Number 96* was made at a cost of $10,000 per episode, and its success turned the fortunes of the 0/10 Network around.

‘Number 96, pro rata of population, at 8.30 at night, was the highest rating TV show in the world. That’s quite something.’

TED JOBBINS: There was one stage where — around about the period when *Number 96* came in — there was talk of taking one of the three commercial channels away. The government was saying there were too many channels and people were saying we've got to get rid of one, the papers were saying that. But because with *Number 96* the ratings evened out across the board there was no way of getting rid of the 0/10 Network by that stage, which became the 10 Network right across the country. *Number 96* established 10 as a major network in Australia.

In February 1974, Crawford's *The Box* began on the 0/10 Network. Set in a fictional television station, *The Box* followed *Number 96*'s emphasis on sex and nudity and enjoyed very high ratings. During its three-and-a-half-year run its popular cast included Belinda Giblin, Lois Ramsey, George Mallaby, Paul Karo, Judy Nunn, Ken James, Barrie Barkla, Fred Betts, Peter Regan, Briony Behets, Jill Forster, Ken Snodgrass, Cheryl Rixon, John Stanton and Tracy Mann. Screening right after *Number 96*,

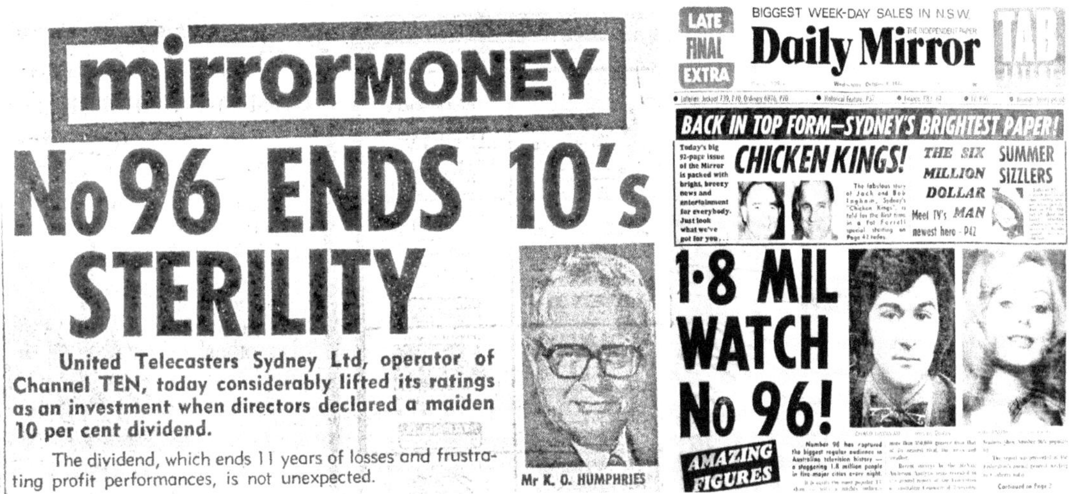

mirrorMONEY

No96 ENDS 10's STERILITY

United Telecasters Sydney Ltd, operator of Channel TEN, today considerably lifted its ratings as an investment when directors declared a maiden 10 per cent dividend.

The dividend, which ends 11 years of losses and frustrating profit performances, is not unexpected.

Mr K. O. HUMPHRIES

LATE FINAL EXTRA

BIGGEST WEEK-DAY SALES IN N.S.W.

Daily Mirror

TAB

BACK IN TOP FORM—SYDNEY'S BRIGHTEST PAPER!

Today's big 52-page issue of the Mirror is packed with bright, breezy news and entertainment for everybody. Just look what we've got for you...

CHICKEN KINGS!

THE SIX MILLION DOLLAR MAN

Meet TV's newest hero - P42

SUMMER SIZZLERS

1·8 MIL WATCH No 96!

AMAZING FIGURES

Number 96 has captured the biggest regular audience in Australian television history — a staggering 1.8 million people in five major cities every night.

above: More articles on *Number 96*'s ratings success

it was another major factor in the network's continuing success. Often described as a rival to *Number 96*, the series is more accurately seen as a stablemate.

TOM GREER: I had a version of the Southern Aurora take both the cast of *Number 96* and Crawford's *The Box* to Brisbane for a street parade and their 'Channel 10 is 10' celebrations. That was also a hoot. I even got to drive the train. 'My two shiny bands to destiny,' I called the tracks from the driver's seat.

Number 96 triumphed when the *TV Week* Logie Awards were announced. Having won the Logie for Best New Drama in 1973 it went on to win Logies for Best Australian Drama in 1974, 1975 and 1976. Pat McDonald's personal success at Logies time saw her win Best Actress awards in 1973, 1974 and 1976, as well as the coveted 1974 Gold Logie Award for Most Popular Female Personality on Australian Television. In 1975, the year Pat missed out on the Best Actress Logie, the award went to Bunney Brooke. It is largely believed Bunney received the award in particular for scenes involving bride-to-be Flo being jilted at the altar.

left: From left, Sheila Kennelly, John Wayne, Bill Harmon and Pat McDonald at the 1975 *TV Week* Logie Awards. Courtesy Sheila Kennelly

right: Bunney Brooke as Flo, jilted at the altar

PETER BENARDOS (director): I remember shooting in a church when Bunney Brooke, Flo, was getting married, but the groom didn't turn up and that was a very sad scene, with this poor little figure holding onto a little posy of flowers. It was one of the best things Bunney ever did — I cried and so did she. It was beautiful.

BUNNEY BROOKE (actress): That was only a fifty-second scene, but with those fifty seconds I had to get across the heartbreak that Flo was going through, and it was done almost wholly without a word being spoken.[9]

JILL FORSTER: I didn't have too much to do with Bunney's character, but I used to love watching her work. I thought she was a quintessentially fine actress, and she was the one that I would watch more than any of the others.

CAROL RAYE: In real life Bunney Brooke was a fabulous character, a fabulous person. She was a very good actor and had a great deal of experience, and she was a great strength in that whole soap opera.

As *Number 96*'s star continued to shine, attempts were made to cash in. There were several novels based on early storylines from the show, but only one title, *Bev & Bruce & Maggie & Don*, featured cast members on its cover. After ruffling some actors' feathers due to lack of remuneration, the follow-ups all featured unknowns.

TOM OLIVER: I think I saw one, one day, and you don't complain. You just ring up your agent and ask what he can do about it. That's what they get paid ten percent for. If I did make a fuss it's all forgotten now and gone. Comes under the heading, 'Exploitation', probably.

PETER BENARDOS: We introduced a *Number 96* t-shirt and so I wore one somewhere, in the garden mowing the lawn or whatever. Everybody stopped and said, 'Where can I get one of those?'

Long before anyone ever heard of Kylie Minogue, or countless other soapie stars who have attempted recording careers, eight *Number 96* cast members released records. These ranged from novelty songs by Johnny Lockwood with 'In My Deli on the Telly/No. 96' and James Elliott's version of 'The Streak', to a contemporary album, *New World*, by Joe Hasham, a ballad by Norman Yemm called 'Darlin' Vera', and an album of duets by Ron Shand and Pat McDonald called *Old Fashioned Way*, which went gold. Abigail and Chard Hayward also released albums following their exposure in *Number 96*. And that's not all. *TV Times* magazine released an album of TV themes as voted for by viewers. Performed by Eric Jupp and his orchestra, the *Number 96* theme 'Paperboy' was included alongside the themes of other shows such as *Skippy*, *Division 4* and *Aunty Jack*.

NORMAN YEMM: I wanted to write something about Elaine Lee because she was wonderful to work with: 'Darlin' Vera, I am so lonely because I'm lost without your love.' It fitted in with *Number 96*, but I tell you where it was funny —

As well as novels based on early storylines and a cookbook featuring cast members' favourite recipes, there were *Number 96* t-shirts and records galore writing: 'You made me go away from 96.' We were promoting this single and Channel 9 wanted me to sing on this show, but we had to change the words: 'You made me go away from 96.' They were so paranoid about promoting another channel.

JAMES ELLIOTT: Denis Whitburn came to me one time and he said, 'Listen, we've got a record here and we've got the rights to it and we wonder if you could sing it for us.' I said, 'I'm not a singer.' He said, 'Oh it doesn't matter, you don't have to be a singer.' It was a thing called 'The Streak' and because I had been associated with the streak through the dining car of the Southern Aurora I would have some expertise in this area — streaking. Doug Ashdown was involved in it too. He played the banjo and perhaps some other musical instruments. It was recorded in Glebe. I can't recall the name of the studio now. It was Col Joye's studio.

JOHNNY LOCKWOOD: I wrote 'In My Deli on the Telly' but it didn't sell in the shops. I used to sell it at my clubs, which sold a few. There's another song on the other side: 'Number 96, Number 96, we're all a lovely bunch of happy lunatics.' Remember that one? That's on the other side of it.

JOE HASHAM: I enjoyed making the album, especially working with Ron Falson, musical director. The album was actually a joint idea of Channel 10 and my management team, and was structured around the TV Special *Hasham* directed by Ron Way and produced by James Fishburn. It was a lot of fun. Hard to believe it was over forty years ago.

Shops across Australia with a street address of 96 emblazoned their businesses with the *Number 96* logo, and for some of those directly involved with the show life started imitating art, and vice versa. Nancy Cash had a dress boutique in Sydney's Double Bay called The Tapemeasure, as did Vera Collins in the show. Chard Hayward opened a hairdressing salon in Cremorne called Dudley's, while Dudley opened one on-screen, and Tom Oliver and Lynn Rainbow opened a bar.

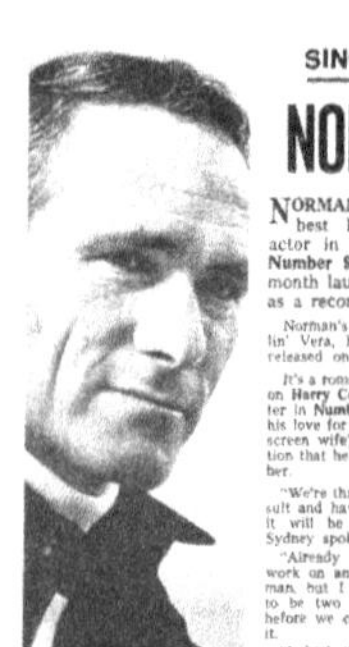

SINGLE NOW AND AN ALBUM SOON

NORMAN YEMM GOES POP

NORMAN YEMM — best known as an actor in **Homicide** and **Number 96** — will this month launch his career as a recording artist.

Norman's first single, Darlin' Vera, has already been released on RCA.

It's a romantic ballad based on **Harry Collins,** his character in **Number 96.** It tells of his love for **Vera Collins** (his screen wife) and his realisation that he is "no good" for her.

"We're thrilled with the result and have no doubt that it will be a hit," said a Sydney spokesman for RCA.

"Already we have begun work on an album for Norman, but I would expect it to be two months at least before we consider releasing it.

"I think the single will be in the charts for that long."

The single, Norman's first, features Jean on the flipside.

TELE DISC with TONY FAWCETT and IAN DOUGALL

He will also begin a tour of the Riverina soon.

"I will be making television appearances to promote the record, but I probably won't have time for any acting," said Norman.

"I'm tremendously excited about the way RCA has greeted Darlin' Vera.

"I didn't want to put out

duced in all areas with the tracks He's Part Of Us; Summer (The First Time); If'n I Was God and She standing out. He also does an excellent version of Killing Me Softly With Her Song. Goldsboro plays rhythm guitar, 12-string guitar and the harmonica on the album.

★ ★

FAIRPORT CONVENTION has released a new album titled Fairport Convention Nine (Festival). This punchy album follows through with their original sound and style. The tracks, The Hexhamshire Lass, Bring 'Em Down, Pleasure And Pain and Polly On The Shore all stand out.

★ ★

JOHN BATTERSBY, trumpeter with the **Daly Wilson Big Band** gets a solo airing on a new and exciting album called *Love Is A Feeling*. It's on the Copperfield label and features brassy

BAN ON ALDO'S SAUCY RECORD!

A RECORD made by **Number 96's** Johnny Lockwood has had an unofficial ban placed on it by most radio stations throughout Australia.

The stations are refusing to play the record, Number 96, because they believe its lyrics may offend some listen-

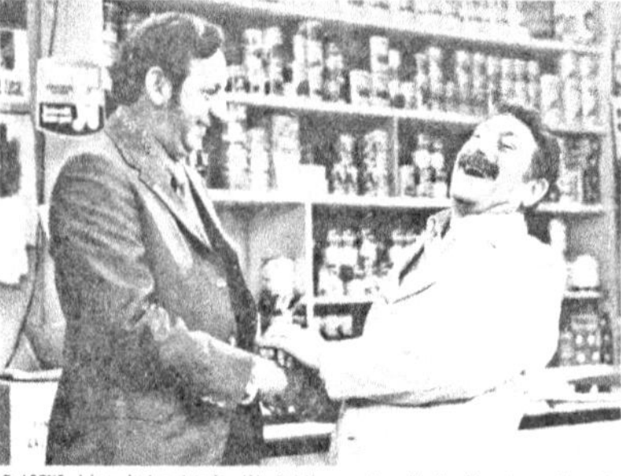

● ABOVE: Johnny Lockwood in his Aldo Godolfus gear from Number 96, enjoys a joke with Queensland TV man Les Harmon of RTQ7, Rockhampton.

offensive in this beautiful the slightest bit dirty is Number 96 was written for

TOM OLIVER: I had this idea because on the foot of the *Number 96* building was a wine bar that Jack Sellars owned. So I got the Cash Harmon permission to open one in reality, with exactly the same decor, and we approached Penfold's wines. It was just a wine bar and damn good steaks. We had a property on a corner in Kensington. It was okay with Sheila Kennelly too, to do a copy of the famous nude painting of her. It was the same decor as the one on the show, so people felt they were part of the show, which was the whole purpose of the place to start with.

opposite: Several *Number 96* stars released records

above left: *Number 96* stars took their on-screen businesses into the real world

above right: Norma's Bar inspired Tom Oliver to open his own version called Jack's Cellar in Sydney's Kensington

LYNN RAINBOW: We would go there at least probably three or four times a week for dinner, and be seen and talk and socialise and be there to sign autographs if necessary, but people just liked to come up and say, 'G'day, love the show.'

TED JOBBINS: When Tom opened that bar in Kensington everybody went along to that to give him support.

TOM OLIVER: It was called Jack's Cellar, as in wine cellar. So Jack Sellars became Jack's Cellar. The whole thing was there to exploit the character, and it was full of people who would come from the airport having flown from Perth. They'd still have their suitcases with them. They'd stop off at Anzac Parade on their way into the city to have a drink in Jack's Cellar. They were fans of *Number 96*. It worked a treat.

Magazines and newspapers ran competitions offering fans the chance to win a role in the show. One such competition was won by eighteen-year-old Robyn Weingott, whose father Owen and brother Paul had already made their mark on the series.

ROBYN WEINGOTT: I won a role in *Number 96* when I was eighteen. I ended up not taking up the offer as I was sitting for my Higher School Certificate and the filming fell on the day I

THREE GIRLS ON THE WAY TO FAME

The three girls (above) who could be going on to stardom, are Robyn Weingott, Vivien Stacy and Charmaine Vakanas.

They are among the 11 people who won roles in Channel Ten's nightly serial, Number 96.

A competition was run by the Daily Mirror to find personalities to appear in the series.

Thousands of entries were received. Everyone, it seemed, wanted to be a part of the curious activities that occur in Number 96.

The finalists were shown scenes of the serial being taped at the Ten studios and met the stars of the show.

They now wait their call to go before the cameras.

YOU could star in Number 96!

YOU could be a TV star—simply by filling in this coupon. The Mirror and Channel 10 are offering 10 people of any age, the chance of a role in Number 96. Simply fill in your name, age and address, then give a description of yourself in about a dozen words. ADDRESS your entry to: TV PARTS, Box 7066, GPO, Sydney 2001.

telephotos

WHEN Tom Oliver, Number 96's Jack Sellars, opened a bistro in Sydney, Number 96 cast members were prominent among the first night crowd. Above: Enjoying themselves were, from left, Jeff Kevin, Thelma Scott, Elaine Lee, Bettina Welch and Chard Hayward. At left, others in the cast attending were, from left, Sheila Kennelly, Oliver, Bunney Brooke and Ron Shand with a visitor, Judy Lake, at front. Below: A moustachioed Robert Bruning was there with Pamela Garrick and the couple were greeted by Joe Hasham.

was sitting my English exam. Once I received my results, Dad said perhaps I should have filmed the episode.

If fans still weren't satisfied, they could always go on an overseas package tour with their favourite *Number 96* stars.

TOM OLIVER: During *Number 96*, American Express asked the cast to accompany parties of people; some to Europe, some to the States. I had done this American Express ad for them and I said I'd go along with that, but Lynn and I chose to go to the States.

opposite top left: Robyn Weingott (left) and two other competition winners pose for the press. Courtesy Robyn Rowlison

opposite bottom left: A competition run by the *Daily Mirror* to win a role on *Number 96*

opposite right: Celebrating the opening of Tom Oliver's bar, Jack's Cellar

above: A promotional brochure for a European package tour with the stars of *Number 96*. Courtesy Elaine Elliott

SHEILA KENNELLY: I had a free trip to Europe on a Tele Tour organised by American Express — a whirlwind trip to England, France, Switzerland, Italy, Austria, Germany and Holland in December 1974. Also travelling were Johnny Lockwood, Bettina Welch, Philippa Baker and James Elliott.

TOM OLIVER: So we did all that. We didn't actually take them. They had tour guides, but they advertised it inasmuch as you could come to America with Jack Sellars or you could go to Europe with Aldo, Johnny Lockwood's character. That sort of thing. That's how they promoted it.

"N U M B E R 96"

ORIGINAL SCREENPLAY BY

DAVID SALE

and

JOHNNY WHYTE

PROPERTY OF: CASH HARMON TELEVISION PTY.LTD.,

293 PACIFIC HIGHWAY,

CROWS NEST 2065
'Phone: 926836

Chapter 8

On the Big Screen in Colour

In 1973, Cash Harmon unveiled a bold plan: a feature film version of *Number 96*.

DAVID SALE (writer): We were all so swept away by the extreme success of the show. Nobody was really thinking about anything else but getting the show on. When it did come time for the movie, well, of course Johnny Whyte was the story editor by that time, and with myself as creator and head writer we were asked to collaborate on a script.

JAMES ELLIOTT (actor): It was just an idea to make money, I suppose. The producers made a lot of money out of it, I'm told, and the actors made some pocket money.

PETER BENARDOS (director): Well the show was so successful. Who suggested we try and do a movie version called *Number 96: The Movie* I really don't know. It could've been Bill's idea or it could've been Channel 10's management, but it sounded good.

DAVID SALE: The idea for the movie? I don't know. I can't remember. It was probably Bill Harmon's. It happened very quickly and very economically too.

ELISABETH KIRKBY (actress): It was announced in no uncertain terms that we would be paid a flat fee for the film, a fee that reflected Bill's assessment of the value he placed on our character in the film. The choice was ours — we either agreed to the fee offered or our character would not be in the film at all.

SHEILA KENNELLY (actress): We just did everything in those days, whatever we were asked, pretty well. I remember it was very hot, there was nowhere much to change and there wasn't seating. That's right, I do remember I was cross about that. It was all done on the run, everything was done in such a ruddy hurry, and on the cheap as well.

above: A daybill for the *Number 96* movie

DAVID SALE: It was done very cheaply because, of course, it was done on the studio sets. The actors were paid their regular salaries and it was done in two weeks.

ELAINE LEE (actress): It was done in two weeks and we were paid exceedingly badly for it. The actors wanted to hold out for more money and it was Pat McDonald — I was angry about the whole thing because Pat McDonald said, 'We'll do it, we'll do it,' and she being the hottest thing in the show we didn't have a leg to stand on. So we all did it, but actually I thought the movie was good. It was fun. It worked.

DAVID SALE: We knew everything back to front, so what we did was just say, 'Well, you take scenes one to twenty and I take twenty-one to forty,' and we knew that they would link up because we were so in-tune with everything. So we just decided then, between the two of us, on the plotlines that would use all the characters to the best advantage.

PETER BENARDOS: Bill said, 'You and Brian will be directing.' I said, 'That's fine.' He said, 'You do the studio side of it and Brian can do the outside broadcasts.' There's a bowling segment and so forth.

KEVIN POWELL (production manager): It had to be started on the Monday after we finished shooting on the Friday. Johnny McLean did the camera operating on the film. We shot that on three 16mm cameras. It was like multi-cam, but instead of multi-cam they were all independently mounted Arriflex cameras shooting at different positions.

TOM OLIVER (actor): It was shot in ten days over the Christmas break. They put 16mm cameras on television dollies, controlled from the one source again, and used them like ordinary video cameras. That's why they were able to shoot the lot in ten days, but oh God it was awful.

LYNN RAINBOW (actress): Doing the film was a bit like a day on the set, really, because it was how we worked doing the series.

DAVID SALE: The only departure from doing the regular episodes were two days that were allotted for location shooting, something we'd never done before then. All the cast knew their lines; they knew their characters. There weren't many retakes as there are in regular movies, and it was just rushed through.

'here the audience had a chance to see their favourite characters on the big screen in colour for the first time.'

CHARD HAYWARD (actor): It was a stroke of genius. Remember, the TV program was in black and white at the time so here the audience had a chance to see their favourite characters on the big screen in colour for the first time. The script had already been written when I joined the cast, but my character became so popular very quickly that they decided to write me in.

JEFF KEVIN (actor): We made it in about a week-and-a-half. There's some really funny stuff, but it was so badly done. It's got a cult following. I had a small role, I didn't have a huge part to play.

SHEILA KENNELLY: I was just one of the background characters in that. I didn't really have a storyline.

LYNN RAINBOW: It was good, and my character was actually one of the main characters in the film. They tried to murder me and Tom Oliver came to my rescue.

JOHN ORCSIK (actor): I was in Melbourne shooting *Petersen* and while I was shooting that a script arrived from Sydney,

MORE NUDES, SEX SCENES, RAPE AND VIOLENCE...

96 MOVIE SHOCKER!

● ABOVE: James Elliot (Alf Sutcliffe) dressed as a swagman in the Number 96 movie. In this scene Lucy (Elizabeth Kirkby) is sending up her husband.

● BELOW: Claire Houghton (Thelma Scott) and Dorrie Evans (Pat McDonald) in some of the elaborate costumes used in the film.

NUMBER 96 shocked the television masses and now its big-screen equivalent, the Number 96 movie, should do the same with theatre audiences.

For the movie — featuring the same cast as the television series — can match it nude scene for nude scene and sensation for sensation. And there are plenty of both.

The movie opens with a brutal rape scene and is followed by drama upon drama.

Though, producers still hasten to add that it's all no more revealing or shocking than everyday life in a typical suburban block of flats.

Like the series, it is heavily laced with humor.

But, unlike the series, it's all in glowing color and the nude scenes are more explicit — due to the more liberal censorship of movies compared with television.

One of the first to doff her clothes is attractive actress Rebecca Gilling, who plays an air hostess called Diana Moore.

She is joined by Tom Oliver (Jack Sellars), Elaine Lee (Vera Collins) and newcomer John Orcsik, who plays Simon Carr.

While Joe Hasham makes a first in his homosexual role of Don Finlayson by appearing in bed with another man.

On television, the Broadcasting Control Board's strict rulings on such subjects as homosexuality barely allow Don Finlayson to even shake another man's hand.

The movie was made in a record 11 days in a new film studio at Sydney's TEN10 where the television serial is produced.

It was written by Johnny Whyte (96's regular editor) and David Sale (the creator) and directed by Peter Bernardos and Brian Phyllis, both regulars on the series' production.

Its producer was Bill Harmon, the man who, with the late Don Cash, first brought Number 96 to Australian television.

If it's successful, a follow-up movie will almost certainly go into production. #

● BELOW: Vera Collins (Elaine Lee) is kidnapped by a bikie gang intent on rape.

● RIGHT: Claire Houghton (Thelma Scott), Herb Evans (Ron Shand) and Dorrie Evans (Pat McDonald) at a fancy dress ball.

● ABOVE: Dorrie Evans and Flo Patterson wait for their scene in the 96 movie.

MAY 11, 1974—TV WEEK—Page 11

above: Details of the movie were fed to the press to hype the *Number 96* movie's release

which was the *Number 96* film script. I remember reading it, going, 'Are you kidding me? This is tantamount to porn.' There was this one section where Elaine Lee was meant to go down on me. And I said, 'I'm not doing this.'

> *'I remember reading [the script], going, 'Are you kidding me? This is tantamount to porn.''*

ELISABETH KIRKBY: I was quite genuinely taken by surprise when I saw the *Number 96* movie. I had no idea how risqué some of the situations were.

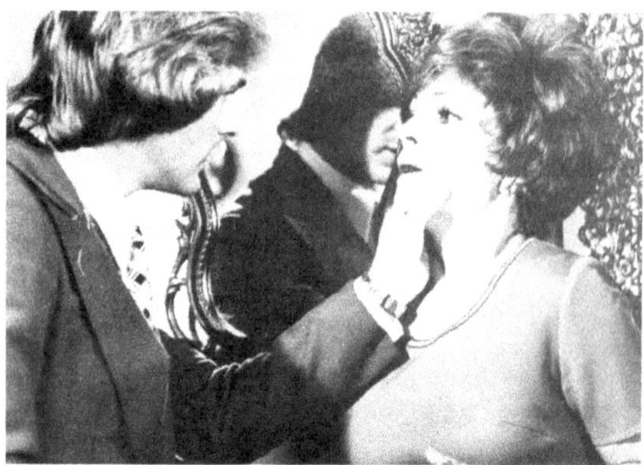

left: Patrick Ward as Tony Brent threatens Elaine Lee as Vera

right: Elaine Lee as Vera in bed with John Orcsik, who reprised his role as Simon Carr from the TV series

DAVID SALE: It started off with Elaine Lee being raped. Her frock was ripped off and her breasts were shown and she was raped by these bikies — that was before the titles! We kidded that we put that in right off the top so that the audience would know they hadn't walked into the wrong cinema.

ELAINE LEE: I do remember the opening scene of the film where Vera's driving a motorcar along this lonely road — she was never known as a driver — when she suddenly gets a flat tyre or something was wrong with the engine. She saw these headlights coming towards her and she stepped out onto the road to stop them. They were a team of bikies and there were about four or five of them, I suppose, and the inevitable happened, of course.

PATRICK WARD (actor): There were a few people I knew who played the other bikies. Phil Avalon was one of the extras. There were quite a few of them that I knew so we became just like a little bikie pack, and there was Elaine screaming her tits off as I'm ripping off her dress.

JOHN ORCSIK: I had a hysterical time with Elaine Lee, being naked with her in bed. The whole thing was just an absolute riot. Unbeknownst to me, during all those scenes everybody was upstairs viewing the whole thing.

‘The whole thing was just an absolute riot.’

JOHNNY LOCKWOOD (actor): If you remember the film, I was supposed to accidentally burn the money up that was meant for the tax people. I think that was the idea. And to get extra money I got myself a job running weddings in a wedding reception, right? Well, that idea came because I *did* own a big wedding reception place.

TOM OLIVER: I do remember Thelma Scott sitting in a swimming pool and the butler wading in to serve her a drink. That was so Thelma. She loved that.

THELMA SCOTT (actress): That little chap, Mutashi — in the pool: ‘Oh Mutashi, you've bruised the gin.’ I was in a swimming pool. But that little fellow who played Mutashi, he was about five foot; he wasn't tall. He reached to my hip. You know about the rehearsal scene? I met him and said hello and then I said, ‘There seems to be a smell of anaesthetic.’ He said, ‘I'm sorry. It's me.’ Alarmed, I said, ‘Have you been hurt?’ ‘No, I've just come from the university. I'm studying to be a head surgeon and I've been cutting up cats.’ So that scene was played out reeking of anaesthetic.

DAVID SALE: We thought the idea of a threatened wife would be good and Lynn was a good actress, so we thought let's bring Lynn back.

LYNN RAINBOW: I shot all my scenes in one day — eighteen scenes — and I finished just in time. They promised they'd have me out because I was doing a play. I wasn't just doing a bit part in a play, I was playing Elvira in *Blithe Spirit* at Marian Street for Alastair Duncan, who directed it. And it was the day my in-laws had arrived from England and Tom was bringing them to

left: Thelma Scott in one of the movie's more surreal scenes

right: Sonia being urged to leap from flat 5's balcony

opposite: Patrick Ward. Courtesy Patrick Ward

the theatre. It was the last night of the play, my in-laws had just arrived and I finished eighteen scenes, but I hopped in the car and rushed to the theatre.

Lynn Rainbow wasn't the only former cast member of the TV series to return for the movie.

JOHN ORCSIK: Originally, when I'd auditioned for *Number 96* — when I was actually in the series — Tom Oliver and I were going for the same role of Jack Sellars. Tom Oliver got the role obviously, and then they actually wrote something for me in it, which was Simon Carr, a designer of some kind, the same character they wanted to write into the film. Then suddenly I'm having this bloody sex scene with Joe Hasham, and I went, 'No way, I'm not doing it.' Bill kept insisting and I kept saying no, so Bill upped the money but I kept saying no. Bill could not relate that it did not have anything to do with money. He was a lovely guy, but his mentality was that I was trying to screw him for more money. Nothing could be further from the truth. In the end my agent said, 'Look, please do me a favour and get him off my back.'

Actors James Condon and Patrick Ward had also appeared in the TV series at one time or another. Towards the end of 1972, James Condon portrayed Don's uncle Sir Arnold Ashton. In the movie he played politician Nick Brent, father of Tony Brent, the bikie rapist played by Patrick Ward.

PATRICK WARD: James Condon. I remember him from years ago. He did a Barossa Pearl commercial or something and I think he had a patch on one eye. In the ad he was carrying a sword — this was when I was about nine or ten — and I thought, *my God, what a dashing looking man*, and now he's playing my father.

ELAINE LEE: Jimmy Condon played the soon-to-be prime minister that Vera falls in love with.

Harry Lawrence, who had unsuccessfully auditioned for the role of Alf Sutcliffe, appeared in *Number 96: The Movie* as drunkard Horace Deerman, but during the run of the series he played two different characters, including John Vernon, a mate of Harry Collins' from AA. In 1972, Patrick Ward had played Mike Parsons, a colleague of Don Finlayson, in the TV series.

PATRICK WARD: All I remember about that is I was there to try and blackmail Don out of the office by telling people that he was homosexual, and I think I was in for about two weeks or something.

Of the rest of the guest cast, Alister Smart appeared in the movie as Duncan Hunter and then joined the series as a different character towards the end of its run, while Rebecca Gilling, who played Diana Moore, only ever appeared in the big screen version. Uncredited performers include Paul Chubb, as a sauna delivery man, and Caz Lederman and Phil Avalon as bikies.

TOM OLIVER: There's a clip where Rebecca Gilling is in the shower and Jack gets home and sticks his head in the bathroom. We talk, and while we're talking I'm quietly taking my clothes

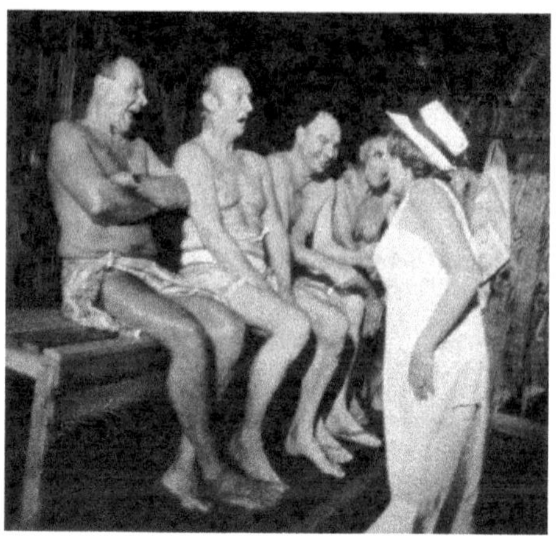

off and slide the shower curtain back, and the famous line is, 'Move over sweetheart, and watch where you put the soap.'

'the famous line is, 'Move over sweetheart, and watch where you put the soap.''

Rebecca Gilling spent a lot of her time naked in *Number 96: The Movie*, but the blokes got their gear off too, especially when Les Whittaker and Herb Evans opened a men's sauna in the basement. This storyline allowed for a lot of laughs, particularly in one scene when Dorrie Evans unwittingly comes face to face with a sauna full of naked men. It was one of many memorable scenes throughout the movie.

DAVID SALE: I wrote Claire's drunk scene where she rambles on, and she gets drunker and drunker and rambles on and on. I remember doing that with great pleasure.

JOHN ORCSIK: Then came the big moment with Joe. Joe and I had talked about it. 'Look, Johnny Whyte and David Sale, the entire PR department,' I said, 'I hear that they're all going to sneak up onto the set even though we've said it's going to be closed.' He said, 'Yeah, I heard.' I said, 'Right, well this is opposite left: Rebecca Gilling as Diana Moore

opposite right: After a wild chase scene, Dorrie ended up trapped in the all-male sauna in the *Number 96* basement

right: Thelma Scott and James Condon in *Number 96: The Movie*

what we're going to do in rehearsal. I'm meant to be putting sunscreen or something on because I got burnt and I haven't got any clothes on, and you come in out of the shower,' or whatever it was. 'I'm going to grab hold of you and throw you down onto the bed' — totally nothing to do with the choreography or anything like that — 'and we're going to roll around,' and he said, 'Okay.' 'And we'll give them a fucking eyeful.' So that's what we did. It was hysterical: 'Cut, cut, cut!'

JOE HASHAM (actor): Yeah, I remember kissing John Orcsik — good fun!

JOHN ORCSIK: So then we did it properly. It was hysterical. We just couldn't stop, we laughed and laughed and laughed. We were friends, we were men. It didn't bother me at all. I've had gay friends all my life through the theatre. That wasn't the issue ever. I didn't have a problem with any of that.

LYNN RAINBOW: David tells me there were things cut from the film, scenes that were cut and now they've been lost. It was about the Joe Hasham character and John Orcsik.

DAVID SALE: The kiss was cut out after the initial run.

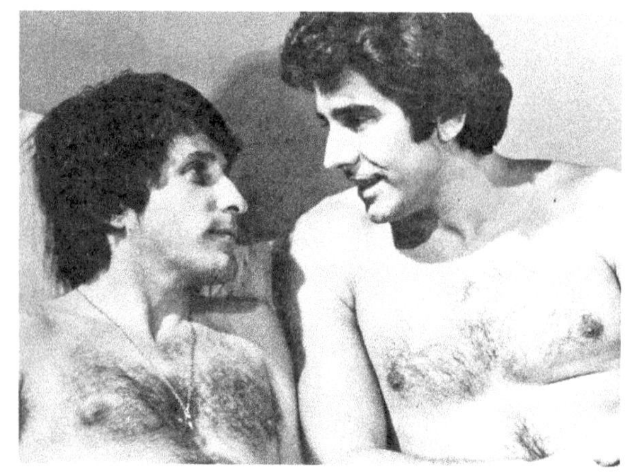

JOHN ORCSIK: It was there. Why would they cut it? It was there in the cinema.

Simon and Don's kiss mysteriously ended up on the cutting room floor, but there are plenty of other outrageous moments, which still cause shock and laughter. One major storyline centred on Dorrie and Herb's ruby wedding anniversary, which culminated in a fancy dress party.

DAVID SALE: I can remember Johnny Whyte coming out to Bilgola Plateau for the weekend while we were writing it, and we spent one very drunken dinner just deciding on what the fancy dress costumes would be and which characters would wear which. We had an absolute ball just deciding on what they'd all wear. It makes me laugh now to think of it.

'we spent one very drunken dinner just deciding on what the fancy dress costumes would be and which characters would wear which.'

SHEILA KENNELLY: I remember the poor white horse that had to carry me in when I went as Lady Godiva at the end. And I thought, *oh this isn't right, I shouldn't be doing this* because Abigail had done something similar at some charity event or something.

DAVID SALE: Lady Godiva! We put an in-joke there. Alf says, 'My God, it's Abigail.'

ELAINE LEE: I loved the last scene of the movie and the writers did a lovely, beautiful send-up of Vera waving like the Queen

opposite: Don and Simon in a bedroom scene from *Number 96: The Movie*

top left: Claire Houghton crosses verbal swords with Herb and Dorrie at the ball

top right: Herb, Lucy and Alf in fancy dress

in this Rolls Royce. Suddenly she was the first lady of Australia, which was a hoot. They hired this Rolls Royce that was kept for royalty when they came to Australia, like the Queen. It was a bit of a send-up. I was dressed in a duplicate of what the Queen wore. That was David and his sense of humour. It was an incredibly hot day. So we were driven in this Rolls Royce from wherever we picked it up from — can't remember now — to Double Bay and the bloody Rolls broke down. Bill was funny. He said, 'Goddammit, bloody Rolls Royces.' He said, 'This wouldn't have happened if it was a Cadillac.' So the royal Rolls broke down.

'It was a bit of a send-up. I was dressed in a duplicate of what the Queen wore.'

Number 96: The Movie was given an M rating as the change to colour came with a lot more sex and nudity. Despite this it premiered in Sydney in time for the May school holidays of 1974, and went on to be a huge success all around Australia.

DAVID SALE: I remember the opening night was a Sunday night at the Regent Theatre in Sydney. It had all the fanfare with

the full red carpet and everything you could imagine. There was even a brass band.

SHEILA KENNELLY: I remember Barry Humphries came along in a flowing cape and a big hat, carrying a packet of Jaffas.

JOHN ORCSIK: Limos were taking us down George Street and there were all the lights and everything else. I'd said to Jinx Huber, Bob's wife, I said, 'I want you to make me a caftan. I'm going to the opening of this film in a caftan. And I'm going to kiss Bill Harmon when I get there.' Which I did. He looked at me when I got out of the car and he said, 'What's that you're wearing?' I said, 'Well, I'm playing gay, Bill,' and I kissed him. We became friends and I did a bit of writing for the show after that.

'I'm going to the opening of this film in a caftan. And I'm going to kiss Bill Harmon when I get there.'

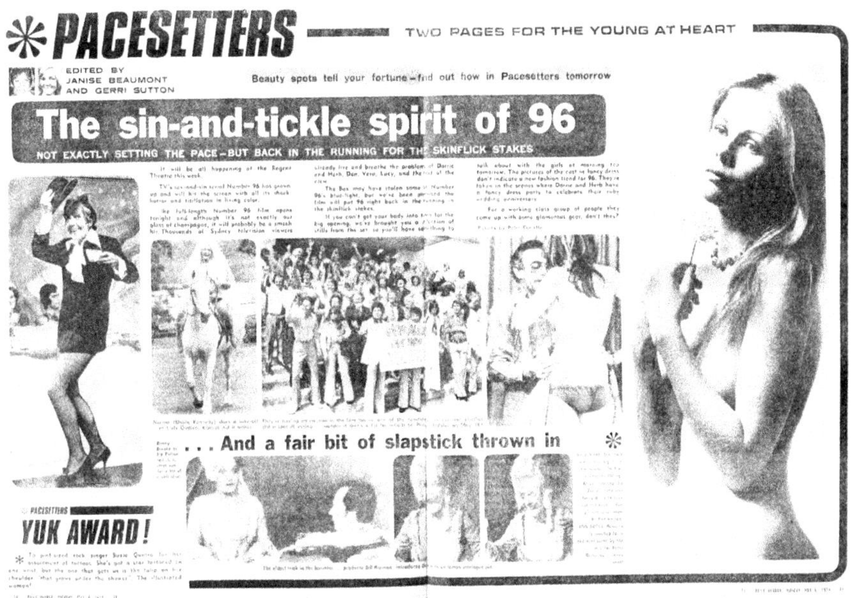

PACESETTERS — TWO PAGES FOR THE YOUNG AT HEART

EDITED BY JANISE BEAUMONT AND GERRI SUTTON

Beauty spots tell your fortune — find out how in Pacesetters tomorrow

The sin-and-tickle spirit of 96

NOT EXACTLY SETTING THE PACE — BUT BACK IN THE RUNNING FOR THE SKINFLICK STAKES

It will be all happening at the Regent Theatre this week.

TV's sex-and-sin serial Number 96 has grown up and will hit the screen with all its shock horror and titillation in living color.

The full-length Number 96 film opens tonight and although it's not exactly our glass of champagne, it will probably be a smash hit. Thousands of Sydney television viewers already live and breathe the problems of Dorrie and Herb, Don, Vera, Lucy, and the rest of the crew.

The Box may have stolen some of Number 96's blue-light, but we've been promised the film will put 96 right back in the running in the skinflick stakes.

If you can't get your body into town for the big opening, we've brought you a [illegible] of stills from the set so you'll have something to talk about with the girls at morning tea tomorrow. The pictures of the cast in fancy dress don't indicate a new fashion trend for 96. They're taken in the scenes where Dorrie and Herb have a fancy dress party to celebrate their ruby wedding anniversary.

For a working class group of people they come up with some glamorous gear, don't they?

. . . And a fair bit of slapstick thrown in

PACESETTERS YUK AWARD!

opposite: Abigail's appearance as Lady Godiva at a charity event inspired the writers to dress Norma Whittaker in the same costume

above: Newspapers were keen to capitalise on the promise of *Number 96*'s usual 'sin-and-tickle'. Courtesy Elaine Elliott

JOE HASHAM: The most outrageous of the many premieres that we attended was in Newcastle. I remember Tom Greer dropping me off at the hotel after the huge party and reminding me to behave myself. When I arrived at my room there was a little surprise waiting for me — a set of twenty-year-old twins. Two delightful sisters who had followed me from Sydney and just wanted to spend some time with me.

CHARD HAYWARD: As for the premieres, I think Jimmy Elliott and I attended nearly all of them. It was so much fun.

ELAINE LEE: When we saw it, there weren't rave reviews, but the public just couldn't get enough of it; they couldn't get enough of it and the gay community, particularly, seemed to just take it to their hearts. I don't know why. It's still popular with the gay community. I'm delighted about that.

TED JOBBINS (producer): They could've just had them standing there singing *Mary Poppins* and people would've flocked to see it because the show was so big.

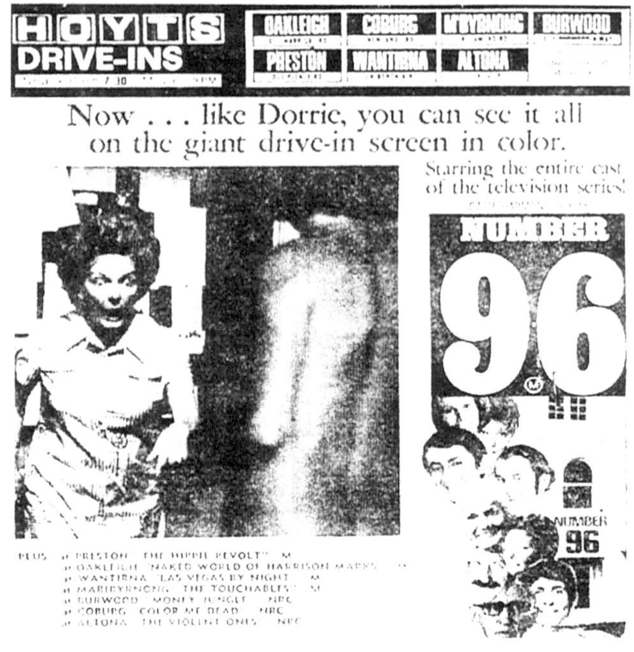

above: Promotional material for screenings of *Number 96: The Movie* at cinemas and drive-ins around the country

PATRICK WARD: The quality of it was not good at all, but I guess all the publicity from the TV show really made it work.

SHEILA KENNELLY: It was dreadful, just dreadful. It was made to make money in the heyday of *Number 96*, and it did.

JOHNNY LOCKWOOD: It had a longer run than most of the films on in Sydney. It had a nine or ten week run in the big cinema there.

DAVID SALE: It had a very healthy run at the Regent, which was the biggest cinema — unfortunately gone now — but it was the biggest cinema in Sydney. I can't remember the length of the run, but it was very healthy.

JAMES ELLIOTT: It must've been successful; it must've made a profit. People were queuing right along the street and right around the corner to get in.

ELAINE ELLIOTT (wife of James Elliott): At the end of 1973, after twelve months overseas, I moved to Sydney to live. There, in a flat without a television, *Number 96* had little impact on my life … until the release of the *Number 96* film. My walk to work took me past the Regent Theatre, which then stood near the corner of George and Bathurst streets. I remember being astounded at the long queues of people, often stretching around the block, before nine o'clock in the morning. I had the impression that many of them had been there several hours.

'People were queuing right along the street and right around the corner to get in.'

DAVID SALE: On the Monday morning I got up and I put the news on, and one item on the news — this was the 7am news — was that people were already queuing round the block at the Regent Theatre for the first public session, which was at 11am. And they were queuing at 7am.

PETER BENARDOS: It was very cheaply done, and it was so successful that I remember Bill coming in one day and saying, 'You should see the queues outside the movie theatre — they run for three blocks.' So what a success that was — really wonderful. So people made a lot of money out of that and we made an extra week's salary or whatever it was, but that's fine [*laughs*].

ELISABETH KIRKBY: I have no idea how much the film made for Cash Harmon, but I have been told that it made all the production costs back in the first week at the old Regent Theatre in George Street. It is still shown at cinemas in Sydney and Melbourne, as it has become a cult film with certain audiences.

JOHN ORCSIK: The film opened and it was a huge success. By the way, I think it's one of the most successful films, still, dollar for dollar in Australia's film history.

> *'I think it's one of the most successful films, still, dollar for dollar in Australia's film history.'*

TOM OLIVER: There was no cut of the box office for us or anything like that.

JAMES ELLIOTT: We all got the same amount no matter which character we played, and we were all sworn to secrecy at that time as to what they were paying us, which is not surprising because it was such a rotten, lousy deal we got.

ELAINE LEE: Bettina got $700 for doing it and I got $1200, and the film grossed, in Australia, more than *The Sound of Music.*

opposite: Posters for more recent showings of *Number 96: The Movie*

above: *Number 96: The Movie* made the cover of Australian cinema magazine, *Movie News*

That's where they made their money and good luck to them, but it was disgusting the way we were used in that. It makes me angry.

JOHNNY LOCKWOOD: I, funnily enough, had an agreement with them about a percentage of the money, but I had a very, very bad agent at the time and he was an idiot, this man. He didn't go into it, but I did go in for a percentage — a very small percentage, but a percentage of what the film made could be a lot of money. After it had been going about a year I suddenly got a cheque for about $1300 or something. I knew it had been on television once, and I rang them up and said, 'What about my money?' and they said, 'No, no, actually you shouldn't have got what you got in the beginning. That was a mistake.'

DAVID SALE: Even though it was a huge success, Johnny Whyte and I never saw a cent of any gross profits. It certainly made a mint of money, and only cost $100,000.

KEVIN POWELL: It worked because the people wanted to see their friends in colour. It was cashing in on the fact that this was colour, and we knew that so many months down the track we'd be broadcasting our first colour *Number 96*s. It was a way, also, for us to start looking at people and seeing them in colour, so we knew what we'd have to concentrate on. When you look at the storyline, it's a nice romp for an hour-and-a-half or so. It was great.

McWILLIAM'S
Cream
TABLE
WINES

Chapter 9

Mayhem and Murder

At the beginning of 1974, the new residents of flat 5 were introduced to the viewing public. The McDonald family comprised father Reg, his wife Edie and their teenage daughter Marilyn. Reg, known formally as Reginald P. McDonald, was a public servant set on making his way up the ladder in local government. Both his wife and daughter referred to him as 'Daddy'. He, in turn, referred to his wife as 'Edith' or, most commonly, 'Mother'.

DAVID SALE (writer): I loved all the comedy characters. Eventually new ones came in. Mummy and Daddy — Johnny Whyte thought up those, to give him his credit — and I loved them — they were partly based on his parents.

MIKE DORSEY (actor): Bill cast me in an early storyline as a police sergeant investigating a murder, which I think took place in the chemist shop. About eighteen months later, Bill told me during a golf game that he had a role for me that should run for about ten weeks, playing a character with a rod up his arse and no sense of humour.

WENDY BLACKLOCK (actress): I was in an Australian play by David Williamson called *Don's Party*, which was very successful, and Bill Harmon had been to see it. I was told afterwards he said, 'I've got to have that woman,' which meant he wished me to be in his television series. I said, 'No, no, no, I'm not going into a television series,' and he persisted.

MIKE DORSEY: When I read the script I said to Bill, 'Who's playing my wife?' and he said Wendy Blacklock, and I thought, *oh shit, I've got someone to match up with there*. I think we got on, in terms of what's on screen, extremely well.

WENDY BLACKLOCK: Bill Harmon said, 'I want you to play this just how you are, a Mosman mother,' and I said, 'I'm not playing it like a Mosman mother, Bill, this lady comes from Blacktown.'

top: Mike Dorsey as Reg McDonald. Courtesy Mick Pratt

bottom: Wendy Blacklock as Edie McDonald. Courtesy Mick Pratt

MIKE DORSEY: Daddy. He was an arsehole. Let's be honest. Everything is proper and frightfully, 'TC at the TH,' and all that sort of rubbish. I based him on a character I had met in England who was terribly pompous. Bill Harmon gave me the hair thing and the glasses, and all that shit. That's direction, but the character came from this guy in England who I hated, actually.

WENDY BLACKLOCK: I created a hairstyle and then was stuck with it. I got out those old-fashioned silver clips that you used to stick in your hair. You then couldn't change it because they'd made terrible indentations. I used to have my hair done with these clips and, come the weekend, I couldn't get rid of these terrible waves. I looked like Edie for years. But I just wanted her to be different to me.

MIKE DORSEY: Reg McDonald. He was the TC at the TH with a rod up his arse, and that's how I played him — a pompous prick, pardon my language, and he seemed to go down well. I had to change my appearance because of the fact that I'd already done a role in *Number 96*. So we smoothed my hair down, added the glasses, and always with a suit and tie. As I say, a pompous ass. I don't think I changed the performance from day one till the end. I don't think I had to.

WENDY BLACKLOCK: Edie was a character who took Bex and used to drink gin. They actually took her off the Bex because they said, 'People are seeing you taking Bex and we don't think that's very good.' You know, she'd take a Bex and then swoop it down with a glass of gin, but it kept me amused.

ELEANOR WITCOMBE (writer): I was there when they first started and I was the one who suggested that he talked in all those, you know, 'Going to the TH,' the 'TC', and all that sort of stuff. I said, 'Where could he come from that he thought was marvellous?' 'Well,' I said, 'what's the most boring town you can think of? Blacktown.' So he came from Blacktown, and the epitome of sophisticated living was Blacktown. I had a lot of fun with him. And Wendy played Mother. We decided Mummy was going to get hooked on an afternoon serial so I invented this thing called *Natalie Faces Life* on television, and she couldn't wait to see *Natalie Faces Life*. We had a great deal of fun.

Judy McBurney was originally cast as daughter Marilyn, but having taped six episodes she developed peritonitis and had to be replaced.

MIKE DORSEY: Judy McBurney got sick and they cast Frances Hargreaves who, in my opinion, is the most photogenic actress I've ever worked with. In a certain light she was absolutely beautiful, an angel. And a beautiful actress too. South African. She had not long been in Australia when she joined *Number 96* and we took her under our wing for a while.

WENDY BLACKLOCK: Franny was like a daughter to me. She's a lovely woman. She was a girl then.

With just forty-eight hours' notice, nineteen-year-old Frances joined the show. Her only previous screen experience in Australia had been an episode of the ABC's *Behind the Legend* series.

FRANCES HARGREAVES (actress): It was a lot of hard work, but the thrill of getting the role helped me a lot. I was terrified at first. The cast of the series helped me a lot and that made it easier.[10]

top: Frances Hargreaves replaced Judy McBurney as Marilyn McDonald. Courtesy Mick Pratt

bottom: Pop singer Marty Rhone began on screen in April 1974 as Dean McDonald. Courtesy Mick Pratt

opposite: The McDonald family moved into flat 5 in early 1974. Courtesy NFSA

MIKE DORSEY: Wendy Blacklock and I took a while to get close to each other. I have some old press clippings and in one interview she stated that I was one of two actors she swore she'd never work with! But we became good friends.

WENDY BLACKLOCK: Mike Dorsey and I virtually lived in each other's pockets. We worked together and we'd learn our lines together. He'd come over to my place at weekends and learn lines. I think if you're working day after day after day in a

serial that is on every night, if you don't learn to work well together then you don't last. It's as simple as that. You have to adjust to each other's way of doing things.

MIKE DORSEY: More often than not, Wendy and I would be the last block to be filmed on a Friday because I think both directors and the production people recognised that we were usually take one, take two maximum. I don't think I ever went to take three.

WENDY BLACKLOCK: I can remember that we were sort of like the poor relations to begin with. The show was very settled, very successful and the people were very well known. Abigail had had enormous publicity. Pat McDonald and Elaine Lee had been there since the beginning and I think we came in about two years after it had been playing. So they were all very settled and this was a new couple coming in.

FRANCES HARGREAVES: They were nuts, so the daughter had to be nuts as well.[11]

MIKE DORSEY: We were a very good little team, I think. The producers and the public thought so too. We rapidly caught up with the regulars who had been in it from day one. We were on par with them, I think. That was my impression.

WENDY BLACKLOCK: I think I'm correct in saying that if we hadn't worked as an ongoing storyline they would've gotten rid of us. That's probably why in the back of my mind I thought, *well, six months and we'll call it quits*. Somehow David Sale and the other writers kept writing more stories that suited our life, and people accepted us.

top: Jan Adele as Trixie O'Toole

bottom: Carol Raye as Amanda Von Pappenburg

MIKE DORSEY: During the last year of *Number 96* we took a double act into the clubs, which was extremely popular and very successful for about two years.

WENDY BLACKLOCK: We were really a comedy couple.

Number 96's ability to keep its audience laughing was one of the keys to its continuing success.

TED JOBBINS (producer): I think one of the successes of the show was that even though it was basically a drama, there was so much comedy.

CAROL RAYE (actress): It had that reputation to start with, of being sex and sin. That gradually changed and more and more comedy came into it, which lightened it, and I think people enjoyed the comedy.

DAVID SALE: Although it was called the sex and sin show, it was sixty percent comedy and this didn't come from people trying to write funny scripts; the comedy was inherent in the characters.

CHARD HAYWARD (actor): The promise of nudity probably got people to watch initially, but basically I believe it was just a fun show inhabited with interesting and unusual characters. We always won the Logie for Best Drama and used to joke about that because, as we said, we always thought we were making a comedy.

DAVID SALE: I thought Mummy and Trixie O'Toole were like Laurel and Hardy. All that funny stuff. Jan Adele and Wendy Blacklock were so funny. Trixie O'Toole was based on Jan Adele. When she read my script she said, 'It's me!' When it came to writing Trixie, I wrote all Jan's sayings.

WENDY BLACKLOCK: I don't think I'd ever worked with Jan Adele and we became very good friends because she had my sense of humour, you know, she was as mad as a meat axe. It was a really enjoyable partnership with her because I just found her extremely amusing.

ROGER WARD (actor): A lot of fun was had with Jan, both in front of and behind the camera.

SHEILA KENNELLY (actress): Jan Adele as Trixie O'Toole. She always had a fund of jokes. So whenever she was in a bar scene Brian Phillis, the director, would ask her to tell one of her bawdy jokes so we'd all be genuinely laughing when the scene started and had a good wine bar atmosphere.

CHARD HAYWARD: As most actors will tell you, the comedy comes from the reality of the situation that the character is in. We had some terrific writers that put the more comic characters in some outrageous situations, and playing the truth of these is what made it all so funny.

CAROL RAYE: There was a huge amount of humour creeping in to the series at the time that I was in it, and I think I did about three months and I loved every minute of it. The character had been quite a success so I was asked to come back.

DAVID SALE: We had a storyline, which was one of my suggestions, that the Baroness had a look-alike and was suddenly being presented with bills from the big stores and couturiers for goods, which she'd never bought. Eventually there was a confrontation, and we actually did a scene where they were both in it. It was a big deal for us — Carol playing two parts.

CAROL RAYE: It was just such a fun character written by our writers David Sale, mainly, and Johnny Whyte, who both wrote these lovely situations that they got her into.

ELEANOR WITCOMBE: We all loved Carol Raye. She was fantastic.

left: ***Number 96*** **had an abundance of comedy characters. From left, Aldo, Roma, Herb, Dorrie and Flo**

right: Johnny Lockwood, Jeff Kevin and Philippa Baker shared comedic chemistry. Courtesy NFSA

opposite: Josephine Knur as Lorelei Wilkinson. Perhaps it was deliberate when, years later, Paula Duncan played a character with the same unlikely name in ***Prisoner***

CHARD HAYWARD: I was infatuated with her like everyone else who came under her spell. She was a delight. Full of fun and energy, much like her character.

JOE HASHAM (actor): I fell in love with her on the very first day she walked onto the set. Sexy, sophisticated and at all times a real lady.

The humour in *Number 96* was broad, ranging from high camp to slapstick to farce, and as well as plenty of funny individual characters there were great comedy teams.

TOM GREER (publicist): It had to have comedy — hence the Dorrie, Herb and Flo storylines, and the Whittakers.

SHEILA KENNELLY: Les and Norma were much more about comedy. That was their main function, though we could touch on other areas.

PAT McDONALD (actress): My own sense of fun is in Dorrie. But Dorrie is actually without humour and it's her lack of humour that makes her so stupidly funny to others.[12]

PHILIPPA BAKER (actress): Over time the character of Roma altered, what with changing writers and the exigencies of plot; she became less classy and more comic.

JEFF KEVIN (actor): I learnt such a lot from Johnny Lockwood in terms of comedy. And Philippa Baker as well. I also learnt a lot about the chemistry between performers and how important that is. When it clicks you can almost instinctively know what the other's going to do. So Johnny, Philippa and I had that, all three of us. We worked easily together and enjoyed what we were doing.

PHILIPPA BAKER: I had not known what to expect when I found out I would be working with Johnny Lockwood — a big name from a quite different branch of show business — but it was an unexpected pleasure working with him, and indeed, without exception, with all the cast and crew. I think that's one of the things that made the whole show work.

JOHNNY LOCKWOOD (actor): I think that was the success of *Number 96* — they had comedy characters. Although Aldo didn't tell jokes he was a funny character.

The writers regularly introduced new characters to keep the comedy and storylines fresh.

JOSEPHINE KNUR (actress): I was introduced to the series in 1974. My character, Lorelei, was a naïve country bumpkin who came to the big city to find a rich husband. I found the role difficult because her way of speaking was somewhat unnatural. Her lines were not easy for an inexperienced actress like myself. I always felt I was miscast. But Dudley and Lorelei scenes were definitely fan favourites. I enjoyed working with everyone and learned from everyone, especially Chard Hayward and Pamela Garrick. Most of the comedy in *Number 96* was clever and very funny.

ELEANOR WITCOMBE: They were all, basically, pretty nice people. Except Mummy and Daddy were a bit of a worry!

In 1975, Mike Dorsey co-starred alongside Pat McDonald in the first outdoor colour scene ever shot for *Number 96* — a comedy dream sequence.

above: One of Dorrie's wild dreams featuring Daddy

opposite: Studio B control room

MIKE DORSEY: I think the dream sequence with Pat was probably more of an embarrassment than anything else! Frankly, my recollections of much of that part of things is somewhat hazy.

BOB HUBER (producer): Colour was a real pain in the ass. The studio wasn't ready for it.

TED JOBBINS: It was like the millennium bug. It was going to be doom and gloom. The art department kept going around saying everything would have to be colour coordinated and all different things would have to be done; we'd have to take more notice of the coordination of this, that and the other. It lasted for about two weeks and then we just went back to where we were before. Colours of costumes, it really didn't make that much difference, and most of the flats were beige, neutral colours. We never really had any bright, bright colours. Even the flats that were wallpapered, from memory, were in dark beiges and maroons and darker colours. I think the whole lot were painted beige because, see, the fact that we were changing the same flat backwards and forwards meant we couldn't have

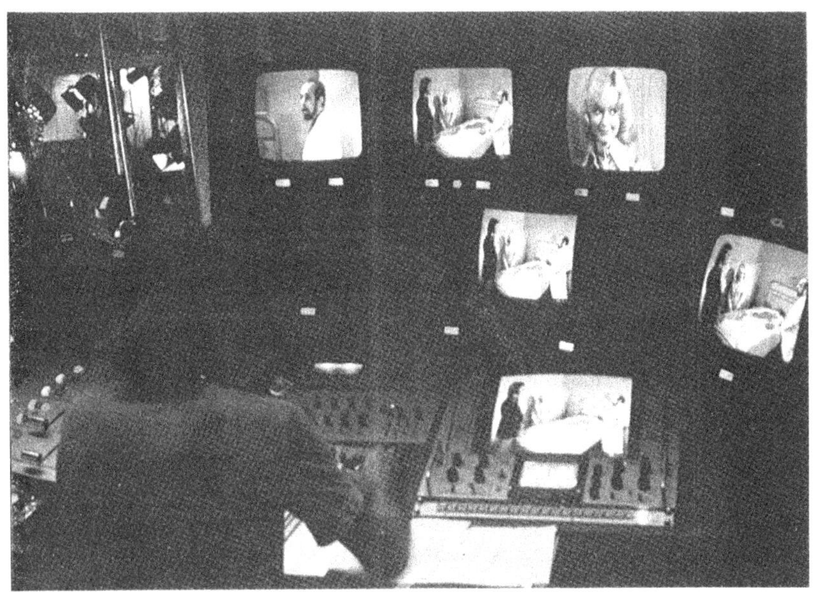

exotic wallpapers, because if you did they were special panels that had to go on. So it never really affected us that much.

SHEILA KENNELLY: When the show went to colour we all looked fatter, and Elaine went on a grapefruit and water diet. I thought about it.

TED JOBBINS: We'd moved to studio B. We moved over there when colour came in. We had a couple of problems because it was smaller than studio A. What we lost was a lot of the working room we had around the set. It had been an empty studio up until that point. So we went in there. They sound-proofed it.

PAT McDONALD: In fact *Number 96* was the first thing to go to colour because we actually shot a scene of us all sitting down, waiting for colour television.[13]

TED JOBBINS: When we went to colour, Tom Greer — again, he was a very astute young man — knew that the Broadcasting Control Board said that you went to colour at midnight on a certain date, and Tom had this promo made where all the cast of

Number 96 were in Dorrie's flat, or someone's. It was someone that had a colour set. They all went there to watch colour, and they sat down and looked at the set and the television set went to colour. From there the whole thing just went out and showed the whole scene in colour. But Tom made sure that it went to air so that when we were supposed to go to colour at midnight he went like ten seconds earlier. Out of that, for many years, Channel 10 was known as 'Channel 10: First in Colour'. It was the first colour station in Australia only by ten seconds.

CHANTAL CONTOURI (actress): This role came up for *Number 96* and I went and auditioned — I got this very dull role of Tracey Wilson, who was just a nurse. I didn't sign a nude clause. I wasn't going to be nude. But I went in at a fortuitous time. They were just starting colour. So I didn't do any of the black and white episodes. It was a new era.

The first colour episodes were compiled in 1974, with episode 649 being the first of a few test screenings before Australian television switched permanently to colour on 1 March 1975. *Number 96* was now produced in colour, and as well as the show's regular doses of comedy, drama, sex and nudity there was still some good old-fashioned romance to keep viewers watching. But not all love affairs run smoothly.

JEFF KEVIN: Marriage on television soaps produced huge ratings. The first one, where I was married to Pamela Garrick, Patti, I think was at a church in Chatswood. There were crowds of people outside while we were filming the exterior stuff. And it rated its socks off.

PAMELA GARRICK (actress): It was the first time such an event graced the covers of both *TV Week* and *TV Times*. My parents and brother were in town and allowed to sit at the back of the church to watch filming. I recall in one of the shots they can be seen briefly, sitting in the pew at the back of the church.

above: Magazine covers featuring Arnold Feather's wedding to Patti

DAVID SALE: When Arnold got married and Johnny Whyte took a dislike to the wife, he had her murdered by the pantyhose murderer at the first opportunity.

JEFF KEVIN: I don't think that was quite true. I think they realised they'd made a mistake, in a sense, by marrying him off because the character was better if he was mothered, if you like, and freer. He was the sort of character who worked better if he wasn't content.

PAMELA GARRICK: I was called into the production office and told by a panel of writers they had run out of ideas, so I would be written out in upcoming episodes.

The pantyhose murders meant the show lost some popular female cast members, but once again viewers were hooked on a whodunit storyline. Josephine Knur as Lorelei was the first to go on a Friday night in November 1974. Less than three weeks later there was an attack on Tracey Wilson, who survived. Patti Feather's murder was discovered in the final moments of the last episode of the year, providing yet another season-ending cliffhanger.

JOSEPHINE KNUR: I do remember when Bill Harmon came to the studio and told Pamela and I that we would be written out. He thought we would be devastated, but was surprised to find that we had both already planned on quitting. Bill said he was sorry that I was being written out as he hadn't realised how popular my character was until it was way too late to change the storyline.

SHEILA KENNELLY: On the first night we screened in colour, David Sale told his mother he'd come to dinner and watch the show with her. The climax of this episode was the discovery of the death of a much loved character at the hands of the pantyhose strangler. Norma, having been to a ball, was elegantly gowned with mountainous coiffure from our hairdresser, Gail Edmonds. She opened the door and screamed at the sight of lovely Lorelei, played by Josie Knur, dead on the couch. End of episode. David looked for his mum's reaction and she approvingly commented, 'Doesn't Norma's hair look *lovely.*'

top: Josephine Knur as Lorelei Wilkinson was an early victim of the pantyhose murderer. Courtesy Mick Pratt

bottom: Pamela Garrick as Patti, another victim of the pantyhose murderer. Courtesy Mick Pratt

CHANTAL CONTOURI: I think I only had a thirteen-week contract. I wouldn't sign a longer contract with anybody because I didn't want to do television. I just thought television was my training ground. I thought film. If you were signed up they wouldn't let you out of that contract to do a film in those days. So thirteen weeks was good because then that thirteen weeks would finish and I would be free again. They either had to ask me to stay on or they had to get rid of me — one of the two — and so that storyline, the pantyhose killer, was around and I was one of the victims as well.

But it was all part of the audience guessing game and another clever plot twist.

CHANTAL CONTOURI: She was attacked and supposedly an attempt was made to strangle her. They found her with pantyhose around her neck. Well it was evidently explained later to her boyfriend, who was played by Peter Adams, that she had feigned that so she could take suspicion off herself. At the time that I did it I thought, *oh whoa, she was nearly a goner* [*laughs*].

JOSEPHINE KNUR: None of the actors were told who the murderer would turn out to be. That was a big secret. Perhaps not even the writers knew till it was written in.

ELEANOR WITCOMBE: When we started these murder things nobody had a clue who the murderer was. Not a clue. So when we'd run it and milked it as much as we could — and this took a lot of ingenuity; we did really squeeze dry our minds over it — we'd think of the different combinations and things we could do with it. When we'd done that then we had to decide who the murderer was.

CHANTAL CONTOURI: I absolutely didn't know it. The whole cast didn't know it.

PAMELA GARRICK: People were upset and kept asking what happened and who the murderer was, but I didn't know myself till I saw the episode the next year.

CHANTAL CONTOURI: What happened was, for a week before we had to film it — because we were a couple of months ahead, airtime. So it was before Christmas 1974 because then I went on tour with *Alvin Rides Again*; promotions right around Australia with the film coming out. So I know that we finished *Number 96* in November and what happened was I got the script, they called me and they said, 'You are the pantyhose murderer, but you're not allowed to tell anybody.' So I wasn't allowed to tell.

JOSEPHINE KNUR: When it was finally revealed we all thought it was pretty weak and nonsensical.

CHANTAL CONTOURI: It was in the laundry, somewhere, and it was with Marilyn, yeah, the character Marilyn, and it really was uneventful. They just gave me some gloves and some pantyhose — they weren't going to reveal my face. So my hands had to hold the pantyhose in these leather gloves and you still couldn't tell who it was.

Towards the end of January 1975, episode 679 provided yet another highly dramatic Friday night cliffhanger. Was beloved Marilyn McDonald about to become the pantyhose murderer's next victim?

CHANTAL CONTOURI: Frances Hargreaves had to say this thing that has become a classic with my gay friends — when she says, 'Oh, it's you,' [*laughs*]. 'Oh no, it's you.' Everybody mentions it. I've had a lot of gay people across the room saying, 'You, it's you,' doing the Frances imitation. So that's what I remember. And then they swung the camera around and did a reveal.

above: Alf and Marilyn in the laundrette, the scene of the pantyhose murderer's unmasking. Courtesy Elaine Elliott

opposite: Chantal Contouri played Tracey Wilson, the infamous pantyhose murderer. Courtesy Mick Pratt

In the opening minutes of Monday night's episode the police arrested Tracey in the laundrette and saved Marilyn. In a final plot twist, Tracey managed to escape custody and returned to *Number 96* where, by the end of the episode, she had leapt to her death from a bedroom window of flat 6.

DAVID SALE: Chantal was lovely. Chantal Contouri is a delightful lady — gorgeous — and worked very well in the show.

CHANTAL CONTOURI: I didn't ever think that I would be remembered for a very long time. Forty years later I'm still remembered for something that I said to my sisters: 'I'm going to go to Sydney and be in *Number 96*,' and they said, 'Oh yeah, right. She thinks she can do anything.'

The pantyhose murders remains one of the most memorable storylines in the history of Australian television drama, and one of the two most talked about plots in the entire run of *Number 96*. The other most talked about plot twist came abruptly and at a very high cost — in more ways than one.

KEN SHADIE (writer): I'd been working flat-out so I went in to Bill and said, 'I'd like to have a week off.' No worries. So

I'm home about a day and the phone rings. It's Bill. 'Can you come in?' I said, 'You just gave me a week off.' He said, 'This is important, please come in. It's very important. I can't tell you until you get in here.'

DAVID SALE: Bill called us and it was an emergency meeting, and he said the ratings had gone down and we're landed with all these characters. Johnny said, 'Well, we'll start to write them out.' Bill said, 'We're eleven weeks ahead; we could lose a thousand viewers.'

BILL HARMON (producer): I had just returned from overseas to find that the ratings had dropped dramatically. So we decided that there should be a gigantic blow up and that way we would get rid of those characters for whom we were finding it difficult to write.[14]

DAVID SALE: I must confess I'd had a couple of drinks and I said, 'Well we could always blow 'em up,' being my usual facetious self, and Bill jumped on it and said, 'That's it.' We just looked at him and said, 'What do you mean?'

JAMES ELLIOTT (actor): This was when the show sort of began its slide downwards. Bill Harmon came back from a long trip abroad and ratings had dropped, so something had to be done quickly. So it was decided they would do something spectacular, such as blow up the building. Well, that *was* spectacular. It got rid of a lot of people, but then they realised that they'd made a mistake.

KEN SHADIE: I got to write the top episode of the storyline, where the building blows up with the time bomb and the whole thing. So we blew it up. At the time I thought, *okay, but who's going to be blown up with it?* And for some bizarre reason they started to blow people up that were the favourites, you know, like Les.

PETER BENARDOS (director): Brian did the bomb episode and he did it beautifully, there's no doubt about it.

BRIAN PHILLIS (director): When preparing for the scene a week before, I made a point of asking Bill what he would prefer for the bomb's trigger device: the traditional cartoon-style alarm clock with wires coming out of the top or a digital clock showing minutes and seconds ticking away. I recommended the digital because seeing seconds passing before the detonation heightened the tension rather than inanimate hands of a clock face. Bill readily agreed.

TED JOBBINS: We had a props boy working at the time. 'Oh yes,' he said, 'I've worked with explosives. I can do it.' We said, 'Now, are you sure? This has got to look good,' and we worked with him for weeks before.

BRIAN PHILLIS: On the morning of the shoot — a Saturday, which was most unusual — there was high expectation and nervousness. No-one knew what to expect, least of all myself. Wires and cables ran everywhere across the floor and a big NO SMOKING sign. Bill in his lazy way of walking, casual, putting a cigarette to his lips, putting out his hand for someone to give him a light, stumbling over fuse wires. 'Bill!' exclaimed the prop man, 'No!' By this time the prop man was so nervous he had consumed half a bottle of brandy to steady his nerves. The previous day I had asked him how much blast powder he was using — after replying I said, 'Double it.' This was a one-take scene so there could be no compromise.

TED JOBBINS: Everybody else was out of the studio. He had worked all night preparing the explosives and everything. We had two fire brigades standing by. Everything was fine till just before the scene was to be shot. I found the props boy now behind one of the flats guzzling down some brandy. I said, 'What's this for?' He said, 'I just hope everything works.' I said,

'This is a lovely time to tell me you *hope* everything works,' and I got the impression he hadn't worked with explosives too much before.

BRIAN PHILLIS: Meanwhile, Bill's glance fell on the digital clock device for the bomb. 'Brian! What the fuck is that? I wanted the traditional bomb, y'know, the one with bells on top.' I politely remonstrated with him and reminded him that he favoured the digital and besides, it was too late to change. Bill lit another cigarette and went up to the control booth. 'Okay,' I yelled, 'let's do it.' Everyone crowded into the booth — there could be no-one allowed to stay in the studio. Many of the people peering over my shoulder were unknown and I don't know where they came from. The moment came. I said, 'Roll tape.'

TED JOBBINS: We had a camera set up close to the front of the deli behind shot-proof glass. There were several cameras in all varying positions and every camera was then locked onto a videotape. So there was no editing, no cutting, nothing. I think there were two or three cameras, but most of them were locked in behind glass, behind things to protect them. So we had everything covered and the big countdown came. I thought, *well, the only one in the studio is the kid with the explosives*, and I thought *if he blows himself up it's his own silly bloody fault. It's either going to be spectacular or we're going to have nothing.* Anyway, all the tapes were rolling.

BRIAN PHILLIS: There were three VTRs rolling simultaneously to get multiple angles. I ran through the ten-second countdown, like Cape Canaveral. The blast shook the big glass window of the booth to near breaking point.

TED JOBBINS: There was this most God almighty crash and the glass in the control room — I was standing near the glass — the whole glass vibrated and I thought it was going to go, and then we saw all the effects coming on and it just looked fantastic.

left: a promotional advert for the bomb episode

right: the explosion in the deli

BRIAN PHILLIS: The double entry doors leading into the studio were thrown open by the percussion, the cast-iron table and chairs in front of the deli moved inches off their marks. At first there was stunned silence until, with a grunt of satisfaction, Bill promptly left the booth; he knew it had worked the way he wanted.

Episode 839 is arguably the most infamous in the history of *Number 96*, and went to air on Friday night, 5 September 1975. With two minutes to spare, Les Whittaker finds a note left under the door of flat 7 that reads: 'DEAR MRS CAMERON, BOMB IN NUMBER 96 WILL BLOW AT 6PM'. Les races down the stairs in an effort to warn everyone as the screen splits into four different locations.

PETER BENARDOS: Brian montaged it with Les running down the stairs saying, 'Fire, fire, there's a bomb in the building, there's a bomb in the building, get out of the building.'

TED JOBBINS: It took a long, long time to assemble that scene; just to get the composite of the different pictures took a long time. We devised things as we went along. I went with Brian and we said, right we'll put so-and-so here, then we worked out what was going to go where; what he wanted in the scene. We just put Chinagraph lines on my monitor and then as we shot different composites different things had to be kept within the area inside those lines. Now when we got to the control room to put it together, it meant many runs because what you had to then do was put one scene down and then put another scene down over the top of it — key that in. It took a while just to make that little composite up, which lasts all of three or four seconds. Les was running down the staircase in one. I think we saw the bomb ticking — the numbers ticking over — in another one; the deli and the wine bar in the others. It took us as long as it does to do a whole episode, just to make up that one scene, which ran about two or three minutes.

Les sounds the warning in the wine bar, then runs next door to the deli. With seconds remaining he tells Aldo and Roma Godolfus and Miles Cooper that there's a bomb in the building and it's going to go off at six o'clock. As the clock strikes six the bomb explodes in the delicatessen, where it was hidden in a box of olives. The scene then cuts to the wine bar where Norma Whittaker is thrown to the floor by the blast.

SHEILA KENNELLY: That was me. It was all done in slow motion. I think I must've had a mattress to fall back on, and I just sort of reached up and fell back as the shelving fell away the other way.

Viewers had to wait until the following Monday night to learn the identities of the dead.

DAVID SALE: It was very depressing, but it worked. I've never seen anything like it. The papers treated it like a real tragedy. They had lists of dead and dying and everything, as if real people had been killed.

Bang go the No. 96 stars

Uproar over 'death list'

Number 96 blasted back into the top TV ratings last night with the release of the names of the four stars "killed" in an explosion.

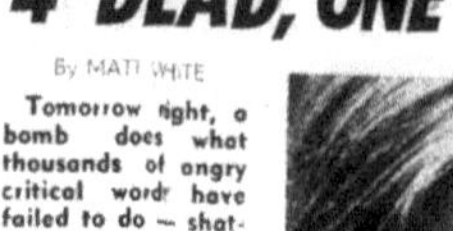

BOMB BLAST AT 96 — 4 DEAD, ONE CRITICAL

Tomorrow night, a bomb does what thousands of angry critical words have failed to do — shatter Number 96.

Vivienne Garrett . . . return to 96.

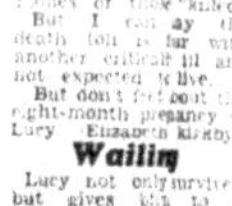

JOHNNY LOCKWOOD: I was shocked. I wasn't told that I was going. I was told that I was going to be back in it in two or three weeks. Then when I read the script and it said I was blown up, I thought I must get better or something in the next scripts.

PHILIPPA BAKER: Some people seem to think the cast members who were blown up should in some way have been upset, but I had never expected the show to last the time that it did. To me, the four years was a bonus.

JOHNNY LOCKWOOD: We talked about it, said, you know, that we were all professionals and it's the nature of the business. You're liable to be a big success one day and not the next. I don't think Gordon was as surprised at getting out of it as me.

GORDON McDOUGALL (actor): When I was written out I was disappointed, but the long run in the show had allowed me to put a bit aside so it wasn't as if I was suddenly destitute. I had plenty of notice to organise other things — a season with the

PETITION WANTS 'DEAD' 96 CHARACTERS TO RETURN

A Sydney cake shop owner has drawn up a petition to bring back her favorite characters killed off in Number 96 last night.

By WAYNE DARWEN

Lamenting the violent deaths of Les Whittaker (Gordon McDougall) and Aldo and Roma Godulfus (Johnny Lockwood and Phillipa Baker)), Mrs Wyn Garner said

petition last week protesting over the Number 96 "killings."

She placed it on her shop counter for customers to sign.

Mrs Garner and her shop assistant, Mrs Rita Richards, eagerly watched the long-awaited disaster episode last night.

"We both felt very sad after the show," Mrs Garner said.

"We watch the show together every night."

LES, ROMA and ALDO . . . Number 96 victims.

Outraged fans blast network

opposite: The identities of the dead were revealed in a one-hour presentation of *Number 96*. The following day's newspapers reported on the tragedy

above: An article about viewers' anger at so many favourite characters being killed off

South Australian Theatre Company first, then various bits and pieces in television and movies.[15]

SHEILA KENNELLY: Double J did a radio series on it. So they interviewed, supposedly, Norma in hospital, not knowing that Les had died. Well, it was hilarious. That was an interesting thing to do, all in character. A lady sent me a spare wig, she said in case I needed a spare wig, and I got flowers and condolence notes.

ELEANOR WITCOMBE: They got rid of Les, which I think was a shame because a lot of people like failures, you know, they like someone like Les. He never gave up, never gave up and he was a good character.

SHEILA KENNELLY: I was very upset, I remember, and there was something else — it was really weird being sort of left when he had gone. I felt a bit uncomfy about it.

JEFF KEVIN: I think that was a huge mistake, killing off people that were so good, like Philippa Baker, Johnny Lockwood and Gordon McDougall. It was crazy and I said so. I really spoke up at a meeting and said it's the most stupid thing I've ever heard.

KEVIN POWELL (production manager): I think that the biggest mistake that ever happened, which was really a kneejerk reaction to the ratings dropping, was the blowing up of the building because in that one fell swoop we blew out six or seven of the people's favourite characters. There were so many people who said, 'Oh, you've killed off my favourite friends.'

above: Scott Lambert as Miles Cooper was one of four cast members killed off in the bomb blast. Courtesy Mick Pratt

opposite: A promotional advert hyping Lucy's on-screen discovery of the tragic news

TOM OLIVER (actor): They made a big mistake because they killed off, I think, four very, very popular characters; three or four. You don't do that in good soap. Kill off somebody else, but not three or four of your favourite characters because if they're your favourite characters it means a lot of people watch it for them. If you kill 'em off they're not going to watch and your ratings drop, and they really, really were good ratings.

KEVIN POWELL: I was once under police protection for two weeks straight. I got a phone call late at night. It was a Friday night at my apartment in Neutral Bay and this person said to me, 'You're Kevin Powell,' and I said, 'Yes I am.' He said, 'You're responsible for killing off my friends. I'm going to get you. You're going to be killed off too.' *Click*. So I rang up Ross Hawthorn, who was our general manager, and I said, 'Ross, I've had this strange phone call.' He said, 'Forget about it.' Later I told Bill about this and Bill went absolutely mad: 'Why didn't you tell me? Jesus Christ.' Ian Holmes, the general manager at Channel 10, had his front door blown up with such power, from what I was told, that the bolt was embedded up the staircase in the wall. It was kept very low-key. Tom Greer managed to get all that kept very quiet. They eventually got the person.

SHEILA KENNELLY: People were profoundly affected. I mean, the ratings went down to billy-o after that. People didn't like losing so many of their favourites. There was a nice, very good young actor, Scott Lambert. Now, he went as well and he was a sympathetic character.

CHARD HAYWARD: It was a terrible idea. The stories per se were not important. What was important was what was happening to one's favourite character. That was the subtle difference. Then, in one episode, they got rid of so many.

BOB HUBER: It was Bill's decision and he stood by it, but it was the wrong decision.

JEFF KEVIN: I do remember Carol Raye and I begging the producers to change their minds. It wasn't just them. It was also Johnny Whyte and David Sale, I think, too. You know, the writers were stuck on this idea that they had to do something dramatic.

TED JOBBINS: We'd shot all of our stuff leading up to it. We had to leave it. Just put the fire out, make sure everything was safe and leave it because Peter Benardos was coming in the next week. The deli blew up — he was then left with picking it up from that point on. So he had to rehearse all his scenes around it, with all the devastation that was there because they had to be the first scenes shot. The chaotic set made it a little bit awkward for Kevin in production to get people around. Peter had to follow through with all the sidewalk operation. It looked good. I was surprised when I saw the next lot of stuff come through, how well they did it considering the space that they had to work in.

PETER BENARDOS: On my week, the following week, I had the aftermath, which I think was just as bad because suddenly you had two ambulances in the studio, which was quite small really, let's face it. All the other sets are still up, but we still had to manoeuvre vehicles and a police car on top of that with flashing lights and so on.

ELISABETH KIRKBY (actress): One of the questions I have been asked most often is what happened to Lucy in the explosion. I have vivid memories of shooting those scenes. Lucy, heavily pregnant with her menopausal baby, was on the stairs trying to escape to the street. So, I was lying in rubble and broken woodwork while ambulance and emergency workers tried to extricate me. It looked very realistic at the time and was filmed with the usual *Number 96* economy.

MIKE DORSEY: When you're in a series, deep down, every actor is insecure. You expect to be written out and I think it's quite a pleasant surprise to read the script and find that you're

above: The *Number 96* cast, a third of whom departed in the wake of the bomb blast

opposite: A promotional advert announcing Jack Sellars' return to *Number 96* and his intention to set a trap

not written out. We knew there was a bomb going to go off and I thought, *hello, there goes me and I'm back on the skids again*, but it wasn't me.

DAVID SALE: We all knew which characters would go. Les Whittaker was getting irritating. All these inventions of his had run their course and I don't know — the delicatessen. We'd run out of things for the delicatessen. We just thought it would give it a fresh start.

JAMES ELLIOTT: They thought new talent would be the answer and half the established talent suddenly disappeared.

JEFF KEVIN: After the bomb happened there was a very big void in the show and everybody felt it. You also felt insecure because you didn't know when the next axe was going to drop or who it was going to drop on.

In a move characteristic of good soap, the writers, perhaps in a bid to compensate for the loss of so many popular cast members, brought back Tom Oliver and Vivienne Garrett for a couple of crucial episodes.

TOM OLIVER: They ring up — I get it via my agent. They'd like you to go back for two or three episodes to clear up some loose ends, like with Bettina's character. She's got to go to gaol and blah blah blah. Sure, I'll do that, just for old time's sake.

VIVIENNE GARRETT (actress): I was married off to the nice Jewish doctor and sent away to New Guinea, but they did say that I had to go back at some point. They had an idea that they were going to blow up the delicatessen. So they did contract me to go back and reappear from New Guinea, and I agreed to it.

TOM OLIVER: I had a bit of a punch up with Bettina Welch's character. She tried to do the dirty on me, or something, because we were a company, we owned the whole apartment block.

Having already axed Johnny Lockwood, Philippa Baker, Gordon McDougall and Scott Lambert, it also looked like the end for Bettina Welch as Maggie Cameron.

KEN SHADIE: Once again, nobody knew. We were sitting around the table — who could've planted the bomb, anybody got any ideas? And you know, well, Maggie Cameron did it. Why did she do it? Well, you know ... and off we'd go.

DAVID SALE: I didn't like that at all, frankly, because she was a darling lady and a very, very good actress and had worked very well, but she seemed to be the only culprit. I mean, it just seemed to work that she wanted to get everybody out, to do something with the building. So, poor Bettina.

ELEANOR WITCOMBE: Poor Bettina. When she discovered that she was the bomber she was absolutely flabbergasted. She kept coming up with ideas. What if it was all a mistake and she was doing it to hide somebody else's guilt? What if, really, she had a wicked twin that came back from America?

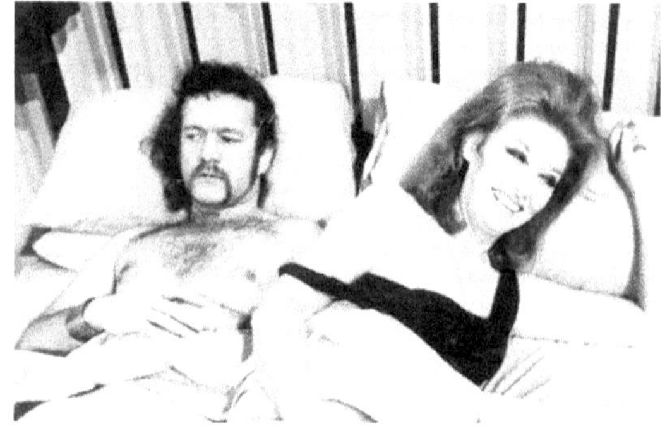

LYNN RAINBOW (actress): She was frightened. She loved the show. The theatre was her world and she really didn't have too many interests outside and she was really worried. I don't know if she talked to Bill, but he was approachable.

ELEANOR WITCOMBE: David said, 'We'll give her a wonderful send-off.' So they hired an old courtroom and gave her a big courtroom scene. It turned out, in the ultimate, that there was no other person who could've done it.

above: Bettina Welch as Maggie Cameron in an early scene with Vince Gil

opposite: Original cast members Elisabeth Kirkby and James Elliott left *Number 96* shortly after the bomb. Courtesy Mick Pratt

BETTINA WELCH (actress): I was in Dymock's Arcade and suddenly found myself surrounded by about twenty-five people shouting, 'Bitch, bitch, bitch,' at me. It was most upsetting.[16]

ELEANOR WITCOMBE: The old theatrical thing is it's only the nicest players who can play these bitches. Bettina was one of the favourite people of everybody. She was a darling woman.

MIKE DORSEY: The most professional actress in every sense of the word 'professional' that I've ever worked with. Every young actress should've shared a dressing room with Bettina. She was the epitome of absolute professionalism. I loved Bettina.

Just a month or so after the bomb blast, more beloved cast members were to depart.

ELISABETH KIRKBY: I wasn't told that I was to be written out. There had been various problems that made me think it would be a good idea to be written out. It was partly that I had various problems with Bill Harmon. I was the Equity representative on the show. He didn't approve of unions and was asking for certain things that I couldn't agree with, so it made things a bit tense. But the main problem was the fact that my husband found my involvement in *Number 96* annoying. I think it was likely that Bob Huber had told Bill I wanted to leave because

of the distress over the breakdown of my marriage. Bob was a personal friend as well as being part of management. There was no discussion with Bill Harmon, and I think they were too busy trying to invent ways of rescuing the ratings to worry too much about the old characters.

JAMES ELLIOTT: I was at home and Kevin Powell rang me and told me I'd been written out. I said, 'Well, that's a silly thing to do.' His exact words were, 'I've just come from a script meeting, Jim, and you've been written out.' I said, 'I'll see you tomorrow night; we'll have a beer then.' The next morning I was doing a scene with Lis and during a break in this scene she leaned forward to me and said, 'Did you get a phone call last night?' I said, 'Yeah, Lis, I sure did.' And that's how each of us were broken the news.

ELISABETH KIRKBY: I know Jimmy was very disappointed. He did say that he had hoped to be in *Number 96* for the rest of his life! Lucy and Alf had a storyline after the explosion. There was the kidnapping of the baby.

JAMES ELLIOTT: It didn't work because a lot of characters had been killed off or sent off elsewhere and they were going to replace them with new, young actors, but it was the beginning of the end.

JEFF KEVIN: They had tried the bomb in an effort to improve the all-important ratings, but only succeeded in blasting away the chemistry that existed within the company; the axe fell in the wrong area. Removing major characters in one fell swoop was folly and the show never recovered.

ELEANOR WITCOMBE: They killed off all the characters I was interested in writing. I didn't want to go into tits and bums.

CHANNEL TEN & CASH HARMON CELEBRATE

NUMBER 96

1,000th EPISODE

NANCY CASH & FRIEND.

are invited to Studio A, Channel Ten, North Ryde
Friday, 28th May, 1976. Cocktails & Buffet 8pm

RSVP 20th May. Publicity 888 5555

Chapter 10

Celebrations and Spin-Offs

The idea behind the bomb was to clear out some of the well-worn characters, make way for some fresh ones and get the ratings back on track. And while the bomb did boost the ratings to high figures once again, the results were short-lived. Viewers tuned in to see who got blown up, but they didn't stick around once the dust had settled. Prior to the explosion there had already been an injection of new, young faces, including Margaret Laurence, Pamela Gibbons, Vince Martin, Anya Saleky and Ashley Grenville. Carol Raye had once again returned to *Number 96*, only this time she was working on the other side of the camera.

preceding: An invitation to the 1000th episode party. Courtesy Nancy Cash

below left: Vince Martin as David Palmer

below centre: Margaret Laurence, Joe Hasham and Pamela Gibbons

below right: Anya Saleky

opposite left: Michael Ferguson returned to *Number 96* after the bomb blast

above right: An article on the new cast members

CAROL RAYE (producer): My role was Creative Producer for Cash Harmon. The brief was to come up with ideas and also help with the storylines and do the casting. So it was that side of things I was involved with.

In the wake of the bomb a new family was introduced and a familiar face returned.

MICHAEL FERGUSON (actor): My return to the series in August 1975 was directly after, and as a result of, the bomb. My father in the show, Les, was killed, heroically trying to warn everybody to evacuate the building. I wasn't expecting to return to the series and wasn't following the storylines, so it was a pleasant surprise

After that blast — a new family at 96

☐ **A NEW family is moving into bomb-blasted Number 96.**

Mrs Eileen Chester, a seamstress who works for Vera Collins, will move into a vacant flat with her two daughters, Jane and Debbie.

Patti Crocker will play Mrs Chester; Suzanne Church will play Jane, a theatre usherette, and Dina Mann is Debbie, a high school pupil.

Patti (no relation to Barry Crocker) began her show business career at 11 in the ABC radio Youth Show. She spent four and a half years there and was the original Mandy in Blue Hills.

She retired from show business to marry and raise a family before making a comeback on cake-mix commercials and doing voice-over work.

Patti did a pilot for Casualty Ward, which wasn't taken up.

PATTI . . . from Blue Hills to Number 96.

She also had a part in Luke's Kingdom.

Suzanne Church, 23, said: "Basically my 96 mother is a nice, little soul. She is working and I'm the favourite daughter.

"I'm quite happy with the part. It's very good experience for me."

Bill Harmon, head of the Cash-Harmon organisation which prduces Number 96, said: "A few others are coming into the series. Gordon Glenwright (janitor Hubbard in Class of 74) will play Arthur Partridge, a retired railroad man.

"Don Philps is coming back because of the death of Les Wittaker."

Latest additions to the O-10

SUZANNE . . . plays the favourite daughter.

DINA . . . will be the high school pupil.

network's serial will be seen in Melbourne and Sydney in early October.

when my agent called me and said they wanted me back in the show indefinitely.

DINA MANN (actress): The new characters, who in this instance happened to be my mother, whose character's name was Eileen, played by Patti Crocker, and Suzanne Church, who played my sister, Jane Chester and myself were introduced very strongly.

SUZANNE CHURCH (actress): I had a first audition for another role in which I was required to take off my top. I did it, but cringingly and I think they were more embarrassed than I was. Not surprisingly, I was not cast in that role. A few months later I was working in Hong Kong and received a call from my agent to say there was a part for me in *Number 96* and would I return to see Bill Harmon. On the day of the casting I arrived back in Sydney at 5am not having slept. I just had time to shower, change and get to the casting wearing no make-up but with my sunglasses on. They of course asked me to remove them. I refused, saying I was too jetlagged, but I got the part of Jane Chester.

above: From left, Dina Mann, Suzanne Church and Patti Crocker as Debbie, Jane and Eileen Chester respectively. Courtesy Mick Pratt

opposite: Mary Ann Severne as lawyer Laura Trent, and Roger Ward as Weppo the garbo. Courtesy Mick Pratt

DINA MANN: I auditioned for a role in the show, but didn't get that role. That role went to Margie Laurence and then not very long after that, I think, I got a call from Carol Raye. Obviously, from the audition I'd done previously, they felt that I had the acting capabilities, so I didn't actually have to audition for Debbie Chester. I just got it, which was great.

The Chester sisters' names were straight out of Hollywood.

DAVID SALE (writer): It was Johnny Whyte's idea, of course. The sisters were named for Debbie Reynolds and Jane Powell.

SUZANNE CHURCH: I think I met Patti Crocker and Dina for the first time on-set. It took a good six months for me to settle in. I had previously only appeared in one episode of *Alvin Purple* for the ABC and I was relatively inexperienced.

DINA MANN: When I first went into it they were still shooting five half-hours and that's a lot of scenes to be shot in one week. And our characters suddenly seemed to be in lots of episodes because they wanted to establish us.

SUZANNE CHURCH: I found the established cast extremely welcoming and supportive. Sheila Kennelly was always jolly and calm. Jeff Kevin and Wendy Blacklock, again, extremely solid. As a new girl it was always easier to work alongside the confidence of a more experienced actor, particularly at the beginning. Dina Mann was wonderful. Despite playing my younger sister Dina was a little older than me and had a background of conventional acting experience. We stuck together through thick and thin, and I think for both of us it was a case of being thrown into the deep end. We were cast as sisters and that quickly became our relationship, which still exists to this day.

‘I found the established cast extremely welcoming and supportive.’

DINA MANN: Joe Hasham was always absolutely gorgeous to me and really, really lovely to work with and really did become, in a way, a bit of a mentor like his character was for Debbie.

MARY ANN SEVERNE (actress): I auditioned for Carol Raye. Henri Szeps and I had returned from living in England only a few months before. I did a play at Nimrod then *Number 96*. I didn't know much about the show. The speed with which it was done was a bit of a shock after working in England for four years. I don't remember how long the contract was for, but I ended up with the show for eighteen months. I think it was always intended to be a long-running part. My character was named Laura, and she came into the show as both a lawyer in the office of the character played by Joe Hasham and also to share his flat.

ROGER WARD (actor): My involvement in *Number 96*, at least as far as the character of Frank 'Weppo' Smith was concerned, began near the end of September 1975, although I had played various other parts — detectives mostly — in the years prior to that. I discovered the character was a simple garbage collector who had a great knowledge of and a penchant to quote

Shakespeare. My initial contract was for three months, and the first of these episodes featured Edie and Weppo as rock'n'roll dancing champions. Wendy was fabulous in the part, and we often rehearsed well into the night to get the moves and the comedy that followed just right.

'the character was a simple garbage collector who had a great knowledge of and a penchant to quote Shakespeare'

MICHAEL FERGUSON: The writers began to involve me in some comic scenarios with Weppo, played by Roger Ward. Absolutely *loved* working with him; a funny lunatic.

ROGER WARD: My initial contract expired in early December 1975, and I remember being in the Channel 10 canteen on my last day when Bill Harmon went by and said, 'You're doing great, kid, keep up the good work.' 'Thanks, Bill, but it's a bit late for that. This is my last day.' 'It's what?' 'My last day, I only had a three-month contract.' 'Shit,' Bill said, and wandered away mumbling.

Ward returned to his home and family in the Adelaide Hills.

ROGER WARD: I was only there a week when a telegram arrived. I had been offered a further contract for *Number 96*, this time open-ended, but I was enjoying my home and family so much I refused to accept the offer. A few days later another telegram arrived. This time there was a substantial increase in my fee, and I was informed the writers had been instructed to write in a romantic interest if I deemed to come back. The latter interested me more than the former because all through my career I had seldom played the romantic lead. So I accepted and returned to Sydney and *Number 96* early in 1976.

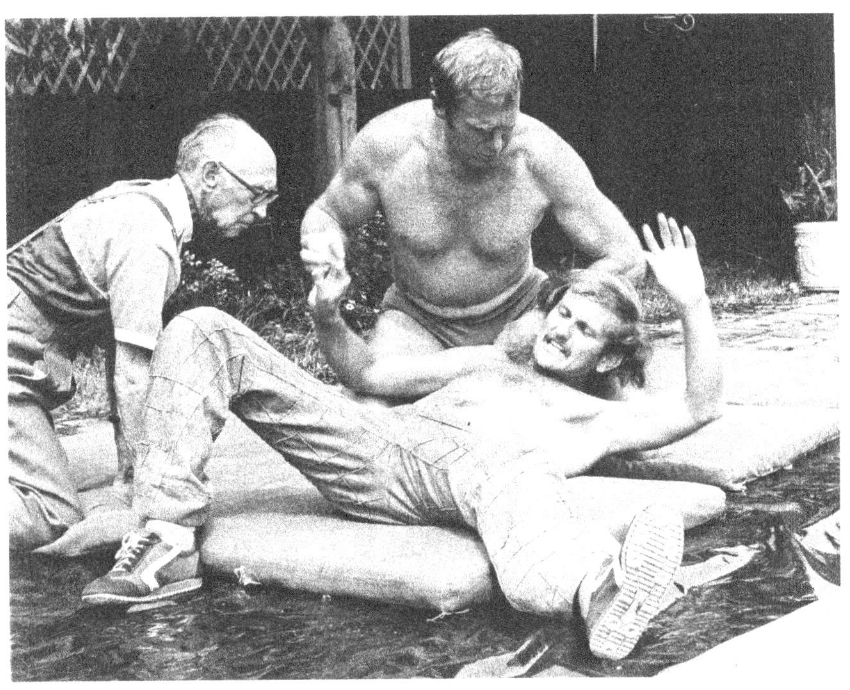

above: Ron Shand looks on as Roger Ward teaches Michael Ferguson a wrestling move. Courtesy Michael Ferguson

The writers developed a romance between Weppo and the recently widowed Norma.

ROGER WARD: Sheila was vivacious and brilliant, yet an easygoing actress. I was fortunate to be able to share some lovely scenes with her.

SHEILA KENNELLY (actress): It was always a pleasure to work with Roger. I remember Carol, working in the production office at the time, asking me one day what sort of men I liked. My reply was 'big men', and the next thing, Weppo turned up in Norma's storyline, played by one of the biggest men in the industry.

'When we did drugs we got the drug squad in to show us how to do it properly ... it was educational and a warning.'

DAVID SALE: We were asked by the police if we would do a storyline where a school girl was doing drugs and her mother didn't even know. That was with Dina Mann. There was a policeman on set for the preparation and everything. Now, people said we were being sensationalists, but we were doing that at the request of the police.

DINA MANN: The heroin storyline. They brought in Julieanne Newbould to play a school friend of mine, a fellow student. I think we were doing this heroin thing together. And we had a dealer. I can't remember who played that now. I think it might have been Terry Camilleri.

TOM GREER (publicist): People were being educated. When we did drugs we got the drug squad in to show us how to do it properly. So it was done correctly, but the storyline always ended in tragedy. So it was educational and a warning. We were very responsible, it was never promotion, but it was life.

DINA MANN: I do remember doing a telethon at the end of 1975, and getting people ringing me up and particularly wanting to speak to Debbie. They were actually kids that were having problems on heroin. I found it terribly difficult. I felt unqualified to be … you know, all I could do was listen and give heart and say to them, 'Can I take your number and I'll try to find someone who can help you. I'm really just an actor.' It was really quite confronting. I did have one person ring up — it could've been a joke — and say they wanted to know where to get drugs [*laughs*].

Not all storylines were inspired by real-life events. Some came straight out of Hollywood.

‘In the early days the stories were make ups of old Warner Brothers and Metro movies’

above: Lorrae Desmond, the first female to be awarded a Gold Logie, was one of many big-name stars to make a cameo appearance in *Number 96*

TED JOBBINS (producer): Everybody contributed to the show. In the early days the stories were make ups of old Warner Brothers and Metro movies; 20th Century. The writers would take an idea and they'd just twist it and turn it around.

In episode 450, a courtroom scene involving Carol Raye's character, Amanda, is an unabashed rip-off of a scene in the Gertrude Lawrence biopic, *Star*, with Julie Andrews. The same was true of other storylines and characters.

CAROL RAYE: My Amanda character was really 'Auntie Mame'.

DAVID SALE: Lorrae Desmond was in the show. She had the best line, what Johnny Whyte and I considered the best line in the whole series.

When her attempted seduction of Arnold Feather ends in a case of premature ejaculation, Lorrae's character, Mrs Carlton, phones for a taxi, prompting him to ask, 'Do you think it will come quickly?' She replies, 'If the rest of the evening's anything to go by it should be here before you've got your tie on.'

DAVID SALE: She delivered it perfectly. She was marvellous in that scene. We called that the Mrs Robinson scenario — *The Graduate* — the older woman with Arnold.

TED JOBBINS: There was a funny scene that was shot with Johnny Lockwood and Jeff Kevin. We were working on the scene, and Brian and Johnny worked out a routine that was basically W. C. Fields. He'd come up with the routine in a movie, and Brian and Johnny worked out a similar routine where Aldo hit Arnold on the head and got this sticky paper stuck to his golf club and everything. It was basically pinching ideas that people had seen.

BRIAN PHILLIS (director): When the hit movie *Jaws* came out the writers decided to do a *Number 96* version as a way of writing a character out of the show. The scene was to be complete with oblivious swimming extras and a looming shark fin cutting through the water just off Balmoral Beach. The stuntman had an aqualung and a ridiculous Styrofoam fin affixed to his back. He also needed to be in at least five feet of water so he could remain submerged. I ran the cast through their paces up on the beach and Patti Crocker, whose character was being written out, dutifully said her lines, and then we were ready to shoot the scene. Meanwhile a veritable armada of small vessels, gawkers, extras, technicians etc. were floundering about in the sea. Some distance away I noticed a Channel 10 executive keeping a sharp eye on us, making sure we weren't wasting money. I called out to Patti to get ready for the action — when you're about to be taken by a shark there's not much else to say. So I took Patti by the arm and guided her down to the water when, abruptly, she turned to me, almost tears in her eyes and stuttered, 'I–I can't swim.'

'I took Patti by the arm and guided her down to the water when, abruptly, she turned to me, almost tears in her eyes and stuttered, 'I–I can't swim.'’

96's shark puts the bite on us viewers!

DINA MANN: A character was brought in called Ian, played by Stewart Finch, who was my long-lost father. You'd get your scripts and you'd open them up and see what the hell's going to happen to you now. I opened them up one week and I went, 'Oh, for God's sake.' Debbie, her mother and father hired a boat and went out and they were having a lovely time together. Then her mother decided to go off the side of the boat and have a swim, and along came a shark to attack her. So my father dove in to save my mother and the shark attacked him too. So, my mother and father were eaten by a shark in front of my eyes.

(clockwise from top left) Stuntwoman Kathy Troutt watches as the shark fin is prepared; Patti Crocker (in blue dress) and Stewart Finch (with beard) wait with crew before filming; director Brian Phillis and crew prepare to shoot the 'shark attack' scene; the 'shark' enters the water. Courtesy Dina Mann

Then I turned to the next script and it says, 'Debbie has been struck dumb by the sight of both her parents being eaten by a shark.' So it went on for two episodes where I didn't speak, but was sitting there in this catatonic state.

January 1976 saw a change in format from half-hour episodes five nights a week, to one-hour episodes twice a week.

PETER BENARDOS (director): Luckily, towards the end of a five-and-a-half-year period, or whatever it was, instead of doing five half-hours a week we ended up doing two one-hours, which was therefore four episodes. Gee, that made a difference.

above: Peter Whitford as Guy Sutton (top) and Harry Michaels as Giovanni Lenzi (bottom) joined the cast in 1976. Courtesy Mick Pratt

BILL HARMON (producer): I wanted to cut it down. I thought it had gone far enough at five episodes a week and I wanted to cut it back to three. Then I was talked into two hours a week.

DINA MANN: After the Christmas break, in 1976 it then went to two hours a week, which meant that you had slightly less workload and they did a little bit more of it outside; outside broadcasts. So they actually filmed outside the *Number 96* building, which was in Moncur Street, or they'd do OBs on beaches or whatever to try and get a little bit more variety into it, I think.

PETER WHITFORD (actor): So they were going to write in a character called Guy Sutton. Guy Sutton was a racing car driver who'd lost his nerve on the European circuit so he'd come back to Australia. They were looking at different people to play Guy Sutton the racing car driver. So my agent told me to go and be seen by the people who made *Number 96*, Bill Harmon. So I go into this absolutely famous serial. It was fun. Once again it was a regular paycheque. It was already worked out that I was to be Vera's new romantic interest.

ELAINE LEE (actress): Peter played Guy Sutton, a racing car driver, and we became firm, firm friends.

Episode 932, which screened in February 1976, saw the introduction of a new assistant in the deli, an Italian boy named Giovanni Lenzi. The role went to aspiring actor Harry Michaels, who was in fact Greek.

HARRY MICHAELS (actor): One day I got a phone call from my agent at Telecast in North Sydney and they said, 'There is a part going at the moment for a young Italian to be involved in the deli with Arnold Feather. And I think you'd be ideal for the part. We're putting you up for it, so can you please quickly get to Cash Harmon's offices for an interview and if they like what they see they'll give you an audition script.'

At Cash Harmon he was interviewed by Carol Raye, Bill Harmon and Johnny Whyte.

HARRY MICHAELS: They interviewed me; they gave me a script. It was Friday, I remember, and they said, 'Go home, learn your lines and come back on Monday.' It was the longest bloody weekend of my life.

Michaels won the role and was signed for thirteen weeks, but it wasn't his first visit to *Number 96*.

TED JOBBINS: After the bomb blast — that's when Harry Michaels came into the show. He was in the deli. The funny thing with Harry — Harry had come into the show earlier in the piece to do just a one day extra part. This Greek boy arrived and he was so enthusiastic, he was driving everyone nuts — trying to keep him down until the time came for his part. Anyway, he came in and he did his little part and that was it.

'I come in, dancing Greek style and running around and making all these noises.'

HARRY MICHAELS: I came in as an extra, being a Greek National Guard, and Daddy and Mummy picked me up from a nightclub. They invited me in to the flat, so I come in, dancing Greek style and running around and making all these noises.

TED JOBBINS: The producers were looking for someone to go into the deli. I think he was Italian — the part Harry Michaels played — and I said, 'Well, if you're looking for an Italian, we had a Greek boy in the other day; he'd be ideal to play it.' And Bill Harmon said, 'Well go and find him.'

Joining the full-time cast was a dream come true for the young, impressionable actor.

HARRY MICHAELS: I went into *Number 96* and I looked around me and I was like a kid in a candy bar, with all those people that I admired. All those people that I was watching on television — now I'm rubbing shoulders with them, and I thought, *this is not fucking true, no way.*

As the character of Giovanni became established, other members of his family were introduced. Austrian-born actor Joseph Furst played Carlo Lenzi, Giovanni's father. They would eventually be joined by New Zealand-born actress Arianthe Galani as Aunt Maria Panucci.

HARRY MICHAELS: Joseph Furst came in about four weeks later. He was an actor of all actors. I mean, a guy who was in one of the James Bond movies. I was so lucky to be working with Joseph. He made everything look so simple. And because of my inexperience I couldn't understand how this guy can come on, do his lines like that and walk off. He was unbelievable. To say that I learned a lot from him is an understatement.

'He was an actor of all actors. I mean, a guy who was in one of the James Bond movies.'

opposite: Harry Michaels takes a break with Suzanne Church, Dina Mann, Ron Shand and Pat McDonald

above: From left, Joseph Furst as Carlo Lenzi; Arianthe Galani as Aunt Maria; Karen Petersen as Christina. Courtesy Mick Pratt

ROGER WARD: Joseph brought a touch of European class to the cast. It was nice to have him to chat to during breaks.

KAREN PETERSEN (actress): Working with Joseph Furst was a European pleasure. He was Austrian, playing an Italian. I was German, playing an Italian. Both of us also spoke fluent Italian, so there was no problem with the Italian accent. Sometimes in the canteen, while going over our next scene, we would start discussing it in English, then involuntarily switching to German, much to the amusement of other cast members.

Joseph Furst and Karen Petersen were two of many international performers to join the cast of *Number 96*. Throughout the years, others included Indian actor Beverley Roberts as pharmacy assistant Brian Banerjee, and Americans Natalie Mosco, Harry Harris and Alfred Sandor.

KAREN PETERSEN: An opportunity offered itself at a plotting session: 'Giovanni Lenzi, Harry Michaels, needs to settle down

left: Justine Saunders makes the cover of *TV Week*

right: (left to right) Justine Saunders, Pat McDonald, Karen Petersen and hairdresser Gail Edmonds in the make-up room. Courtesy Karen Petersen

and have a bride' was the theme. His father Carlo Lenzi and Aunt Maria Panucci decided to bring out a bride from Italy for him. David Phillips suggested the Italian import should be the opposite of expectations. Instead of a demure bride-to-be from Sicily, a blonde, blue-eyed, self-possessed firecracker enters. I auditioned for Bob Huber. He told me on the spot that I was Christina Vettare. The established cast made me feel very welcome. I already knew Dina Mann from *Petersen*, Mike Ferguson, Roger Ward and Sheila Kennelly.

When Justine Saunders joined the cast in mid-1976 it was yet another groundbreaking moment for Australian television, and Indigenous actors in particular. She said at the time:

> Justine Saunders (actress): At last I have the chance to act and not to be just an Aboriginal being killed off. I'm sick to death of dying! It will also be good for black actors.[17]

KAREN PETERSEN: One actor I bonded with was Justine Saunders. One morning, panic in the studio. Justine hadn't turned up for her 7am call. Frantic phone calls to her agent and her flat brought no results. Justine went missing for two days. She arrived on the third day, nonplussed about all the fuss. 'I went walkabout,' she explained. It was accepted, respected and included in future scheduling by Cash Harmon.

JEFF KEVIN (actor): Justine was a wonderful actor and *Number 96* was one of her first on-screen roles. She found the strict timetable daunting, if my memory serves me well, but then she wasn't the only performer in that category.

JUSTINE SAUNDERS: I was terribly nervous when I walked into the studio for the first time, but without exception every cast member welcomed me in a matter-of-fact way. They were never patronising, but always kind and helpful, and straight away I felt one of the gang.[18]

DAVID SALE: Justine Saunders. You see, we decided to bring in an Aboriginal girl, but we didn't want her to be brought in as 'an Aboriginal girl'. What she was brought in as was a hairdresser's assistant who *happened* to be an Aboriginal girl. And I don't think the race thing cropped up all that much in it. In fact, she just evolved in other ways. She got raped by the masked rapist, but then so did everybody else. But it was marvellous because that was Justine's first major part and she went on to so many great things.

The hooded rapist storyline became the latest in a long line of mysteries, and lasted six or seven weeks before Lenny Fisher, an employee in Norma's Bar, played by Terry Peck, was revealed as the rapist.

SUZANNE CHURCH: Jane Chester was a victim in the hooded rapist storyline. Brian Phillis taught me a valuable life lesson when I questioned the reality of the scripted scene where Jane opened the door to her flat to a man who would, in thirty seconds, render her powerless on the sofa. Brian spoke to me from the control box saying, 'Okay Sue, just try it once. When

you hear a knock, open the door. I will play the rapist.' I was flat on my back on the sofa before I knew what had happened. Brian just grinned and said, 'Now do you believe it?'

The most bedded character throughout the series would have to be the 'unlucky in love' Vera Collins, played by Elaine Lee. Starting with Norman Yemm, Elaine's list of on-screen romances included Max Cullen, George Assang, Tom Oliver, Julian Rockett, Kit Taylor and Peter Whitford.

ELAINE LEE: There was really only that one actor, Bill's mate who I really couldn't stand. The rest were all terrific, but I can't remember them all!

PETER WHITFORD: Elaine Lee — Vera — she'd gone through boyfriends, engagements, marriages, affairs, rapes. I mean, Vera had done the lot and Elaine was amazing. She's been a close, personal friend. She was great to be with. In due course they'd run out of storylines for the Vera character.

After more than four years, 992 episodes and countless lovers, Elaine Lee said goodbye to Vera and *Number 96* in June 1976.

'Vera – she'd gone through boyfriends, engagements, marriages, affairs, rapes. I mean, Vera had done the lot'

ELAINE LEE: In a way I was disappointed, in another way I thought that yes, we had come to the end of the tether with her. Mixed feelings, really, mixed feelings. I mean, I had enjoyed every second of it and I missed it when I first left.

Number 96 reached a milestone when episode 1000 screened on 21 June 1976. To celebrate this achievement Cash Harmon packaged a retrospective special.

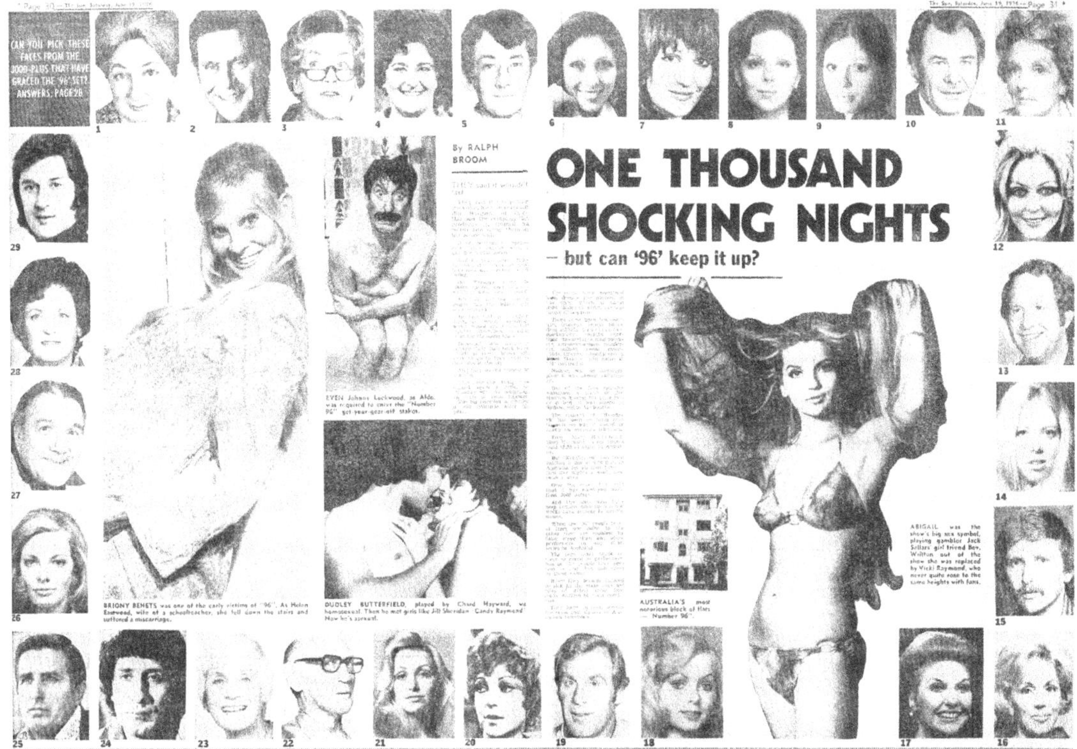

CAN YOU PICK THESE FACES FROM THE 1000-PLUS THAT HAVE GRACED THE '96' SET? ANSWERS, PAGE 28

ONE THOUSAND SHOCKING NIGHTS

— but can '96' keep it up?

By RALPH BROOM

EVEN Johnny Lockwood, as Aldo, was required to enter the "Number 96" get-your-gear-off stakes.

BRIONY BEHETS was one of the early victims of "96". As Helen Eastwood, wife of a schoolteacher, she fell down the stairs and suffered a miscarriage.

DUDLEY BUTTERFIELD, played by Chard Hayward, wa homosexual. Then he met girls like Jill Sheridan (Candy Raymond). Now he's asexual.

AUSTRALIA'S most notorious block of flats — Number 96".

ABIGAIL was the show's big sex symbol, playing gambler Jack Sellars' girl friend Bev. Written out of the show she was replaced by Vicki Raymond, who never quite rose to the same heights with fans.

opposite: An advert for the *Number 96* retrospective special, 'And They Said It Wouldn't Last'

above: A special newspaper feature for *Number 96*'s 1000th episode

PETER BENARDOS: We did the Special with Johnny Whyte, called: 'And They Said it Wouldn't Last'. We had snippets of all sorts of characters and scenes, and so on.

DAVID SALE: The Special was mostly done by Johnny Whyte. It was Johnny Whyte's baby. He wrote the linking stuff and he took a chance with Abigail, saying she 'remained a virgin, well on-screen anyway'. He didn't think she'd say that, but she did.

ABIGAIL (actress): I first worked with them again on the 1000th episode special Cash Harmon made, and I suppose that was an indication that the hatchet had been completely buried.[19]

Along with Abigail, other former cast members Johnny Lockwood, Philippa Baker, Gordon McDougall, Bettina Welch, James Elliott, Elisabeth Kirkby and Elaine Lee came back to introduce highlights from the series.

right: Peter Armstrong's stunt crew with the actors (clockwise from front left) Harry Michaels, Karen Petersen, Joseph Furst, unknown, Peter Armstrong, Karen Petersen's stunt double and Harry Michaels' stunt double. Courtesy Karen Petersen

below: From left Michael Howard and Stephen McDonald as brothers Grant and Lee Chandler and Lynne Murphy as their mother Faye. Courtesy Mick Pratt

opposite: Thelma Scott, the 'grand dame', as Claire Houghton. Courtesy Mick Pratt

ELAINE LEE: We did the Special and I introduced a lot of the segments for the 1000th episode. I suppose they gave us a party. I can't remember.

BOB HUBER (producer): The 1000th episode was the best party of all, I think. It was held in the Mike Walsh studio at Channel 10.

The storyline of the 1000th episode included a jewel heist.

KAREN PETERSEN: The storyline leading up to the jewel robbery was a direct steal from *To Catch a Thief*. David Phillips, responsible for it, had a motto: 'Read everything, watch everything, steal everything.' Bill Harmon used to add, 'These Hollywood people spent a lot of time and money on their movies. Who are we not to steal their plots?' Carlo and Christina rescued Giovanni when he was trapped after stealing the Moritza Diamond. Part of this sequence took place on top of a high-rise building in North Sydney. It was a freezing night, and the abseil action challenged my acrophobia, but Peter Armstrong's brilliant stunt team kept us safe. We filmed all night. Finally, at 4am, it was a wrap. Our director, the lovely Peter Benardos, took us to Bill Harmon's office, just around the corner. Bill had given instructions: 'Take them there to warm up. There's a fine scotch to help.'

This milestone episode also saw the introduction of a new family, who moved into flat 7. Lynne Murphy was cast as Reg McDonald's sister Faye Chandler, and her sons Lee and Grant were played by Stephen McDonald and Michael Howard.

DINA MANN: There was Suzy and I and then not long after we arrived there were the Chandler brothers, who were Michael Howard and Stephen McDonald — we were all 'the youngsters'. I was playing sixteen and Stephen and Michael were late teens/ early twenties, and it was all kids' stuff.

Around this time, Thelma Scott as Mrs Claire Houghton returned to the series. Still based in Point Piper, the writers involved her with Michael Howard's character.

THELMA SCOTT (actress): This boy Grant Chandler. Nice kid; liked him a lot. He worked with Claire; he was her toy boy.

TED JOBBINS: I loved working with Thelma, but she was the worst as far as lines are concerned. She held the all-time record for the number of takes on a scene but she was so much fun, and everybody knew if they were in a scene with Thelly then don't think you're going to do it in one take. So everyone came prepared for it. I think we got up to about thirty-two takes on a scene, and she was working with Michael Howard, one of the young kids that came in towards the end. Everybody kept prompting her and in the end she said, 'Everyone knows the fucking line except me.' But we loved working with Thelly because she made the day, she brightened it up. She was the grand dame.

Despite working flat-out during the run of *Number 96* Cash Harmon made a few attempts at other series.

KEVIN POWELL (production manager): There was *Bonner and Clyde*, a pilot we did for Channel 9, which was about two lawyers living in Kings Cross; that sort of sitcom-type stuff. Kerry Packer apparently liked it and he wanted thirteen story outlines, but for some reason or other Bill wasn't prepared to go that far without a commitment from them. When Channel 9 is prepared to pay for the outlines, I would've thought it would've been worthwhile putting the effort in and saying yes, we'll do it, but for some reason Bill decided we wouldn't put our energies into coming up with thirteen storylines.

BILL HARMON: I said you either like it or you don't like it. Then Packer wanted to buy *Number 96* for Melbourne, away from Channel 10, which we wouldn't allow. I guess Don Cash was gone by that time. Maybe he would've convinced me to do the scripts, but I just felt there was no-one there who could judge them anyway, and we just never went ahead with it. *Bonner and Clyde* were two crazy legal kids. These kids were breaking all the rules to win the cases. It was a comedy. It was an idea I had. I think Johnny Whyte wrote that. It would've gone ahead, I guess. I just didn't want to do more scripts. We were so busy.

KEVIN POWELL: We did things like the *Gloria* special. We also did a telemovie that Terry Bourke directed called *Murcheson Creek*, and that was shot down towards Narellan and Camden.

ITALIAN STAR FOR AUSSIE TV SERIES!

ITALIAN actor Walter Chiari will move to Australia with his family next year and is tipped to star in a new television series.

The series is **Melting Pot**, a program set in an Australian migrant hostel.

Last week Chiari was in Australia having talks with Cash Harmon Productions, the company which is planning **Melting Pot**.

He is expected to buy a house in an exclusive Sydney suburb and return with his family either later this year or early next year.

A pilot episode of **Melting Pot** is being made for the Nine Network and a decision on its future will be made soon after.

It is one of several new projects being launched by Cash Harmon Productions, the company which makes **Number 96** for the 0-10 Network.

The other projects are:

● A drama series called **The Palmer Affair** all about a reporter who is blinded after having acid thrown in his eyes by a small-time thug.

● **McManus MPB**, a movie about the investigators of a missing persons' bureau and intended as the pilot of a pos-

● **Jill**, a new variety series to star entertainer Jill Perryman.

Last week Cash Harmon's executive producer, Bill Harmon, said Walter Chiari was only one of several actors planned to be used in **Melting Pot**.

"The series will be a whole new concept in serials," he said. "We will have a regular cast of people who play the staff of the hostel and then we will have others passing through.

"Every four weeks there will be new guests as the people in the hostel change. It will almost be like an anthology."

Walter Chiari will play an interpreter in the hostel.

Bill Harmon said he would probably come to Australia "when I call for him". No shooting date has been set.

The Palmer Affair — if it goes ahead — is envisaged as one of the most dramatic and ambitious drama series ever made here.

The Seven Network has commissioned a pilot episode and scripting is currently under way.

The hero of the series will be a young reporter who has been blind for four years

● ABOVE. Walter Chiari . . . coming to Australia.

pays a thug to throw acid in his face.

His only hope to regain his sight lies with a research doctor working on eye transplants. The doctor has had moderate success with animals, but has never attempted a human eye trans-

A friend persuades him that he should be the first human guinea pig.

The operation, performed illegally, is only partially successful and at any time he can again lose his sight.

All the while the reporter

above: Walter Chiari worked with Don Cash and Bill Harmon in the NLT film *Squeeze a Flower*. He was tipped to star in a new series for Cash Harmon called *The Melting Pot*, but it never eventuated

JAMES ELLIOTT (actor): It surprised me that Lis and I would be chosen to leave the show to help it on its way, but that's what happened. I was sorry at the time, but actually, Bill Harmon rang me one day and said he was doing another series and asked if I'd like to be involved in it. I think *Murcheson Creek* was what it was called, and I said, 'Well, Bill, you should've told me earlier because I've already signed something with the Queensland Theatre Company and I'm going to do it.' It was *Equus*. Bill said, 'It's always the way, isn't it?'

BILL HARMON: We did the pilot for *Murcheson Creek* and then that never got off the ground either, although we did sell it to Paramount. It was about a country doctor. We did an hour-and-a-half pilot. Each episode was supposed to be an hour.

JOHN ORCSIK (actor): My friend Terry Bourke directed *Murcheson Creek*. I was going to be in it down the track, as an actor. Terry did a great job. Everyone had high hopes for it, and the pilot, I thought, was very, very good. I had a little input into it. I really liked the whole idea, the concept. The feel that Terry had for that was very good, and we were all very disappointed that it didn't go on at least to one series to sort of see what might happen.

above: A promotional advert for Cash Harmon creation, *The Unisexers*

The *Murcheson Creek* pilot was produced for the Nine Network in 1976. The cast consisted of Mark Edwards, Cornelia Frances, Sandra Lee Paterson, Keith Lee, Gordon McDougall, Dennis Miller, Philippa Baker, Abigail, Lew Luton, Rowena Wallace, Anne Louise Lambert and Robert Quilter.

KEVIN POWELL: We did *McManus MPB*: a nice hour-and-a-half telemovie with Peter Sumner, directed by Max Varnel, which was based on the Missing Person's Bureau of the New South Wales Police.

BILL HARMON: *McManus*. That was a police show. It was based pretty much on a *Detective Story* idea that everything happens in a police station. It was a serious thing like *Detective Story*. We did an hour and a half but it was also intended for an hour each week. That one, I think, was written by Bob Caswell and it never got off the ground.

As well as Peter Sumner, the cast of *McManus MPB* included Arna Maria Winchester, Pamela Stephenson and Chantal Contouri. It was produced in 1976 as a pilot for Channel 10.

BOB HUBER: Another series that began on Channel 9 under the Cash Harmon banner was *The Unisexers*. I left *Number 96* to do that. It was a disaster. David Hannay joined me and we tried to save it.

‘Bill had a couple of ideas for new programs, which didn't quite get off the ground.’

CAROL RAYE: When I was with Cash Harmon, behind the scenes, Bill had a couple of ideas for new programs, which didn't quite get off the ground. *Unisexers* was one of them. It was going to be about a lot of youngsters and that was going to be a soap opera too.

***The Unisexers* cast members, Josephine Knur (top), Patrick Ward (middle) and writer David Phillips (bottom)**

BILL HARMON: Channel 9 approached us to do *The Unisexers*. Now, we did a pilot of that — an hour and a half. They bought it and then proceeded to say we couldn't do what we originally intended. They'd bought it and we'd started production. We had scripts done when they decided they couldn't have any of the boys and girls in rooms together — because they were putting it on at six o'clock — unless the door was open. They couldn't have wine on the table. A lot of comedy was predicated basically upon boys and girls being together. Well, hell, we had to knock all that stuff out; any sex connotation was gone.

DAVID PHILLIPS (writer): In 1974, after thirteen years of continuous professional acting, I sent a sitcom script to the ABC, Crawfords, Grundys and Cash Harmon. I received no reply from Grundys, a seven-page response from Crawfords telling me how to turn it into a *Division 4* episode, a three-line answer from the ABC telling me they didn't understand my script, and a telegram from Cash Harmon offering me a job.[20]

KAREN PETERSEN: The job was to write for *Unisexers*, for which we moved to Sydney. To be precise we moved to number ninety-six Greenwich Road, Greenwich. Number ninety-six? Coincidence? Perhaps not. Old friends shared a house in Carlotta Street, just around the corner, namely Mike Ferguson, James Kemsley — Ginger Meggs cartoonist — and Mick Pratt, who worked on the *Number 96* crew.

PATRICK WARD (actor): *Unisexers* was quite interesting. It had an amazing cast. It was a commune of kids, and 'Unisexers' referred to jeans; jeans that were unisex, so girls could wear them and guys could wear them. So that's basically what it was about, making jeans, and it was a commune because it was the 1970s.

Along with Patrick Ward, *The Unisexers* impressive cast included Josie Knur, Scott Lambert, Steven Tandy, Michele Fawdon, Tina Bursill, Tony Sheldon, John Paramor, Jessica Noad and Walter Pym.

JOSEPHINE KNUR (actress): I didn't know I'd go into *The Unisexers* after *Number 96*. I decided that I'd do that series before going to the US so I could build up a nest egg. Unfortunately, the show didn't last long. It was very expensive to make at that time — $100,000 or more an episode every week is what I heard — so replacing us with *Happy Days* for $7000 or $10,000 an episode was a no-brainer for the TV station.

The Unisexers debuted on the Nine Network in early February 1975. With low ratings and a canning from critics it lasted just three weeks on screens before being dumped.

KAREN PETERSEN: David Phillips managed to write one episode of *The Unisexers*. Sadly, it folded. Before David could pack up his portable typewriter and meet me at the 729 Club St Leonards to drown our sorrows, Bill Harmon moved him on to *Number 96*. We still linked up at the 729 Club, and celebrated!

BOB HUBER: Channel 9 cancelled it and I went back and became executive producer of *Number 96*.

DAVID SALE: Bill also wanted to do spin-offs from *Number 96*. Again, none of them worked.

BOB HUBER: They thought that might be a way to stimulate some more sales, but nobody really wanted to know. I think some of the pilots were quite ludicrous and crazy.

WENDY BLACKLOCK (actress): At one stage they were talking about doing a spin-off and they asked us to do a pilot for our own show. I remember thinking at this time that we didn't spend enough time, or there wasn't enough time allowed, to think through where the characters could go and if there was enough breadth in them to support their own show.

DAVID SALE: They tried to do a spin-off with Mummy and Daddy, but the scenes were tailored to be put in *Number 96* and

‘They tried to do a spin-off with Mummy and Daddy, but the scenes were tailored to be put in Number 96 and you just can’t do that.’

you just can’t do that. If you’re going to do a spin-off it has to be totally away. Keep the characters, of course, but totally away from what they’re doing in the series.

MIKE DORSEY (actor): We shot the pilot. God, who was in it? Jan Adele, Wendy, obviously, and myself. Johnny Ewart. We shot the thing. It was a different storyline to *Number 96*, which made it interesting. I’m surprised it didn’t work. That’s just my ego talking.

The spin-off was called *Mummy and Me* and was set in an advertising agency. Joining Wendy Blacklock, Mike Dorsey, Jan Adele and John Ewart were Lorna Lesley, John Allen and Jacqueline Kott.

below: Mike Dorsey and Wendy Blacklock extended their roles as the McDonalds for a spin-off called *Mummy and Me*

DINA MANN: There was another spin-off with the three girls, with Elaine Lee. And they brought in Lynette Curran and they brought Abigail back.

ABIGAIL: Bill Harmon asked me if I would consider going back into *Number 96*. I refused the offer. So Bill went away and came back with the idea of the spin-off series, with me playing an entirely different sort of character — an older lady, more mature than Bev was and with more brains, I suppose. This time I was interested. The idea appealed to me because there were elements of comedy in it and I felt the character, Eve, was so very different to Bev Houghton.[21]

PETER WHITFORD: After all the years Elaine had been in the serial, they wrote her out by marrying her to Guy Sutton. More

above: From left, Lynette Curran, Abigail and Elaine Lee in another spin-off, *Fair Game*

below: Chelsea Brown had appeared in the US comedy series *Laugh-In* before settling in Australia

opposite: Joe Hasham and producer Ted Jobbins

than that, he then regained his nerve and had the courage to go back to Europe and she, the faithful wife, went with him. So both of us got written out at the same time. That was fine. So they got rid of me, but they realised they needed her back because she was one of the great characters.

ELAINE LEE: In the series Vera actually goes off with Guy, supposedly to live happy ever afters, but when the show was starting to flag a bit, Bill Harmon had the idea — and it was a very good idea — to see if there could be any spin-off series. So he did one with Wendy Blacklock and Mike Dorsey as Mummy and Daddy. He did one with Dorrie, Herb and Flo, and he did one with me and Abigail and the lovely actress Lynette Curran. We were supposed to be three divorcees flatting together. It was a nice script and everything, but none of them ever got off the ground, which was sad. So Vera came back from Europe — apparently her marriage had floundered — and we did the spin-off series.

The sitcom was called *Fair Game*, and others in the cast included Terry O'Neill and Peter Flett, who'd previously been seen in *Number 96* as Michael Bartlett.

‘of course he went back on his word and it was fed into Number 96’

DAVID SALE: Bill asked me to do a pilot for Chelsea Brown, the beautiful black actress with a flair for comedy and who could also sing. She had been in *Laugh-In*. I said, ‘If I write a pilot for Chelsea Brown, it’s not to be fed into *Number 96*.’ So I wrote the pilot, and of course he went back on his word and it *was* fed into *Number 96*, and of course never got sold.

The pilot was for a proposed sitcom called *Hope’ll Help* with Chelsea Brown in the starring role.

DAVID SALE: The pilot was sort of based on the American musical *Bells are Ringing*. It was an answering service, a personal telephone answering service, with Chelsea Brown, June Salter and Lorna Lesley.

KEN SHADIE (writer): The comedy thing was coming out in me with Dorrie, Herb and Flo because they were always fun. I had

a good time with them and Bill said to me, 'Can you write a sitcom for them?' I said, 'Yeah, I'll have a go at that.' And I did. I put them in a restaurant, running a restaurant, and wrote the half-hour episode, but it never happened.

There was also a proposed hour-long drama series spin-off, *A Law Unto Himself*, with Joe Hasham, Dina Mann and Suzanne Church.

DINA MANN: The pilot that Suzanne Church and myself were involved in was the one with Don's character, as in Joe Hasham. He had a kind of solicitor agency and we were to be his assistant sleuths. So it was sort of going to be a detective kind of thing. I don't actually know how they could've done it, but they shot all these scenes and then seemed to incorporate them into the actual series of *Number 96*, which to me seems like they must've compromised the storylines of the pilots somehow. Ours was actually a serious drama. I think that Joe did a really good job and there could've been potential there.

'None of the spin-offs worked because Bill seemed to think he could save money by feeding them into the episodes of Number 96.'

JOE HASHAM (actor): It was basically a spin-off of Don's character, only more physical. Still gay, but very able to look after himself. I took up boxing again — used to box as a junior — to get into shape. It was Bill Harmon's idea. I really enjoyed the pilot; don't know what happened. I do know that it was not picked up.

DAVID SALE: None of the spin-offs worked because Bill seemed to think he could save money by feeding them into the episodes of *Number 96*. So Don suddenly starts to act like a private eye because the spin-off was that he was going to be a lawyer who solved murders. The storylines were threaded through *Number 96*. This could've also led to the decline in popularity of *Number 96* because there was an incomprehensibility about these plotlines that really had nothing to do with the regular *Number 96* characters.

Back at *Number 96* it was business as usual, with various characters coming and going. In October 1976, a much loved, and missed, actor returned.

SHEILA KENNELLY: Of course, the viewers were so upset that Gordon McDougall was written out that the producers had to immediately do something, and they brought him back as his own twin brother, which was lovely — Scottish brother.

DAVID SALE: We'd had Aunt Amanda's double and then we had Les's. Gordon McDougall was Scottish so it seemed quite normal for him to assume a Scottish accent. It filled in a bit.

‘Everybody liked Gordon McDougall and was glad to see him back, but it didn't really work.’

BRIAN PHILLIS: After the bomb blast killed off Les, Bill Harmon realised the show had written out one of its assets so the writers created Les's long-lost twin brother, Lord McCraddanow from Scotland, complete with highland regalia, kilt, sporran, dirk etc. Gordon was meticulous about being correct in every detail of his outfit and it took some time to put it on. Some weeks later, Gordon was well into his new role, Scottish brogue and all — in short, a true Scot. On this particular morning Gordon was all decked up, ready to do his scene, when disaster struck.

GORDON IS BACK... AND BEARDED

above: Sheila Kennelly and Gordon McDougall reunited on the set of *Number 96*

For reasons I can't recall, we had to reschedule another scene. Gordon was not impressed. Ted informed Gordon that he had to change into street clothes for this next scene. This he did, but no sooner had he done so, yet another mini-crisis. Ted advised Gordon that he had to change back into the highland rig. There was a ponderous pause; Gordon showed signs of an imminent meltdown, but went ahead with the change. Golden minutes ticked by before he was ready. Time lost is never regained. By then everybody's temperature was rising as though sensing something in the wind. Then it hit. There was another crisis, this time a technical glitch, necessitating yet another change. This time Gordon was to revert to street clothes. Ted told Gordon, who exploded. I have never witnessed a man having such a meltdown. I promptly called a coffee break, but as the saying goes: beware the anger of a patient man.

DAVID SALE: Everybody liked Gordon McDougall and was glad to see him back, but it didn't really work. It was sort of winding down at that stage.

The on-screen chemistry between the various characters who teamed up was one of the drawcards of *Number 96*. The success of these teams was due to a combination of the way the characters were written and the actors who portrayed them. Although Sheila and Gordon as Norma and Les had a successful chemistry, this wasn't matched by Norma and Andrew. It was the same with Don and Dudley. Over the years Don would have his fair share of lovers, starting with Paul Weingott as Bruce, and subsequently, characters portrayed by David Whitford, John McTernan and Stephen O'Rourke. But it was Don and Dudley who became the most popular, and the best fit, with viewers.

Like Norma and Les, they had a special chemistry that worked so well it was hard for viewers to accept anything different. Chard Hayward as Dudley was the perfect foil for Joe Hasham's Don, but eventually they would separate, and the writers even turned Dudley straight.

Despite this big change the one thing that remained the

same over the years was the nudity. There were always plenty of naked bodies, only now the producers were ready to push the boundaries even further.

‘Towards the end of the five years, yes, we had a naked lady run down the stairs, but in those early days nothing.’

PETER BENARDOS: They all said Abigail revealed her bosom all the time. Rubbish! She had a see-through blouse on one night. We titillated people, as it were. Towards the end of the five years, yes, we had a naked lady run down the stairs, but in those early days nothing.

CHARD HAYWARD (actor): One of my favourite storylines was when Dudley became a TV star. That opened up many great opportunities, including the scene where he was mobbed and disrobed in front of the delicatessen by a bunch of schoolgirls.

DINA MANN: I didn't have the nudity clause even requested. I think that, probably, Bill had decided that she was a sixteen-year-old and I was going to play the schoolgirl role and it didn't come up. It wasn't in my contract.

SUZANNE CHURCH: Despite signing the standard *Number 96* nudity clause I roundly declared to both directors that I was not taking my clothes off and if they didn't like it they could sack me. Dina and I helped each other apply sticky tape to the sheets when there was a dreaded bed scene for either of us.

BRIAN PHILLIS: Few things annoyed me more than actors pulling a fast one. Just another waste of precious time. Anya Saleky, who had signed the nudity clause in order to get the job, had a change of heart and tried to preserve her dignity. She had a scene in bed in which she was to suddenly sit upright,

Reluctant sex symbol Anya Saleky as Jaja Gibson. Courtesy NFSA

causing the sheet to fall away and reveal everything. Anya was stacked and had a good figure. We were all looking forward to it, but when the moment came she sat up and the sheet did not fall one inch. We tried several takes, but nothing happened. There was not a boob in sight. I went down to the studio floor to investigate, then discovered that Anya had double-sided tape under the sheet, with the reverse side against her boobs. We could have gone on re-shooting that scene until lights out at 7pm. I compromised, pulled the lighting down to low-key and shot from a different angle. It seemed to placate Anya somewhat and we finally had a good take.

SUZANNE CHURCH: Director Brian Phillis was great fun, and naughty. In the storyline of Jane's affair with a married man, there was a final scene where her lover left her. This required me to be topless. I insisted on being back to camera. The scene was about Jane feeling abandoned and upset, and I was keen to bring the right emotional edge to this. Brian managed to convince me that a small turn towards camera in the closing shot would end just above my nipples. It was due to Brian Phillis that I inadvertently fulfilled the nudity clause in my contract. Lesson learnt — never trust a director with a camera angle when you are half naked and twenty-three years old.

DEBORAH GRAY (actress): What people do forget a lot, I think, is that every single person had to sign a contract to say that they would be willing to go nude on the show. That was a part of the show. Every actor — at some stage you were going to have to get your kit off and I think just about everybody did, including a lot of the male actors.

HARRY MICHAELS: The thing that disappointed me — everyone passed every fucking nude scene to me, which I thought was very unfair. But towards the end I think they would use Giovanni as a guinea pig.

MICHAEL FERGUSON: I did have the proverbial nudity clause in my contract and like everybody else, especially the girls, dreaded the inevitable scene where you had to get your kit off. My first one was in the shower, thankfully behind frosted glass, but I hadn't seen the set at that stage and I rushed out and bought a full-body stocking. I felt like a complete wally on the day, in front of all the cast and crew. I was very naïve in those early days.

'I rushed out and bought a full body stocking. I felt like a complete wally.'

KAREN PETERSEN: Christina became Gary Whittaker's lover. I remember our first scene in bed, both naked under peach-coloured silken sheets that threatened to slide off. Both giggling, because having been good mates for so many years it seemed funny to have to act passionately. But we did, in one take.

PETER WHITFORD: I think after three weeks of episodes — that was all, three weeks — suddenly Vera and Guy Sutton decided they were deliriously in love and got married quickly, in a rush. So there had to be a bed scene. Now, I didn't like bed scenes. I didn't like them. I didn't have the surf lifesaver's body. I just didn't want to know about it. It was meant to be a passionate night, so when I got out of the bed I was wearing pyjamas. Elaine was wearing a nightie. For a passionate night of a mad woman and her brand-new racing-car-driver husband it was all very prim. We just wouldn't strip off for them.

MARY ANN SEVERNE: Any romantic scenes I did were very modest kisses. I think in those days and in that show a 'lady lawyer' was unusual and a certain type of person — quite proper — and there was no suggestion of doing nude scenes.

DINA MANN: There came, one day, this scene where I was in the shower. I can't remember if it was Brian Phillis or Peter Benardos. It was probably Brian. I said, 'You know I don't have a nudity clause in my contract. It's crossed off.' He said, 'No, no, we won't be seeing anything.' I said, 'Okay, so you won't be shooting below my collarbone, basically?' Then he said, 'No, no, absolutely not.' I said, 'Okay, fine.' He said, 'But so we can see your back we'd like you to be nude. We'll close the set, darling.' All that stuff. Fine. So, remembering Suzy had been told the same thing, what I did was I got those Mickey Mouse band-aids. I got four of them and I put a little cross on my left tit and one on my right tit and I thought, *well, he said they're not shooting that low, so they can't.* So I did the scene and they didn't go that low and I didn't get tricked [*laughs*].

ROGER WARD: My own nudity never worried me, but it apparently did worry the producers of *Number 96*, for in the clauses of my second contract they had written: 'Roger Ward, under no circumstances whatsoever, can take his clothes off during the recording of *Number 96*.' It was a joke of course, but a joke caused by my incessant disregard for clothes during my first three months with the show.

DEBORAH GRAY: In the industry in the 1970s, nudity was kind of a normal thing. You saw a lot of it. It was something that was actually a sign of liberation for women. It was very different because the sixties and seventies brought out a freedom for actresses that they never had before. So an actress could do a nude scene or a semi-nude scene or a love scene and still be respected as a serious actor.

‘an actress could do a nude scene or a semi-nude scene or a love scene and still be respected as a serious actor.’

opposite: *Number 96*'s last sex symbol, Deborah Gray. Her full frontal nude scene hardly caused a ripple. Courtesy NFSA

above left: Ron Shand says farewell to Sheila Kennelly and Mike Ferguson. Courtesy Karen Petersen

above right: Norma's Bar became Duddles disco, and this album was released in an attempt to cash in on the youth market

TED JOBBINS: When it first started there was no complete, full frontal nudity, though by the end of the show Deborah Gray did appear and probably, again, for the first time ever on television — full frontal nudity. It was funny. I was actually working on that scene. She was such a beautiful-looking girl and probably had the most perfect proportions as far as her body was concerned, but nobody, really, took that much notice.

BRIAN PHILLIS: After the initial furore over nudity and Abigail had dissipated, I directed a scene with Deborah Gray in which she showed everything — a full frontal. It was a token closed set, but again, every TV in the place was tuned in.

DEBORAH GRAY: They finalised the script, and that's the first time I'd read that the first scene was going to be 'drops the fur coat' and so on and there was a full nude scene in it. Bill said to me, 'That's the only time you'll be fully nude. For the rest of the time you'll actually get dressed.'

In March 1977, Dave Allenby and Nat Nixon joined the cast as psychiatrist Harold Wilkinson and his grandmother Opal. They lived in flat 7, which Dr Harold used as his consulting room where Deborah Gray as Miss Hemingway was a patient.

DEBORAH GRAY: They wanted to find somebody who had a certain look, who had a sophisticated look, because I was supposed to be a little rich girl who had this compulsion to take her clothes off. It's like wham-bam full-on first scene, and they said, 'From then on, for the rest of the time that you're on the show, as you get better — because you are going to a psychiatrist; you're getting therapy — you will get dressed every time. It's the opposite of what people expect.' So it was very fresh.

As the show headed into 1977, there was yet another cast shake-up. This time viewers said goodbye to the ever-popular Sheila Kennelly as Norma, as well as other favourites Gordon McDougall, Michael Ferguson and Mary Ann Severne.

SHEILA KENNELLY: They wanted to bring in more young viewers — demographics, they call it — because ratings were falling. So they decided they'd let Dudley take over the wine bar and turn it into a discotheque.

'They wanted to bring in more young viewers – demographics, they call it – because ratings were falling.'

CHARD HAYWARD: The executives were always looking for ways to make changes. I don't necessarily agree with some of them. The characters were what made the show and I believe they were what the audience was interested in. Whether the set was a wine bar or a disco was irrelevant.

Chelsea Brown's talents as a singer were incorporated into the show when her character Henri P. Dobb began performing in Duddles disco. This was seen as another marketing opportunity, and resulted in the release of the disco album *Number 96 Party Music*. The producers also tried to inject more action into the storylines.

Jeff Kevin — meet Jeff Kevin!

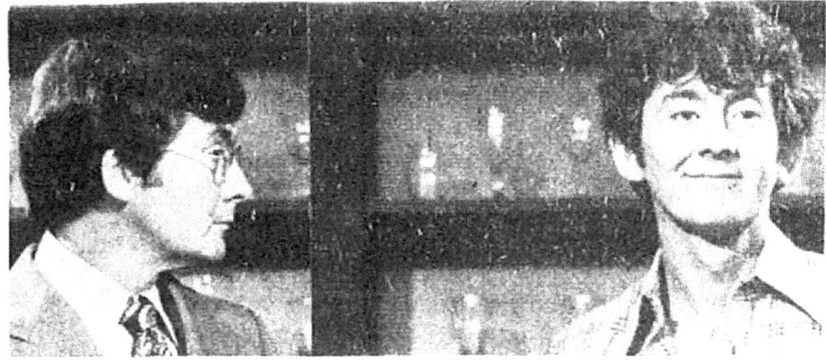

above: Jeff Kevin as both Arnold and his brother 'Chook' Feather

SHEILA KENNELLY: They had bikie gangs and, oh, I don't know what else, but it didn't work that well, you know. It was an attempt to revive a flagging show; that was all.

'he represented a bikie group and that the current storyline resembled them, and they were not happy'

KEVIN POWELL: A storyline involving bikies was introduced to *Number 96*. I was in the office when I was told by an agitated receptionist that a bikie was in reception. I went out and invited him in to my office. He said that he represented a bikie group and that the current storyline resembled them, and they were not happy. After much discussion I suggested that a disclaimer during the show could be arranged, but it would take a week or so. We shook hands and off he went. Some days later I received a telephone call that a group of bikies were coming to the office as the disclaimer had not taken place. Ross Hawthorn took steps to protect the office. Time passed and we were advised that the bikies had turned around after being told their intended destination and business was known.

HARRY MICHAELS: Bikies came to my house and they got very shitty with me because of something that had been said, and they locked me in the house until Bill Harmon apologised and put something at the end of the episode. With the crucifixion, the bikies got a bit of a bad run in the press or something like that, and Bill Harmon had to authorise an apology to go at the end of the show.

DAVID SALE: I was away for a longer period and when I came back I couldn't believe what had happened to the show. Miss Hemingway was flaunting her body on it. There were Nazis. There was Chook Feather, which was totally unconvincing. All this burning of flags and bikies and who was it that was almost crucified? Was it Harry Michaels? I couldn't believe it.

The introduction of Charles 'Chook' Feather, the long-lost brother of Arnold, saw Jeff Kevin playing dual roles.

JEFF KEVIN: I enjoyed the experience of playing something else. It's a pity it was sort of so wacky. I had this dreadful sort of Harpo Marx wig that I wore. I had to do all this split-screen stuff and that was really interesting to do. I really found that fascinating. It took a while, but it was good, interesting stuff. Brian Phillis was the director on most of those.

TED JOBBINS: We had Arnold pouring a glass of wine for his twin. Oh God, that took ages because, again, of the limitations of the technology of split screens, but it actually worked very well. The two of them were in the scene together and to do that the timing was so much on the actor. He was excellent in that regard.

JEFF KEVIN: The opportunity was good, but the character was, I think, extreme. As Arnold was extreme in one way, Chook was extreme in the other. There was never any subtlety. You really know a show's coming to an end when they're introducing your twin.

‘You really know a show’s coming to an end when they’re introducing your twin.’

CHARD HAYWARD: I left because I was offered a game show out of Melbourne and a weekly live variety show in Perth, so I accepted them both, and flew around Australia every week for the next six months. After nearly four years it was time to move on.

DAVID SALE: I think I was away two or three months, and when I came back the whole tone of the show had changed. It had totally got away from the kind of things I had in mind when I started it — and all the way through it — which was audience identification. All these new ideas had nothing to do with the *Number 96* that had gone before, to my mind. I think the thing was once Don Cash died, Bill really lost his direction, in a way. I think at one time, certainly if Don had been alive, they would never have allowed these sorts of things to happen.

After five years the number's up for '96'

SYDNEY. — The long-running television soap opera Number 96 has been axed.

After five years and more than 1000 shows, production of the series will finish on July 15. The last episode will [illegible]

[illegible]

[illegible] yesterday from the general manager of Channel 10 in Sydney, Mr Ian Kennon, on behalf of the 0-10 Network and the managing director of Cash-Harmon Television, Mr Bill Harmon, the producers of the show.

In a statement read to the cast yesterday, Mr Kennon said the show had been rating well in Sydney but disappointingly in other States.

[illegible] phenomenon in Australian television.

"When the programme started five years ago [illegible]

in many social changes and acceptances."

[illegible] replaced by another Australian drama series and the network was considering submissions.

Twenty-five regular actors and a team [illegible] ducers and [illegible] writers are affected by the show's death.

Mr Harmon said last night they had 12 weeks of work left before production finished in which to find work.

[illegible] working on other projects by then.

He thought the decision, which came after "lengthy weekend conferences", was for the good of everybody.

[illegible]

tions of a group of people living in a block of flats in Sydney's Paddington, it fed its viewers on titillation, gossip, trivia — and nudity.

[illegible]

"It's sad because it's like the break-up of a family," one of the two remaining originals, Pat McDonald, said yesterday.

Joe Hasham [illegible] for the pilot episode [illegible] ber of the production crew, Channel 10 staff and everyone else who was connected with the show.

When it finishes the 1218 half-hour episodes will have [illegible]

The axe has fallen but the show must go on. Number 96 stars Pat McDonald, left, Joe Hasham and Bunny Brook study their scripts for the next episode.

Chapter 11

Closing Doors

DAVID SALE (writer): I said to Bill, 'I really don't want anything more to do with this show.' I said, 'I'm sorry, but as far as I'm concerned it's going to be over. It's going to be over and off the air in three months.' And it was cancelled, I think, six weeks after.

PETER BENARDOS (director): Everybody was tired, I felt. Bill didn't want to continue the series. He felt the storylines were getting a bit deflated and so on; ratings had dropped. So it was a situation where management at Channel 10 and the network and the packaging people, and Cash Harmon said, 'Look, enough's enough, let's call it quits. We've had a very successful run.'

BILL HARMON (producer): After four years I wanted to cancel because I wanted to get into films. Ian talked me out of it, Ian Holmes. But it went on. The next year I tried to cancel it too because I wanted it to go out while it was at the top. Then I was overseas for a couple of months and Ian Kennon was running the place. He called me and said they were letting it go, they were cancelling it, and I said fine. There was no argument. I never tried to keep it going. I thought that was enough because I really wanted to get into films.

On Monday, 25 April 1977, Channel 10 Sydney's general manager, Ian Kennon, called the cast and crew into studio B and onto the set of Duddles disco, where he broke the news that *Number 96* had been axed.

BOB HUBER (producer): I was there till the very end. It was very sad. Everybody knew that it was gone and that it should've gone the year before. I think sheer professionalism kept it looking like the ball was in the air when, really, the ball was flat.

JOE HASHAM (actor): It's all about ratings. Actually, we could have continued for another year or so, but I believe the producers made a wise decision in pulling the plug while we were still getting okay ratings. I'm glad they did it that way. In a funny sort of way we could still say that we got out before we were forced out.

‘Everybody knew that it was gone and that it should’ve gone the year before.’

DINA MANN (actress): It was still very successful in Sydney. It was Melbourne that was letting down the ratings. I remember when the announcement was made that day, when we were all told it was going to be axed — we all stood there in silence.

SUZANNE CHURCH (actress): I do remember being told that the show was over, but I think rumours had been rife and it wasn’t a total surprise. I believe we were told the news on the studio floor by the wonderful Ted Jobbins and then I think, officially, by Bill Harmon.

HARRY MICHAELS (actor): It was lunchtime and rumours were going around. After lunch we got a phone call to go in to the wine bar. Ian Kennon, the CEO of Channel 10, comes in and he says, ‘You’ve all been fantastic. It’s been a great show, but unfortunately I’m giving you three months for the show to wind up.’

MIKE DORSEY (actor): I don’t remember the exact occasion. I think it was a sort of disappointment coupled with a little relief. It meant you could go and do other things. I think we all half-expected it. The rest of the leads, I think, were disappointed. They expected it to go on and on and on, as I did. In fact, it didn’t and you very rapidly come to terms with it.

TED JOBBINS (producer): The mood around the studio was funny. A lot of people were saying, ‘Well, you know, it’s run its course.’ Others were saying, ‘It’s a shame.’

WENDY BLACKLOCK (actress): I think I was quite happy. I thought it had run its course.

JEFF KEVIN (actor): Pat and Bunney would have reacted in a similar manner to everyone else when the news of the show being axed was announced: with resolution tinged with disappointment. Personally, I thought that axing the show was an overreaction. The ratings had dropped from high numbers to a middle range; while it wasn't good, it wasn't disastrous. The time had come for a major reworking of the show, no doubt, but to suddenly take it off the air was not warranted. It had become stale but not, I suggest, because of the actors but *for* the writers and producers.

‘I thought that axing the show was an overreaction.’

opposite: The cast and crew of *Number 96* in its final days

above: Pat McDonald, Ron Shand and Joe Hasham made up a trio of cast members who had been there from episode 1 to episode 1218

NANCY CASH (wife of Don Cash): I do think that they all just kind of — including the network — eventually said we can't last forever, and ended it. I think before it needed to be ended, myself. I think that's been proven today, or subsequently been proven by these shows that do go on for a very, very long period of time.

MIKE DORSEY: With *Number 96*, when it finished, I think it was premature. It was, I think, the Australian equivalent of *Coronation Street* in England and should've gone on ad infinitum. It didn't. I don't know, maybe the ratings weren't good enough, but I personally believe it would still be valid today.

HARRY MICHAELS: The show was axed when it was rating eighteens and twenties. You have eighteens and twenties now and you're still on-air.

JOE HASHAM: I know many of the cast had depended on *Number 96* for their living so I assume it would have been difficult for some. I was very fortunate; *Number 96* brought me nothing but amazing success after success. I will forever be grateful.

On the last day of taping, Friday, 17 July 1977, Sydney radio station 2SM did a live cross to the Channel 10's studio to interview actors Pat McDonald and Ron Shand.

> Pat McDonald: It'll never happen again. It was just, that was the time; it happened and the time has gone, but it will live with people for a very long time, I think anyway.
>
> Ron Shand: We'll always be remembered by the people. They'll always remember us, and so the memory of 96 goes on.[22]

During its five-and-a-half-year run, *Number 96* provided an opportunity for dozens of writers and technicians to develop their craft, and became an important stepping-stone for a cavalcade of Australia's top performers. They include Rowena

Some of the familiar faces who appeared in *Number 96* throughout its run: (clockwise from left) Judi Farr, Reg Gorman, Paula Duncan, Moya O'Sullivan, Mark Lee, Henri Szeps, Wendy Hughes and Peter Adams. Courtesy Mick Pratt

Wallace, Judi Farr, Paula Duncan, Jon English, Joanna Lockwood, Dennis Miller, Anne Charleston, Henri Szeps, Reg Gorman, Penny Ramsey, Ray Meagher, Noeline Brown, Tony Martin, Greg Ross, Moya O'Sullivan, Joyce Jacobs, Diana McLean, Pat Bishop, Brian Moll, Penne Hackforth-Jones, Jeff Ashby, Chris Haywood, Tristan Rogers and Mark Lee.

MARK LEE (actor): I had been working as a child/adolescent actor for a while; my entry into the union was 1968. I was with a small theatrical agency called Telecast and it was through them I scored the gig in *Number 96*. I played a high school boy — I can't remember his name — at a prestigious private school, a fictitious one as the storyline would have probably led to a court case otherwise. He began an affair with his maths teacher, who was played by Henri Szeps. It was a relationship that included sadomasochism and other details, which have escaped me, but would probably have a hard time getting on to *Home and Away* and *Neighbours* these days.

CAROL RAYE: We had a wonderful group of actors. People think soap opera is one of the lightweight things of the acting and writing industries, but in fact, to be successful, it's one of the most disciplined things an actor can do, and a writer.

TED JOBBINS: The reaction when the show first started, like with the legitimate actors, was, 'Oh no, I don't want to be in it.' They wouldn't do 'television serials' sort of thing. We had quite a few people who were offered parts but turned them down. Jack Thompson was offered a part. Bill was disappointed that we didn't get some of the people. As the years went on, a lot of people that refused parts in the old days were clambering to get in. Theatre wasn't doing all *that* well, and all of a sudden you had this group of actors that were making a lot of money.

'a lot of people that refused parts in the old days were clambering to get in'

CAROL RAYE: I remember when Bryan Brown first came back. His agent, June Cann, sent me all his photos and his CV. He'd been in England — very attractive, good looking, and we were just looking to cast a new character in the series. So I interviewed him and loved him on sight; he was great. I said to Bill, 'I want you to see this young man. He'd be ideal for this character.' Bill said to me, 'Well he may be a great actor, honey, but he's got an English accent. What good is that?' I said, 'But Bill, he's a Parramatta boy.' I couldn't persuade Bill. Years later Bryan said, 'I've never been more disappointed in my life.' So we didn't have Bryan Brown.

DAVID SALE: The cast, the people who were in it, who are really famous now, like Anne Louise Lambert, who was in *Picnic at Hanging Rock*; she was in it for a time. Wendy Hughes was in it for a little while, as a sort of hippie girl.

DINA MANN: We did get to work with some fabulous actors that came in as guests. I mean, Shane Porteous was absolutely fabulous. John McTernan was a really wonderful actor and it was a privilege to work with him. It was terrific, it was really terrific.

Number 96 also opened its doors to many acting veterans, such as Enid Lorimer, Ben Gabriel, Neva Carr Glyn, Gerry Duggan, Sheila Helpmann, Redmond Phillips, Gordon Glenwright, Diana Davidson, Tom Farley, Les Foxcroft and Aileen Britton.

SHEILA KENNELLY: Aileen Britton was such a darling, yes, and very much a heroine of mine, because when I left school I worked in radio as a secretary and then on casting and then as an assistant. One of the producers there kept on saying, 'Aileen Britton'll be back soon. We'll have Aileen in this,' so this name became very big in my young mind. It was a great honour, later, to be working with her playing my mother. Yes. I always remember her going up in the Murphy bed!

CAROL RAYE: Gai Waterhouse had just come back from England where she'd been at acting school, and her agent sent her along — she was sweet. She wanted to do something if there was a part coming up. We never did find her a role. It was like a magnet to young actors because it was such a showcase. Everybody watched *Number 96*.

With 1218 episodes produced, the series set an Australian television record that remained unbeaten until *The Young Doctors* reached episode 1219 in June 1982.

In Sydney the final episode went to air on 11 August 1977, but *Number 96* continued to screen in other parts of Australia in varying time slots. In Melbourne, where it was screened for an hour each week, it finished on 22 December. The final episode featured an off-screen wedding between Arnold Feather and Vicki Dawson, played by Kay Powell, and the surprise return of Maggie Cameron and Norma Whittaker.

THE PARTY'S OVER FOR 96

above: **An article about the cast of *Number 96* when the show ended. Courtesy Dina Mann**

As the show faded to black, Edie McDonald sat in front of her typewriter upstairs in flat 5, working on a novel based on the building and its residents.

PETER BENARDOS: I was lucky; I did the last episode. Again, that worked very well — the last episode with the typewriter there: 'Once upon a time there was a building …' I thought that was brilliant. I wish I'd thought of that. Marvellous. The only idea I had, my contribution, was Ronnie Shand, who was supposed to be the handyman around the place, in a quick shot of him knocking all the lights out. We put a special little camera up in the grid, way up, trying to get an overall shot. It worked quite well. That was a very sad night, very sad.

When it was all over, cast members past and present were invited to say goodbye in a grand finale curtain call. Those who turned up were paid a $25 appearance fee.

PETER WHITFORD: When it finally finished they had a big episode, where everyone who'd ever been in it was called back for a grand farewell.

'96' RAISES THE DEAD CHARACTERS

THE FINAL CURTAIN CALL

NUMBER 96 will go out in a big way.

Producers, Cash-Harmon Television, are exploring the possibility of re-assembling all major cast members from the past five years for "curtain call" appearances in the final episode, which is taped on June 15 and will go to air early in August.

Executive producer, Bill Harmon, says he wants the series to end on a high note and the idea of re-using most of the past characters was one he was considering for the final episode.

"Even the ones who were killed off," he said.

"We want that final show to be one to remember."

Mr Harmon will meet with network executives this week to discuss plans for production deals.

"Right now, we've signed nothing and we don't have a new deal with the network," he said.

"I believe a deal has been signed with Crawfords for their series Hotel, and I'm hopeful that I'd be able to do something for the network here in Sydney."

Mr Harmon emphasised that he was in no way bitter about the decision to cancel the series.

"Not too many local products have as much success over such a period as Number 96 did," he said.

"But obviously tastes change over a period and lately the series has been falling off in popularity to the stage where it is no longer an economic proposition for the network."

Mr Harmon said his company had several other projects under consideration to fill the gap left when Number 96 finishes production.

"I can't say anything about them until I know exactly where I stand with the network," he said.

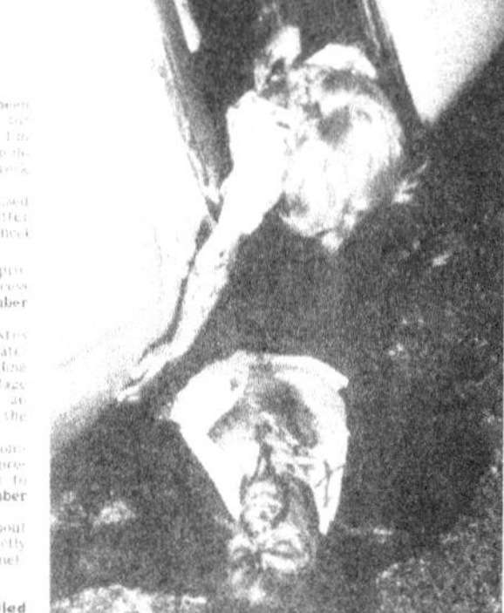

• RIGHT: Joe James and Sophie Vaillant were "killed off" in this car crash, but they may be resurrected for the final episode of No. 96.

Lights have gone out at No 96

BOB HUBER: I thought it was a lovely way to end it, with everybody saying here I am and this is what I played, and bringing back characters from throughout the series.

DAVID SALE: I sat at home alone and watched all those people coming on for that final goodbye. I said goodbye to the show alone and in tears.

TOM OLIVER (actor): The grand finale. I don't remember a lot about it, but I do remember faces that I hadn't seen for a while. It was like visiting family overseas because it was a family.

JEFF KEVIN: The curtain call was high camp and good fun. As for the mood within the company? It was sad, but it was also a celebration of a stunningly successful show, one that I was immensely proud to have been a part of. Whatever was said or written about *Number 96*, its many critics cannot take that away. It outlasted relentless negativity from within the industry and without. Begrudgingly, they came to admit that it was a groundbreaker in the early days of Australian television drama.

'it was also a celebration of a stunningly successful show, one that I was immensely proud to have been a part of.'

VIVIENNE GARRETT (actress): I remember borrowing a dress from Melody Cooper, who was a fantastic theatre designer. I didn't want to do it. Then I thought, *look, come on. What does*

opposite: An article announcing that all actors who had appeared in the series for three months or more were invited back for the curtain call

it matter? Get out there and take a bow. It's been an amazing success story. We didn't say anything in particular, just appeared.

JAMES ELLIOTT (actor): We were all doing our parts with the usual partner; we all had a partner, virtually, the person you did scenes with. More frequently than anyone else I did scenes with Elisabeth and so when we were coming out — there was the base of the building — we came running through, waving our hands to the audience and our presence was announced.

PAMELA GARRICK (actress): It was a long shoot with the director getting everybody in the correct order of appearance — a loathsome task.

ROGER WARD (actor): I do remember the crowd and the positioning for the final cast photo, but the party was just another in a long series of them during those halcyon work-loaded days.

CHARD HAYWARD (actor): I flew back from Perth for the taping of that final episode. The producers in Perth kindly arranged for us to pre-record that week's show the day before airing so I could make it back.

KAREN PETERSEN (actress): I was thrilled to be included in the curtain-call finale. I was in *Young Doctors* at the time and had to get permission to do it. 'No problems,' said Alan Coleman, the producer. Channel 10's facilities were stretched to the limit to house all these actors — make-up and hair working overtime. Everyone was excited, yet sad at the same time. It was a big family reunion. I still have the shooting script.

SUZANNE CHURCH: I remember taking my final bow. It was sad and it felt like leaving a family. At twenty-five years old, for me it had been an invaluable experience and the start of my acting career. It was especially poignant for the older members of the cast.

‘I remember taking my final bow. It was sad and it felt like leaving a family.’

DINA MANN: It felt a bit odd and a bit sad, really. They were just going to dismantle everything and sell all the props, and then afterwards off we went.

On Saturday, 20 August, a week after the final episode screened in Sydney, Channel 10 held a *Number 96* auction, with proceeds going to the showbiz charity Variety Club.

IAN McLEAN (Number 96 historian): Channel 10 hosted an open-air charity auction of some props, set dressings and costumes from *Number 96* in the grounds of the studio. The auctioneer was Joe ‘The Gadget Man’ Sandow. The ninety-minute auction was aired live at noon. The *Number 96* open-top double-decker bus was in view and the top level filled with

opposite: The more than fifty past and present cast members who took a bow in the final episode

cast members. One of the earliest items was Giovanni's green deli jacket. The opening bid was one dollar and it rose by one dollar at a time, until I found myself shouting, 'Five dollars.' Joe said, 'Make it seven dollars and it's yours.' A few items were less interesting. A pair of blue flared denim jeans were held up, supposedly Don's jeans. They also sold off one of Norma's voluminous tent dresses. These items went reasonably cheaply, but I was realising that my early purchase was a lucky fluke. By now the audience had grown substantially. A similar green deli jacket, but with Arnold's name badge on the pocket, went for $70. A small cloth dillybag was opened onstage to reveal several g-strings and frilly knickers, and these were sold off as 'Bev's undies'. Who knows if they were ever actually worn by Abigail. Another questionable item was Arnold's wooden leg, but subsequent viewings identified this leg as part of Les Whittaker's junk pile in flat 1. Flo's bed doll went quite cheaply. One man started buying up lots of items, including Dorrie's famous flower-decorated hat, which received some very competitive bidding, and the Norma painting went for a steal at only $200.

'A small cloth dillybag was opened onstage to reveal several g-strings and frilly knickers, and these were sold off as 'Bev's undies'.'

SHEILA KENNELLY: A guy bought the portrait at the charity auction Channel 10 held with all the *Number 96* stuff, and it was for his billiard room.

Shortly after the axe fell on the television series, the real building, Moncur Flats in Woollahra, was set to be auctioned on 9 June 1977. With the end of *Number 96*, Bill Harmon also began to think about the future of the company he had started with his late friend.

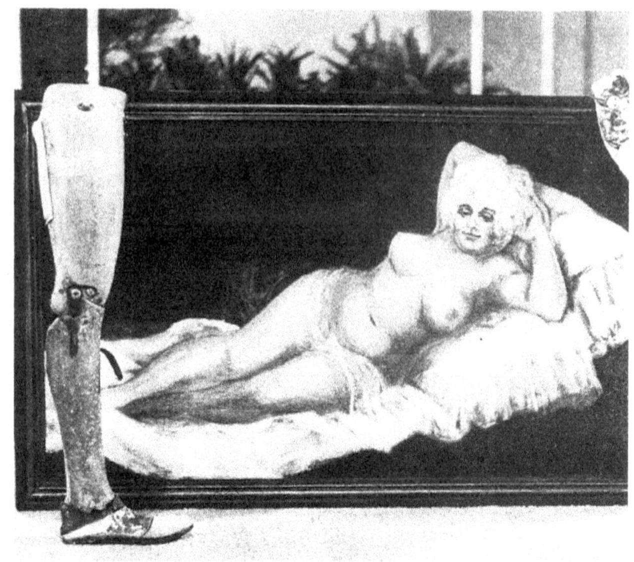

RICHARD ELLIS GROUP

Raine & Horne
Pty. Ltd.

IN THE AUDITORIUM, 7th LEVEL, AUSTRALIA SQUARE

AUCTION SALE DATE: THURSDAY, 9th JUNE 1977

WOOLLAHRA — LARGE TERRACE

"CASTLE TERRACE", 91 JERSEY ROAD
INSPECT: SATS. and WEDS., 11-12
Or by special appointment with the Agents
Three storeys. Rear lane access. Unique design. At present a well-conducted residential of 4 flats. Capable of reconverting to 5 bedrms., 2 bathrms., fine family house
ST. PAULS REAL ESTATE, 36-3449

WOOLLAHRA — CELEBRATED FLATS

83 MONCUR STREET
WELL-KNOWN TO MILLIONS OF VIEWERS AS "NUMBER 96"
INSPECT: SATS. & WEDS., 11-12
Charming and unique block, chosen for its singular style for the famous television series
At last for sale. 2 shops, 7 2 bedroom-plus-enclosed-sunroom flats in superb letting area. Close to thriving and fashionable Queen Street shopping centre and bustling go-ahead Bondi Junction. Harbour amenities close at hand for swimming and sailing. Centennial Park broad acres for jogging, cycling, riding, close at hand. On regular bus route with 10-minute ride to the city heart. In superb order. G.A.R. $27,560.

Watch for further notices or phone
A.H. 32-2827 OR OFFICE NUMBERS
L. W. TAYLOR PTY. LTD., 387-3321

above: The famous painting of Norma and the Moncur Street flats were auctioned off

opposite: Bill Harmon with his all-star cast is honoured on *This Is Your Life*. Courtesy Joanna Lockwood

KEVIN POWELL: I came back into *Number 96* for its last six months. Bill said, 'Look, they've given us notice, it's going to close. Why don't you finish it off?' And that's when I knew he was really saying the company was folding.

BILL HARMON: We never wanted Cash Harmon to be big. It was our intention all the time that we remain … have a few shows and that was it. We started out as a partnership. We didn't know where the hell we were going, but we did it with the philosophy that we would do very few things.

In 1977, following the announcement that *Number 96* was ending, Bill Harmon was honoured on *This is Your Life.*

WENDY BLACKLOCK: I take my hat off to Bill Harmon. He did a very good job. I mean, it must've been difficult in those days to get a show like that — what was almost a cutting-edge show — accepted by Channel 10.

DINA MANN: It was interesting, at those times, when you think about what else was on Australian television: *The Box*,

The Sullivans, *Boney*, *Matlock Police*, *Bluey*. The ABC had *Power Without Glory*. *Certain Women* was still going, and *Bellbird*. You also had *The Norman Gunston Show*. There was all this happening and I think *Young Doctors* started about 1976, something like that. I think *The Box* folded about four or five months before *Number 96* did. So there was this change of guard, and things that continued were *Sullivans* and *Young Doctors*. There was obviously a shift, you know, when you look at *The Box* and you look at *Number 96* and then look at what came after.

TED JOBBINS: Because of the success of *Number 96* and the fact that serials were successful — out of that came the first big blockbusters. What is it the Americans came up with? Was it *Dallas*? *Dallas* and then *Dynasty* and — all of them, basically, are the follow-ons to *Number 96*.

CAROL RAYE: *Number 96* was definitely a watershed show and it will be remembered as such. It showed subsequent things like *Neighbours* and *Home and Away* how to do it.

‘*Number 96* was definitely a watershed show and it will be remembered as such.’

No. 96 goes to Canada

The-sex-and-sin drama, Number 96, has been sold to a Canadian television station, according to a Toronto newspaper.

By
SIMON ROHRSMANN

But Channel 10 is refusing to comment on the sale.

Mr Bill Harmon, the executive producer of Number 96, is on an overseas business trip and is expected to tidy up the details when he visits Canada at the end of the month.

Channel 10's desperate attempts to keep the sale a secret have failed.

The station spokesman, Mr Tom Greer, is usually very talkative, but yesterday gave a stock "no comment" reply to all questions.

Details

magazine printed an article about it.

Since then, Canadian television executives have seen the programme in Sydney and special tapes have been sent to Britain and the United States.

Any suggestion of major overseas sales raises the question of the show being taped in color.

Mr Greer said: "We have a tight schedule with five episodes being produced a week and color would probably knock that back to three.

"The show is made for the Australian market and we are not going to overwork it by trying for overseas sales.

"But if anything does eventuate, then you will be the first to know."

Thanks Tom, but I already do.

Mr Greer

TED JOBBINS: They're all the same — *Melrose Place* — all these things. They're *Number 96* all over again. It's a group of people. We shoved 'em into a block of flats. *Melrose Place* is a block of flats; the same thing except with America they've got more money to use on wardrobe, sets and everything, but it's still *Number 96*. All soaps are exactly the same. It's either stuck on a farm or a ranch, a block of flats, a street. *Neighbours* is a continuation of *Number 96*, as is *Home and Away*; all of them.

KEVIN POWELL: *Number 96* — they did try to sell it overseas. I don't know how it went, obviously not well enough to keep it going.

DAVID SALE: We went to the MIP television festival in 1975, I think — we'd left it a bit late, mind you — and we had composite reels and things like that. Nobody would touch it; too daring. Even New Zealand. Bettina was a New Zealander and she wanted her family to see it. New Zealand wouldn't touch it; far too outspoken for New Zealand, but far too outspoken for everywhere.

ELAINE LEE: I was in Perth years ago and I met this Yugoslav couple who'd just come back from Italy. We were on air there having been dubbed in Italian, so it did play in other places in the world.

In Italy it screened on a soft porn channel and in Canada it turned up on the progressive CITY network. Despite attempts to sell the series internationally, *Number 96* never succeeded outside of Australia.

DAVID SALE: America, of course, was hot to do *Number 96*, but they couldn't because there were so many taboo subjects. They were desperate to do *Number 96* because they

☐ It's true! Cash-Harmon plans to put on a live musical version of their now defunct TV serial, Number 96. The series' longtime script editor, Johnny Whyte, is scheduled to return from his native U.K. in a few weeks to write the singing, dancing version of Number 96.

opposite: An article about attempts to sell the series internationally but *Number 96* never succeeded outside of Australia. Courtesy Elaine Elliott

top left: Despite the claim in this article, the all-singing, all-dancing *Number 96* never went ahead

top right: A promotional advert for the US version of *Number 96*

were desperate for that kind of success. They couldn't do the interracial storyline because of the Deep South. There was also the Bible Belt so they couldn't do any of the homosexual bits, and all that sort of thing.

The Americans tried their own version of *Number 96* without success. It premiered over three consecutive nights on NBC in December 1980, but in early January the following year it was cancelled.

DAVID SALE: They came up with *Number 96: Sunset Boulevard.* I saw the pilot and it was a lot of would-be actors and actresses lolling around the pool in a condominium complex. They could never get it right. You can't duplicate a show and take out all the characters and all the plots, and then say, 'Well, we've got it.'

Back in Australia there was also mention of a stage musical version of *Number 96*. It never eventuated.

An obscure pilot called *Zodiac Girls*, with twelve actresses representing the different signs of the zodiac, was produced in 1977. The cast was made up of many ex-*Number 96* actresses, including Abigail, Deborah Gray, Lorna Lesley and Frances Hargreaves, with Frank Thring playing an acidic male chauvinist astrologer.

BRIAN PHILLIS: I produced and directed *Zodiac Girls*. The concept was a good one. Abigail, so leonine with her flaring blonde hair, was a Leo to boot. But the pilot show had its failings for which I take responsibility. The good doctor who financed it came close to selling the idea, but to no avail.

The *Zodiac Girls* pilot wasn't the first time *Number 96* actors had been used as an ensemble in another production. *The Norman Gunston Show*'s 'Checkout Chicks' sketch was written by Bill Harding and used several cast members from *Number 96*, including Abigail, Anne Louise Lambert, Philippa Baker, Johnny Lockwood and Vivienne Garrett.

VIVIENNE GARRETT: I can't remember too much about it except they wanted me to play some sort of terrorist that blows up the supermarket. That really appealed to me. There we all were: Candy was in it, and a whole lot of people from *Number 96*. It was this wonderful spoof.

CANDY RAYMOND: It was like a send-up of the idiotic aspects of *Number 96*. It was set in a supermarket. The characters were the people working in the supermarket.

In 1977, *The Paul Hogan Show* featured a skit called '96 in 97', also written by Bill Harding, and set in the not-too-distant future: 1997. The *Number 96* building was now a sacred site visited by overseas tourists who, among other attractions, could put a coin in a slot and hear the catchphrases of characters such as Dorrie Evans and Edie McDonald. James Elliott also made a cameo appearance in *The Paul Hogan Show*, reprising his Alf Sutcliffe character and whinging about Australian television. Later, the television soapie *Arcade* — although not a Cash Harmon production — involved many people associated with

above: Many former *Number 96* cast members appeared in the spoof 'Checkout Chicks'

Number 96, from both sides of the camera. Bill Harmon, David Sale, Johnny Whyte, Peter Benardos, Ted Jobbins and Kevin Powell were all involved in the unsuccessful venture.

KEVIN POWELL: I went back to United Telecasters as associate producer/production manager on that *Arcade* series, which lasted six weeks on air and I got something like eight months work out of it. That one failed because I think it was the first one where you didn't have a Crawford's or a Grundy's or a Cash Harmon. It was an in-house production, which meant that every single channel that had an investment dollar in it — their program manager or whatever — became experts in scripts. So you were getting instructions — the producer, I think, was getting instructions — from everybody. It just became unmanageable, and it showed on-screen.

PETER BENARDOS: *The Restless Years* went for … well, I don't know. I was directing it first and then became the producer of it. Then I had the opportunity of doing *Arcade*, which was, quite frankly, more money, and I went to that and shouldn't have; should have stayed with *The Restless Years*.

DAVID SALE: When we got to 1980 and *Arcade*, Bill only agreed to do the pilot. He wasn't interested, by that stage, in doing any more television.

BILL HARMON: I said I didn't want to do *Arcade*, but they convinced me.

Arcade cast members Mike Dorsey, Aileen Britton, Garth Meade, Lorrae Desmond and Patrick Ward had all appeared in *Number 96*.

PATRICK WARD: Bill offered me the role virtually straight away. 'You wanna do this, Pat?' and I said, 'Yeah, Bill, no problems.' Bill Harmon. He was great to me, I must admit. He was just terrific. I went up there, I think, when the auditions were on just to go up and tell him I'd do it. They were auditioning the role of my brother. Jeremy Kewley got that role. That's all I remember about the audition process. I mean, I didn't go through it so it was no big deal for me, but I remember there was an exorbitant amount of publicity and how much Channel 10 had thrown into this deal. As far as I could tell it was something to do with tax write-offs because they'd spent something like a million dollars on the set. They built an arcade, a working arcade in the studio, with all the shops and everything. I thought, *wow, this looks impressive*, but when it came to the scripts I just went, *urgh! They're doing the same stuff. Okay, just grin and bear it. Just do it.* So I did.

JAMES ELLIOTT: *Arcade* was hoped to be another *Number 96*, but it really didn't go that way. I did play a trade union representative and I goofed around with it a bit. I finally had him like an Adolph Hitler sort of character, complete with moustache.

PATRICK WARD (actor): You had Syd Heylen, Aileen Britton, you know, wonderful people. Peta Toppano's mum, Peggy Mortimer and her sidekick — her really good mate, Lorrae

above: ***Wake in Fright*****, a seminal film in Australian celluloid history**

right: Poster for TV show *Arcade*

Desmond. Wonderful, wonderful people. And good mates like Danny Adcock. I enjoyed doing it purely for the bucks and, I suppose, the publicity.

Arcade screened five nights a week at 7pm, but up against *The Sullivans* and other stiff competition its ratings were dismal. After just six weeks the show was taken off the air with several episodes yet to screen, including those featuring James Elliott. For Bill Harmon, *Arcade* would prove to be his swansong. In 1981 he died from cancer, the same disease that had claimed Don Cash less than ten years earlier.

TED JOBBINS: I think Bill was probably looking for other things to do. He had done a lot before. *Wake in Fright*, which was really the very first top-notch Australian drama made in cinema. *Wake in Fright* was the first Australian movie that made people stop and think, but see, he never really got the recognition from that that he should've because I think he couldn't get a releasing agency here, so he sold it to 20th Century or something like that. So they — because they were the releasing people — then got the benefit of it. Bill Harmon's name was just there, but only people in the industry knew it was him.

DAVID SALE: They were participants behind one of the best Australian movies ever made: *Wake in Fright.* Bill and Don were participants and Bill, with the success of the *Number 96* movie, Bill then saw his path; he wanted to make movies. And he never achieved that, but it was what he wanted to do.

DAVID SALE: Bill wanted to do another movie. He was enamoured of *Blazing Saddles* and so he asked me to do a movie that would do for Australia what *Blazing Saddles* had done to send up the western. So I came up with this movie called *Little Neddie Kelly*, which sent up the whole Ned Kelly legend, and it was absolutely wild in the way *Blazing Saddles* was wild.

Chard Hayward was rumoured to be in line for the title role, but media reports suggested he was reluctant to play another gay character. In the end the film was never made. Other proposed Cash Harmon TV projects included a pilot for a series written by Johnny Whyte, called *The Garden of Eden Health Spa* with an episode written by Ross Napier, and *The Palmer Method*, written by Mort Fine. Like so many of the proposed productions, none of these projects saw the light of day.

As for repeats of *Number 96*, in 1973 the TEN Network began screening daytime repeats from the first episode onwards, and then in 1980 screened repeats of the colour episodes late at night in Sydney. Brisbane followed in 1982, with repeats from episode 585. Over the years the special 'And They Said It Wouldn't Last' has screened a few times since its original airdate, but with different introductions. In 1986, David Lyle's *Golden Years of Television* had a salute to Aussie soaps that concluded with a screening of *Number 96*'s bomb episode, and in 2000 Andrew Mercado presented three weeks of assorted episodes on Foxtel's TV1.

SHEILA KENNELLY: I remember we weren't paid residuals. Lis was union rep and she fought, she tried to get residuals, but didn't have any success at all. There were no extra payments.

ELISABETH KIRKBY: I was the Equity deputy for *Number 96*, something Bill Harmon couldn't bear. When fighting for residuals, he told me straight out, 'Who is ever going to repeat a soap?'

Bill Harmon's thinking was partly right, but sadly not for the reasons he thought.

Wendy Blacklock, Jeff Kevin, Elisabeth Kirkby, James Elliot and Bunny Brooke

Number 96 reunion talk

IT was a reunion of the stars who rocked Australian TV to its foundations – five of the faces who launched the sex and sin soap Number 96 in the '70s.

Wendy Blacklock, who played Edie "Mummy" Withers, **Jeff Kevin** (Arnold Feather), Dame **Elisabeth Kirkby** (laundromat owner Lucy Sutcliffe), **James Elliot** (Al Sutcliffe) and **Bunney Brooke** (Flo Patterson) met to talk about old times at the Double Bay Steakhouse where some of the original bar room scenes were filmed.

Watch out for a possible reunion special. A pilot for a two-hour special is believed to be being considered by the networks.

The show, touted on its debut as "the night Australian television lost its virginity", broke all the rules of social convention and introduced viewers to a seedy world of sexual hijinks, homosexuality, sin and scandal.

Number 96 set to re-open its doors!

Ten executives are tipped to resurrect the infamous soapie

above: News reports of a *Number 96* reboot

TED JOBBINS: The big shame was that Channel 10 never kept any black and white episodes. They were hopeless at keeping things. They kept all of *Number 96*, but when they changed to colour their logic was that now we've gone to colour, no-one will ever want to see it in black and white. So they destroyed years and years of work in black and white.

Andrew Mercado subsequently released four DVDs of *Number 96* through Umbrella Entertainment. The National Film & Sound Archive holds all of the colour episodes and a handful of black and white ones, plus photographs, documentation and other artefacts related to the show. Ian McLean runs a website that lists details of characters and synopses of all 1218 episodes. Occasionally, there has even been talk of re-booting the show.

TOM OLIVER: Years later, I think it was Bill Harmon's son, he was going to rehash it and asked me would I be interested. I said, 'No, no thank you.' So many had gone. I mean, Gordon had gone, and Ronnie, Bettina …

There have been various cast reunions over the years, including a tribute to Brian Phillis on *The Mike Walsh Show* in 1981. Also in 1981, Gordon McDougall and Sheila Kennelly teamed up for a series of television commercials for BBC Hardware. In 1983, Pat McDonald and Ron Shand appeared as co-presenters at the twenty-fifth *TV Week* Logie Awards, and ten former cast members reunited for a TEN Network Telethon in April 1986. Other reunions included *Tonight Live with Steve Vizard*, *Sale of the Century*, Peter Luck's *Where Are They Now?* in 1997, and the version hosted by Melissa Doyle and David Koch in 2006. In 2010 some cast members reunited for *Woman's Day* to celebrate Johnny Lockwood's ninetieth birthday.

• • •

Number 96 was the shining light in the relatively brief period of Cash Harmon's existence. Beyond that, there's no doubting *Number 96* was a watershed production in the history of

Australian television. There are numerous reasons for the esteemed place it holds and why people still want to talk about it.

'We were watching an Australian show, not American or British stuff. We were peeping through our own keyholes'

top left: Steve Vizard devoted an episode of *Tonight Live* to remembering *Number 96* in 1993. Courtesy Ian McLean

bottom left: *Number 96* historian Ian McLean with cast members on *Sale of the Century* 'Battle of the TV Classics' in 1995. Courtesy Ian McLean

right: In 2006, some of the cast were reunited on Channel 7's *Where Are They Now?* Courtesy Elaine Elliott

ABIGAIL: We were looking at important issues, but more importantly we were watching an Australian show, not American or British stuff. We were peeping through our own keyholes.[23]

ELAINE LEE: The timing of *Number 96* was extraordinary. The Australian audience really wanted their own show. They'd been spoon fed on American stuff and British stuff; they wanted something of their own. And the writing of the characters was so good because in each flat there was a totally different character. So even if you didn't relate to Vera, all the migrants would've related to Jimmy and Lis, or to so and so. That was the magic of the show.

LYNN RAINBOW: Everybody had a character that they loved. If you preferred the more comic characters, they were there for you, and I think that's what differentiates *Number 96* from all the other serials. All the other series are very heavily into youth — that's fine, but the adults generally seem to just be there because children must have a parent or a guardian or a teacher. *Number 96* had a sense of humour. I think that's why it was so successful, because it had its funny side as well as the heavier side, and it didn't shirk social comment.

JOHNNY LOCKWOOD: I think, personally, the success of the show was the fact that people could identify with the characters, and of course we'd touch on subjects like effeminate men living together and nudity.

'I can look back on it now as one of the most enjoyable learning experiences a young actor could possibly have had.'

JEFF KEVIN: I learnt a lot from both Johnny Lockwood and Philippa Baker in terms of that sense of chemistry. There were others, like Ronnie Shand. You couldn't help but be impressed. Gordon McDougall was good to learn from, and Pat and Bunney, and all those people because they had such a lot of experience. They brought all that experience to bear. Then, as a young actor, I was learning all the time.

FRANCES HARGREAVES: Going into a cast like that of so many professional people — and I was absolutely green — I learnt so much from these people. It was just brilliant.[24]

CHANTAL CONTOURI: Bunney Brooke and Pat McDonald and all those older people were so wonderful to us younger ones. Most of them were theatre trained and had been actors … Pat McDonald had been an actress since the 1940s and was well respected and liked. So for those people to give us their attention and help was a great privilege and honour, you know. And they did.

DINA MANN: The working life of *Number 96* was fantastic. When you work that hard and that fast with a bunch of people and, you know, no matter what one might say about some of the scripts or some of the storylines, the majority of actors that were in that were fine actors. I mean, Pat McDonald, Bunney Brooke, Jeff Kevin, Sheila Kennelly — all of these people were excellent actors and I learnt a lot from them.

JAMES ELLIOTT: We worked well as an ensemble and I think that was one of the reasons for the success.

WENDY BLACKLOCK: What was extraordinary about the show was that it was very, very successful and the people in it became household names. Even though I'd worked very much on the stage I'd never realised the adulation that is given to television, so-called, stars. They had enormous exposure. It was on every night of the week so they were constantly in people's homes.

CHARD HAYWARD: I believe it was the first show to make Australian actors so hugely popular to their audience, and so for Australian television it was clearly a breakthrough. Personally I have been fortunate to have worked on films and television programs in so many parts of the world, so I can look back on it now as one of the most enjoyable learning experiences a young actor could possibly have had.

CANDY RAYMOND: It was the first and, for a long time, only show that did bring public recognition of that degree to a performer. You became a household name. Pros and cons, afterwards, are the tendency for typecasting. I don't think I could've walked out of *Number 96* and immediately be contracted to do *Play School.*

SHEILA KENNELLY: I was a serious actress. *Number 96* was just another role, and I wasn't going to be part of all this sex and sin scene at all. I wouldn't sign the nudity clause. I wasn't embarrassed about being in it, but I didn't like to discuss it too much because it wasn't like doing Ibsen or Shakespeare, or anything serious. Well, who would've known I would spend so many years of my life doing it and I'd make friendships that have endured for decades. It was a very good thing in my life, really.

ELISABETH KIRKBY: I look back on *Number 96* with pride and amazement. It is the thing that people remember me by. I still get stopped in the street or in a pub, shop or wherever. It is forty years ago, but people still want to talk about it. I find that really intriguing. I meet people who remember bits of it that I have totally forgotten. I am also amazed that we were able to present the show as we did; you couldn't do it now!

'I am also amazed that we were able to present the show as we did; you couldn't do it now!'

TOM OLIVER: The wonderful thing about *Number 96* was that it changed the face of Australian television. It truly did and I'm not talking just because you saw boobs in it or anything like that. Joe Hasham's character, for example. Joe played the homosexual Don Finlayson and then there was Norman Yemm. Norman Yemm played Vera's husband, Elaine Lee's husband, Harry, and he was an alcoholic. But the way it was written it showed both sides of the coin.

ELEANOR WITCOMBE: In 2000, I was given an Emeritus Award by the premier. They gave me this and they gave me a luncheon — the Australia Council. So the head of the Literature Board said all the things I'd done in theatre, radio, television and film and made his spiel, and then I had to get up and say something. So I said, 'Thank you very much, that's very flattering that you should say all that, but I think you've left out one of my major credits.' I said, 'You forgot that I wrote for three-and-a-half years for *Number 96*,' and all these big literature people, all dressed up, laughed. I said, 'I'm very proud of it and I think we did a damn good job.' And do you know, from then on, after I'd finished the speech, all they wanted to ask me questions about was *Number 96*, and how they loved this character and what happened to that one. These people wanting to talk about it are great literary names. It was a phenomenon, and it was out of this world.

PHILIPPA BAKER: I wouldn't have missed it for quids. It was tremendous fun!

NORMAN YEMM: I just remember it was fun to be in and a good acting experience too, with Bill and Don. They were terrific to work with. It was like the development, to be part of the development, of an industry, like *Homicide* was, but in a different way. They were fighting new ground. *Number 96* became such a huge success.

CAROL RAYE: *Number 96* was a huge gamble. I think it will be remembered and go down in the history books as, certainly, showing a marvellous innovation by Bill Harmon and Don Cash; boldness from Channel 10 to do it, to pick it up and run with it. And a tremendous accolade to all the people involved with it.

'It was ahead of its time and it broke a lot of the taboo rules on television.'

THE WEEKEND AUSTRALIAN

NUMBER 9943 SEPTEMBER 14-15, 1996 $1.20

AUSTRALIA'S NEWEST STAR
MAGAZINE

40 YEARS OF TELEVISION
8-PAGE LIFTOUT

JURIES ON TRIAL
REVIEW

SYTE MULTIMEDIA'S MILLIONAIRES
8-PAGE LIFTOUT

Telstra jobs axe threatens sale plan

96: The hottest number in 40 years

Hawthorn feud a not so civil war

Number 96 **was still front page news in 1996. Courtesy Elaine Elliott**

MIKE DORSEY: It was ahead of its time and it broke a lot of the taboo rules on television. In that sense it was a novelty and, due to the writing mainly, it took off. In its day — with Abigail and loose tits, and all that sort of stuff; homosexuality had never been seen on television. It brought Australian television into the century.

JOE HASHAM: There can never be another *Number 96*. It has come and gone, but will stay with me forever. As former Justice, the Hon Michael Kirby wrote to me on 12 February 2013, 'God bless *Number 96*.'

DAVID SALE: As for the success of it, nobody can really analyse success. There was a certain chemistry there, which nobody can analyse. Otherwise, every show would be a success if people knew that exact chemistry. It's something that happens between what's going on on-screen and the audience. There is some connection. It's like a meeting of two people who fall in love.

Vale

In memory of those members of the *Number 96* family who are no longer with us:

Don Cash (1910–1973)
Bill Harmon (1915–1981)
Johnny Whyte (c.1926–1985)
Pat McDonald (1921–1990)
Gordon McDougall (1916–1991)
Bettina Welch (1922–1993)
Ron Shand (1906–1993)
Jan Adele (1936–2000)
Bunney Brooke (1920–2000)
Owen Weingott (1921–2002)
David Phillips (1948–2004)
Bob Huber (1924–2005)
Thelma Scott (1913–2006)
Justine Saunders (1953–2007)
James Elliott (1928–2011)
Johnny Lockwood (1920–2013)
Peter Benardos (1928–2014)
Mike Dorsey (1930–2014)
Tom Greer (1942–2014)
Elaine Lee (1939–2014)
Norman Yemm (1933–2015)
Brian Phillis (1939–2016)

And many others mentioned throughout this book, including:

Peter Adams
Michael Boddy
Aileen Britton
Robert Caswell
Max Cleary
James Condon
Patti Crocker
Lynn Foster
Les Foxcroft
Joseph Furst
Mark Hashfield
Sheila Helpmann
Michael Howard
Wendy Hughes
Harry Lawrence
Redmond Phillips

Acknowledgements

Have a look at Lucy Sutcliffe in the throes of labour in episode 840 of *Number 96* and you'll get an idea of what I've been through to bring this book to completion! My sincere thanks to the people who have been alongside me on this wonderful and thrilling journey, going back to when I was a kid watching *Number 96* on the telly: my brother Paul and sister Helen, my late Grandad and my late Aunty Marian; friends Wendy Upstill Kennedy, Jacinta Gallagher and Jeanette Hetherington; my neighbours Billy Banks, Johnny Banks, Gordi Osojnik Featherston and Lilian Osojnik Lloyd-Jones.

Thanks to those friends who, as I've gotten older, have shared my passion and who help to keep the spirit of *Number 96* alive: Christine Critchley, Cheryl Critchley, Marc Coats, the late Darren Coats, Janice Evans, Bruce Thompson, Kerry Power, Tina Rafferty Smallman, Jo Rafferty, Melinda Gladman, Joe Poznanski, Sally Coyle, Cameron Wright, Kate Dermody, Lawrence Johnston, Andrew Mercado, Greg Punch, Kristen Potts, Helen Latemore, James Francis, Andrew Sandham, Suzy Cato-Gashler, and my parents Brian and Carole Giles.

For providing dinner, bed, breakfast and more as I trekked all over the country recording interviews I thank the following supportive friends: in Sydney, the late Megan Tindley, Peter Healy, Catherine Healy, Gregg Ellerton, Lisa Healy and Richard Hinchliffe; in Brisbane, Kerryn Nicks; in Perth, Dan Hatch and Vic Hatch; in Adelaide, Rob Ryan; in Melbourne, Andrew Foster.

Falling into the lap of the National Film and Sound Archive was a gift. Our collaboration has helped keep me on track over the years, and I give thanks to the staff and volunteers for their support and assistance. In particular, my thanks to Ken Berryman, formerly of the Melbourne office, who did a superb job running the Oral History Program and whom, with red pen in hand, gave valuable feedback on my manuscript. Thanks for the boost, K. B. My thanks also to former coordinators of the Oral History Program: Jennifer Thompson, Peter Shaw and Christine Guster. To the past and present staff of the wonderful Sydney office, including: Jane Adam, Simon Drake, Louise Herrick, Tina Fiveash, Carla Teixeira, Jo Fleming, Tara Marynowsky, David Noakes, Anna Kamasz, Frans Vandenburg and Bronwyn Murphy. In Canberra: Dr Louise Sheedy, Cris

Kennedy and staff. To the ever helpful and friendly staff, past and present, of the Melbourne office: Helen Tully, Simon Smith, Zsuzsi Szucs, Maryanne Doyle, Anne-Maree Unkles, Angus Johnstone, Siobhan Dee, Bronwyn Barnett, Michael Herrick and Chris Arneil. For help from other archives I give thanks to Merran Fuller (ABC), Marius (GTV9), Michael Ryan (NAA) and Renee Jurd (Film World).

Heartfelt thanks to each and every one of the generous interviewees who took the time to answer my questions and share their memories (and in many cases provide me with pictures), in order of appearance: the incomparable David Sale who also wrote the perfect foreword, Nancy Cash, the late Bob Huber, the late Johnny Lockwood, Eleanor Witcombe, Elisabeth Kirkby, the late James Elliott, Vivienne Garrett, Paul Weingott, Joe Hasham, Lynn Rainbow, Joe James, Ted Jobbins, the late Brian Phillis, the late Peter Benardos, the late Tom Greer, Rita James, the late Norman Yemm, Sheila Kennelly, Ronne Arnold, Tom Oliver, the late Thelma Scott, Jeff Kevin, Carlotta, Ken Shadie, Wendy Blacklock, Philippa Baker, Michael Ferguson, the late Owen Weingott, Carol Raye, Chard Hayward, the late Mike Dorsey, Candy Raymond, Victoria Resch, Jill Forster, Suzy Hasham, Chantal Contouri, Robyn Rowlison, John Orcsik, Patrick Ward, Josefine Stark, Pamela Gaerlan, Suzanne Church, Mary Ann Severne, Roger Ward, Peter Whitford, Harry Michaels, Deborah Gray and Mark Lee. Thanks for extra special support from the late Elaine Lee, Dina Mann, Karen Petersen, Ian McLean and Elaine Elliott, whose tireless efforts are greatly appreciated.

Sincere thanks also to Kevin Powell, Frances Hargreaves and the late Justine Saunders. In many instances, the generosity of the interviewees extended to the help and hospitality of their families and friends. My thanks to: Pam Borain, the late Iris Shand, Louise Weingott, the late Peg Weingott, Graham Pilgrim, Jay Pillay, Tony Llewellyn-Jones, the late Betty Benardos, Peter Benardos Jr, Greg Benardos, Carrie Phillis, Jodi Phillis, Ben Huber, Peter de Haan, Jan Oliver, Pam Shadie, M. J. Yates, Joanna Lockwood Walker, Simon Orcsik and Dave Debs.

For generously providing many of the images throughout this book I thank Paul Harmon, Mark Harmon, the late Peter Carrette, Ian Whittaker, Keith Wills, Nicola Germaine (Leunig Studio), Chris Keating, Mary Kennedy, Mick Hughes, David Chittick, Don Storey (TV Eye) and Steve Wakely. Special thanks to Dennis Livingston, Mick Pratt and the late Jonathan Duncan.

I would like to acknowledge the work of Albert Moran and Quentin Turnour in recording the stories of Bill Harmon and Kevin Powell (respectively), and thank them for their support of this project. Others who have been invaluable in their support are McKenzie Wark, June Neary, Ginny Hague, the late Victoria

Longley, Moya O'Sullivan, Arianthe Galani, Stephen Lee (Noarlunga Theatre Company), Pauline Lee (ICS), Martin Bedford, Doreen Warburton, Judy McBurney, Peter Cox and Rebecca Bower (The Power House Museum), Darren Gray, Andrew Bayley, Garry Hardman, Piero Pezzopane, Barbara Angell, Neville Phillips, Andrew Nette, Alice Ansara, Peter Flett, Sandra Knur, Bill Harding, John Timlin, the mystery eBay seller who auctioned her *Number 96* scrapbooks (now held by NFSA), Clare Williamson (for your expert guidance), Sally Pryor (*The Canberra Times*), Nick Walker and Wayne Saunders.

Thanks to my colleagues past and present at Reader's Feast Booksellers, especially Mary Dalmau for providing me with a Sunday writing haven.

Love and thanks to John Toogood and gorgeous Rosie O'Connor for delivering my muses, my cats Jasper and Louie.

To the team at Melbourne Books, I offer huge thanks for bringing my baby to life with your talent, patience and consideration: David Tenenbaum, Ellen Yan Cheng, Chloe Brien and especially Raphi Solarsh.

Thanks and gratitude to my Pozible cheer squad for believing in me and supporting this project. It's the truth when I say I couldn't have done it without you. Thank you to everyone who helped me spread the word, too. The generosity and good will of all of you made my dream come true. They include:

> Kristen Potts, Helen Latemore, Rosie O'Connor, Brian Kelleher, Sally Coyle, Danny Maratos, John Orcsik, Janice Northcott, Mirella Manganaro and Alan Pace, Lorna Lesley, Rose Hawkins, Edwina and David Pleasance, Greg Punch, Elaine Elliott, Stephen Tesoriero, Ken and Pam Shadie, Brian Smith, Renee Alford, Robert Connolly and Jane Norris, Joe and Rita James, Elly Hunt and Clive Filtness, Melinda Gladman and Joe Poznanski, Lisa and Gary Burleigh, Trent Davidson, Mary Dalmau, David Ralph, Giusseppe Cipolla, Nelly S Pedavoli, Britt Puschak, Kerry Power, Robert Stomann, Robert and Cris Vajna, Nick Patton, Michael Cole and Donna Melbourne, Kevin and Lorna Powell, Andrew Bayley, Ken Berryman, Steve Healy, David Tenenbaum, Peter Healy, Kerryn Nicks, Michael Hibbard, Cheryl Critchley and Brian, Jess, Bec and Ben Roy, Darren Gray, Andrew Mercado, Bruce Thompson, Jo Rafferty, Chas and Jan Woolley, Helen Hellary, Brian and Carole Giles, Lily and Martyn Lloyd-Jones, Lisa Healy, Marcus Coats, Kristine and Peter Benardos Jr, Greg, Tanya, Zac and Mitch Benardos, Paul Giles, David Sale, Tina Smallman.

Notes

1 *TV Week*, 20 November 1976, p. 34.

2 *Number 96* Publicity Booklet, National Film and Sound Archive, Title No. 419225, c.1974.

3 *TV Week*, 3 November 1973, pp. 16–17.

4 Jerry Fetherston, 'All the Kids Love Dorrie', *TV Week*, 26 May 1973, p. 8.

5 Peter Luck, Abigail and Candy Raymond, *This Day Tonight*, Australian Broadcasting Corporation, June 1973.

6 *TV Week*, 16 June 1973.

7 *TV Week*, 15 March 1975.

8 *This Day Tonight*, Australian Broadcasting Corporation, June 1973.

9 ibid.

10 *TV Week*, 20 April 1973, p. 23.

11 *Where Are They Now?*, 7 Network, 15 December 2006.

12 TEN Telethon, National Film and Sound Archive, Title No. 9415, 4 April 1986.

13 *New Idea*, 11 August 1973, p. 23.

14 *TV Week*, 21 February 1976.

15 *TV Week*, 20 November 1976, p. 34.

16 *Remember When...*, Arnold Earnshaw (ed.), North Ryde, NSW: Angus & Robertson, 1984, p. 32.

17 Michael Hohensee, '96 Opens the Door for New Girl', *TV Times*, 1976.

18 *TV Week*, 17 July 1976.

19 *TV Week*, 20 November 1976.

20 Extract, funeral program for David Phillips, courtesy of Karen Petersen.

21 *TV Week*, 20 November 1976.

22 National Film and Sound Archive, Title No. 548626, 16 July 1977.

23 *The Sun*, TV lift-out, 17 August 1988, p. 3.

24 *Where Are They Now?*, 7 Network, 15 December 2006.

Sources

National Film and Sound Archive of Australia (Oral Histories conducted by author)

Peter Benardos, Wendy Blacklock, Chantal Contouri, Mike Dorsey*, James Elliott*, Jill Forster, Vivienne Garrett*, Deborah Gray, Ted Jobbins*, Sheila Kennelly*, Elaine Lee*, Johnny Lockwood*, Dina Mann, Tom Oliver, John Orcsik, Lynn Rainbow, Carol Raye, Candy Raymond*, David Sale*, Ken Shadie, Patrick Ward, Owen Weingott*, Peter Whitford

Bill Harmon (Oral History conducted by Albert Moran), Kevin Powell (Oral History conducted by Quentin Turnour)

*additional, non-NFSA interviews were also conducted by author

Other recorded interviews conducted by author

Carlotta, Nancy Cash, Tom Greer, Bob Huber, Joe James, Rita James, Jeff Kevin, Harry Michaels, Victoria Raymond, Paul Weingott, Eleanor Witcombe, Norman Yemm

Books

All words attributed to Abigail are quoted from *Call Me Abigail* by Abigail (Petomane Publishing, 1973) unless otherwise indicated.

Letters, emails and phone calls (exchanged with author)

Ronne Arnold, Philippa Baker, Suzanne Church, Elaine Elliott, Michael Ferguson, Pamela Garrick, Joe Hasham, Suzy Hasham, Chard Hayward, Elisabeth Kirkby, Josephine Knur, Mark Lee, Ian McLean, Karen Petersen, Brian Phillis, Kevin Powell, Thelma Scott, Mary Ann Severne, Roger Ward, Robyn Weingott

Bibliography

Byrell, John. *Bandstand … and all that!*. Kenthurst: Kangaroo Press, 1995.

McLean, Ian. 'Do you remember the night Australian television lost its virginity? Celebrating Australia's cult soap opera hit of the 70s'. *Number 96 Home Page*. www.number96.tv. July 2012.

Mercado, Andrew. *Super Aussie Soaps*. Pluto Press, 2004.

Index

H

The Author

Nigel Giles grew up watching television in Croydon, Victoria. He graduated from La Trobe University in 1996 with a BA in Cinema Studies, and since then he has contributed to various newspapers and magazines. He provided research assistance for the books *Super Aussie Soaps* (Pluto Press, 2004) and *Puberty Blues* (Currency Press, 2004) and has contributed to Umbrella Entertainment DVD releases of *Number 96*, *The Young Doctors* and *Sons & Daughters*. In 2006 he was the major contributor to the Sydney Powerhouse Museum's *On the Box* exhibition celebrating fifty years of Australian television. He has recorded close to fifty oral history interviews for the National Film and Sound Archive of Australia. This is his first book.

www.ingramcontent.com/pod-product-compliance
Ingram Content Group UK Ltd.
Pitfield, Milton Keynes, MK11 3LW, UK
UKHW050919270726
13967UKWH00015B/3131

9 781925 556001